ACCESS

Introduction to Travel and Tourism

SECOND EDITION

ACCESS

Introduction to Travel and Tourism

SECOND EDITION

MARC MANCINI, PH.D.

DEPARTMENT OF TRAVEL

WEST LOS ANGELES COLLEGE

DELMAR
CENGAGE Learning·

Australia • Brazil • Japan • Korea • Mexico • Singapore • Spain • United Kingdom • United States

Coventry University Scarborough

Access: Introduction to Travel and Tourism, Second Edition
Marc Mancini, Ph.D.

Vice President, Editorial: Dave Garza

Director of Learning Solutions: Sandy Clark

Associate Acquisitions Editor: Katie Hall

Managing Editor: Larry Main

Product Manager: Anne Orgren

Editorial Assistant: Sarah Timm

Vice President, Marketing: Jennifer Baker

Marketing Director: Wendy E. Mapstone

Senior Marketing Manager: Kristin McNary

Associate Marketing Manager:
Jonathan Sheehan

Production Director: Wendy Troeger

Production Manager: Mark Bernard

Senior Content Project Manager:
Glenn Castle

Art Director: Casey Kirchmayer

Cover and interior designer: Chris Miller,
CMiller Design

Cover credits: Chris Miller, CMiller Design;
hut image ©Shutterstock Images LLC/
Keith Levit

For product information and technology assistance, contact us at
Cengage Learning Academic Resource Center, 1-800-423-0563

For permission to use material from this text or product,
submit all requests online at **www.cengage.com/permissions**
Further permissions questions can be emailed to
permissionrequest@cengage.com

Library of Congress Control Number: 2007922480

ISBN-13: 978-1-1336-8703-0

ISBN-10: 1-1336-8703-2

Cengage Learning
5 Maxwell Drive
Clifton Park, NY 12065-2919
USA

Cengage Learning products are represented in Canada by Nelson Education, Ltd.

For your course and learning solutions, visit **academic.cengage.com**

Purchase any of our products at your local college store or at our preferred online store **www.ichapters.com**

Notice to the Reader

Publisher does not warrant or guarantee any of the products described herein or perform any independent analysis in connection with any of the product information contained herein. Publisher does not assume, and expressly disclaims, any obligation to obtain and include information other than that provided to it by the manufacturer. The reader is expressly warned to consider and adopt all safety precautions that might be indicated by the activities described herein and to avoid all potential hazards. By following the instructions contained herein, the reader willingly assumes all risks in connection with such instructions. The publisher makes no representations or warranties of any kind, including but not limited to, the warranties of fitness for particular purpose or merchantability, nor are any such representations implied with respect to the material set forth herein, and the publisher takes no responsibility with respect to such material. The publisher shall not be liable for any special, consequential, or exemplary damages resulting, in whole or part, from the readers' use of, or reliance upon, this material.

Printed in Canada
1 2 3 4 5 6 7 16 15 14 13 12

BRIEFCONTENTS

CONTENTS

CHAPTER 7

Magic at Sea: The Cruise Industry   145

CHAPTER 8

CHAPTER 9

CHAPTER 10

Making Connections: How to Market, Sell to, and Serve the Traveling Public   227

CHAPTER 11

Techno-Travel: How Technology Has Changed Everything   251

CHAPTER 12

This and That   271

PREFACE

Few careers are as exciting, dynamic, and rewarding as travel. Helping people go places, enjoy themselves, and collect wonderful memories—that's what you'll do on a daily basis if you decide to work in the travel, hospitality, and tourism business.

What makes such a career so attractive? Here are five reasons:

1. **Employment opportunities are excellent.** By many estimates, travel- and tourism-related firms employ more people in the world than any other industry. Although the volume of travel ebbs and flows—prosperity and peace can fuel it, economic recession and political upheavals can dampen it—the trend, averaged out, is always upward.

2. **Advancement comes swiftly.** People employed in travel and tourism quickly discover that upward mobility is the norm for this business. If you perform to the best of your ability, you will probably rise quickly on the ladder of success.

3. **Your options will be plentiful.** Each segment of this industry—lodging, air, cruises, tours, travel agent operations, and more—has its own unique and distinct identity, giving you more choice for career paths than most other businesses.

4. **It's fun.** People in the insurance business don't get excited about insurance. People who work at office supply stores aren't likely to be passionate about office products. But those who choose to work in travel and hospitality? That's different. The best of them take pride in providing travelers with a satisfying experience—and so will you.

5. **It will help your own travels, too.** Industry professionals often get major discounts on their own travels. More important, what you'll learn from this book will serve as insider information, ensuring that you will travel better and smarter.

More About This Book

Access's title conveys precisely what it's about: gaining access to a treasure trove of travel, tourism, and hospitality knowledge. Its approach is highly practical: You'll learn exactly what you need to know about these industries, without extraneous content and details that may be nice to know but won't contribute to your future success.

If you're currently a student, *Access* will open a window onto a vast landscape of possibilities. And if you're already a working professional, you'll learn more about how your job relates to others in this vast industry, explore segments of this business that you once only vaguely understood, and discover others you never even knew existed. No matter where you are on your career path, this book will provide you with those facts, insights, and knowledge that industry professionals *must* know. It uses real-world terminology that you'll actually and regularly employ. And it will form the foundation for all of your courses and career moves to come.

Also, unlike many other introductory texts, *Access* will provide you with an overview of *all* major industry segments. At this point, you may not have yet decided which precise part of this industry appeals to you the most. Remain open-minded. There are jobs in travel that, at this point, you don't know about, yet may prove to be the right, even perfect, choice for you. And no matter which path you take, knowing the *context* of your chosen career—the other parts of the industry that intersect with yours—is vital to your success.

One other hallmark of *Access*: It explores the potential motives behind travel and travel-related purchases. Buyer psychology is essential to understanding why a traveler might, say, rent a car instead of flying or taking a train, or how travelers think of their hotel as a second (and "perfect") home. (Topics like these are rarely covered in other introductory texts.)

We also have tried to create a text that, in the language of publishing, is "evergreen." You'll encounter only modest statistical content, because stats can become obsolete almost as soon as the ink dries on the page. This is especially true of these industries, where dynamic change is the sole constant. You'll read only about those brands that have proven themselves over the long run, that are tried, true, and near-permanent parts of the industry. There will be little about rules, regulations, and prices, because these can change so swiftly. And the Internet permits you to look up such things easily and get perfectly up-to-date information.

Your journey through this book should be a pleasant one, too. That's why you'll encounter all sorts of design elements to help you along the way, such as multiple headings, boldfaced items, bullet points, photos, sidebars, and charts. You'll find the prose to be brisk, airy, and—we hope—a pleasure to read.

Students: **Keep This Book!** Should you resell *Access* after your course is over? (This assumes, of course, that you, not your school, own the book.) In the future, you almost surely will be traveling a lot. And you may very well want to revisit something you remember reading about in these pages... Unlike some textbooks, *Access*'s value to you will extend beyond the class you're presently taking. And if you go into the business, *Access* will be doubly valuable as a reference tool. So, consider this book a lifetime investment. Someday, you'll be glad you kept it.

Some Specific Features

What features will you encounter as you read *Access*?

- A list of **learning goals**, as well as a set of **key terms** to be used launches each chapter. They serve as a roadmap to the content to come.

- **Boldfaced and *italicized*** items underscore the most important words and concepts. This helps you organize and prioritize your learning as you work through each chapter.

- A **Telling Terms** box defines additional and accepted industry terminology that the book's main prose does not cover.

- A **Careers** box tells you about the main jobs available in each industry segment.

- A **This and That** box and a **More This and That** section gather bits of information that go beyond the main text and help fill the gaps in your understanding of the industry.

- **Insider Info** notes reveal information or unusual facts that the average traveler doesn't know about but that industry experts do.

- **Pacesetter Profiles** describe high achievers in the travel, tourism, and hospitality industries—and the paths they took to attain current success. To make these even more interesting for you, we've put them in a social media format.

- **Review Questions** help you test your understanding of key concepts.

- **It's All About You Questions** help you relate the book's content to your own future travels.

- Several **Activities** conclude each chapter and enable you to creatively apply what you've learned to interesting, real-world situations. You can do these activities on your own or as part of a project team, along with other students or trainees.

   Getting into this business was one of the best things that ever happened to me. It can be the same for you. I hope you enjoy *Access*, and I wish you great success in the career and travels that lie ahead.

Marc Mancini

To the Instructor

Thank you so much for selecting *Access* as your textbook of choice. I hope it serves as a solid, stimulating, and entertaining introduction to our industry and effectively supports your efforts to excite your students or trainees about a potentially rewarding and exciting future.

New to this Edition

In response to your feedback, as well as suggestions from students and reviewers, we have:

- Updated content, expanded certain topics, made several changes in chapter and topic order, and added an entire chapter devoted to technology. We've also taken steps to make each of our chapters a "stand-alone." You can assign chapters in whatever order you wish, with only minimal adjustments.

- Added new "It's All About You" questions that require highly personal responses to hypothetical situations, scenarios, and assessments.

- Introduced additional activities, including many tied to the Gale Hospitality, Tourism & Leisure Collection, a vast online database of articles, book extracts and scholarly studies. Instructors have found our activities to be especially useful for online courses, since they encourage creative and personal solutions, rather than the rote learning and open-book testing that can so easily occur online. Instructors, your Cengage Learning sales representative can help you obtain access to this database for yourself and your students. Ask for Gale's **Hospitality, Tourism and Leisure Collection The ISBN is listed in the instructor's companion website to accompany this text**. This database is available at a nominal fee with the adoption of this book.

- Introduced profiles of industry leaders and pacesetters—formatted in a contemporary Facebook-like style. Each profile traces the career path that a noteworthy person in travel and hospitality took to achieve notable success.

- Refined graphics, introduced more full-color photos, and increased use of illustrative and organizing elements to make the learning process easy, effective, and entertaining.

And to support your efforts, we have prepared an *Instructor's Guide* that contains thematic outlines for your lectures, PowerPoint slides, a list of useful Web sites, answers to activities and discussion questions, and an extensive bank of quiz questions. This will make it easy for you to implement *Access* with minimal extra work on your part.

Finally, what educational level is *Access* targeted to? All of them. It condenses a great deal of essential information and analysis into a colorful, easy-to-absorb but academically rigorous package. It works in both a traditional classroom setting and, with its unique activities, in online applications. It goes beyond rote learning and encourages original and creative thought.

Again, my sincerest thanks for adopting *Access* and my best wishes for continued success in your teaching.

Acknowledgments

My sincerest thanks to Karen Fukushima, Rick Scarry, and Glenn Fukushima, my assistants on this project; to the instructors who reviewed the manuscript and provided wonderful feedback; to those at Delmar who carefully shepherded this project; and to the countless travel professionals who, over the years, have educated me on this wonderfully complex industry.

Reviewers

The author and Delmar Learning would like to thank the following reviewers:

Helen Brixey
American Express Consumer Travel
West Palm Beach, FL

David A. Gray, CHE
Sullivan University
Louisville, KY

Marisa Haney
MS Travel Industry Professional
Bradford School
Pittsburgh, PA

Miyoung Jeong
University of Massachusetts
Amherst, MA

Peter Miele
West Los Angeles College
Culver City, CA

Kathleen Reiland
Cypress College
Cypress, CA

Dr. Peter Ricci, CHA
Florida Atlantic University (FAU)
Boca Raton, FL

Nancy K. Roop
CTC Heartland Community College
Normal, IL

Dottie Kohl Sutherland
Pima College
Tucson, AZ

Sandy Tremblay
Johnson & Wales University
Warwick, RI

ACCESS

Introduction to Travel and Tourism

SECOND EDITION

Going Places: An Overview of the Travel Industry

KEY TERMS

- All-inclusive resort
- Attractions
- Business travel
- Centrics
- Charter
- Commodity
- Consortia
- Consumers
- Convention and visitors bureau
- Corporate travel manager
- Demographics
- Dependables
- Discretionary money
- DMO
- Ecotourist
- Escorted tour
- Experience
- High season
- Hospitality
- Incentive trip
- Independent tour
- Intermediary
- Leisure travel
- Low season
- Psychographics
- Shore excursion
- Shoulder season
- Supplier
- Tourism
- Tourist bureau
- Tourist office
- Transportation
- Travel
- Travel agent
- Travel package
- Venturers
- VFR travel

After studying this chapter, you'll be able to:

- Define key terms used in the travel business

- Explain what each major segment of the travel industry represents

- Describe how travel is typically sold

- Analyze different kinds of consumers and what satisfies their travel needs

Photo courtesy of Jennifer Wright

Jennifer Wright

CURRENT POSITION/TITLE:

Account Supervisor, R&R Partners

SHORT DESCRIPTION OF WHAT YOUR RESPONSIBILITIES ARE:

I manage the Norwegian Cruise Line Trade Marketing Account for R&R. I'm responsible for all aspects of our Norwegian initiatives, including NCL University, their online training program.

EDUCATION:

BS, West Virginia University

FIRST JOB IN TRAVEL/HOSPITALITY INDUSTRY:

Account Coordinator, Kaiser Marketing

FIRST PAID JOB (IF DIFFERENT FROM ABOVE):

Waitress at a sports bar/restaurant. I may have been the world's worst waitress. I dropped everything.

FAVORITE PART OF WHAT I DO:

Relationship building. Being in two fields, travel and PR, I get to meet some really amazing people. It feels less like work and more like fun.

THING I WISH I DIDN'T HAVE TO DO:

Daily time sheets.

BEST CAREER MEMORY I HAVE:

Being part of a Second City shoot on a Norwegian cruise. To be around a comedy troupe for seven days is quite an experience.

STRANGEST OR FUNNIEST CAREER-RELATED THING I'VE EVER EXPERIENCED:

Not travel-related but: I was working on the movie, *Cloverfield*. The lead actress was unavailable for re-shoots. They needed a body double. The producer suddenly looked at me. Same build and coloring. And that's why, for a moment, I was the star of *Cloverfield*.

SOMETHING ALMOST NO ONE KNOWS ABOUT ME:

I am a huge science nerd!

f there's something predictable about human behavior, it's this: we love to travel. Some of the greatest adventures of humankind have been fueled by a need to experience fresh, new places.

Many of these journeys were prompted by practical concerns. Asians traveled across the Bering Strait (where, today, Alaska and Russia meet) to pursue food-providing herds. In the process, they eventually populated all of North and South America. Around AD 700, Polynesians from the Marquesas Islands sailed northward across more than 2,000 miles of open ocean to reach a new home in what we now call Hawaii. Some evidence suggests that they may have even visited South America. Still later, the great Italian explorer Marco Polo may have traveled even greater distances to reach China. His purpose: to open trade routes. In the process, he became the most famous business traveler the world has ever known.

But what about travel for pleasure? How far back does it go? Almost surely, the fierce curiosity that's at the core of all journeys motivated even the most practical voyagers. Yet until recent times, leisure travel was something mostly undertaken by scholars, prosperous merchants, politicians, aristocrats, and royalty, not everyday people. For example, the fifth-century BC historian Herodotus journeyed the rim of the Eastern Mediterranean to visit its greatest attractions. Like several traveling scholars before him, he called the

remarkable structures he saw the Seven Wonders of the World. A few centuries later, Emperor Hadrian became the Roman Empire's most energetic tourist. He went as far as Great Britain, where a 76-mile wall he commissioned still stands.

During the centuries that followed, common people increasingly had the opportunity to travel. Their purposes, though, were limited: they went for religious reasons (for example, to visit a shrine), to engage in commerce, or to wage war. The desire to see incredible, exotic places was a strong motive, too, no matter what the official reason for their trip might be.

Beginning in the late nineteenth century, travel became easier. Roads were better,

Wonderful Attractions—Then and Now

Though there were many lists of the Seven Wonders of the Ancient World, this is among the most widely accepted:

- The Pyramids (Giza, Egypt)
- The Hanging Gardens of Babylon (near Baghdad, Iraq)
- The Statue of Zeus at Olympia (Greece)
- The Temple of Diana at Ephesus (Turkey)
- The Mausoleum (Helicarnassus, Turkey)
- The Colossus (Rhodes)
- The Pharos Lighthouse (Alexandria, Egypt)

Source: www.new7wonders.com

In 2007, 100 million people voted online to determine the New Seven Wonders of the World, and the results were:

1. Great Wall of China
2. Colosseum (Rome, Italy)
3. Taj Mahal (Agra, India)
4. Petra (Jordan)
5. Machu Picchu (Peru)
6. Chichen Itza (Mexico)
7. Christ the Redeemer statue (Rio de Janeiro, Brazil)

trains could carry passengers hundreds of miles in relative comfort, and more people could afford the time and expense of taking a holiday. These trends reached full force in the twentieth century, when almost everyone in industrialized nations gained the ability to indulge in travel. The result: travel and tourism soon became the world's largest industry. It still is.

We're lucky to be among the first generations in human history to be able to experience the world in a way only the rich and the adventurous once could, even to *work* in that industry, building careers that others might envy. If you have such goals in mind, though, you must understand how this great, growing industry—and its multitude of parts—works.

Some Definitions

Let's step back and ask ourselves a basic question: what is travel? It seems like an easy concept to define. Yet the term *travel* is actually rather complex, with multiple meanings that overlap one another. A dictionary would describe travel as "going from one place to another." This clearly is too broad for our purposes. Otherwise, driving to the local mall would qualify.

Let's refine the dictionary definition a bit to address what this book is about: **travel** is *going from one place to another—and doing things when arriving there—for* *reasons not associated with everyday life.* This definition isn't perfect (for example, what about travel to relocate to a new home city?), but it's as close as we can come to a universally applicable definition.

Travel is usually divided into two broad categories: leisure travel and business travel. **Leisure travel** is *travel for the purpose of enjoyment.* The person travels to take a vacation, to get away from his or her everyday home life and job. If you decide to go to Hawaii, hang out at the beach, do some snorkeling, go to a luau, or do other fun things, you're clearly on a leisure trip. The same would apply to a trip to Paris to sightsee, eat at wonderful restaurants, and do some shopping. It might even apply to a day trip from home to a local amusement park, tourist attraction, or nearby ski resort.

On the other hand, **business** (also called *corporate*) **travel** is *travel beyond one's general home area for reasons related to work.* If a person must travel from Detroit to Omaha to meet with clients or fly to Mexico City to attend a convention, that would be business travel. Business travelers may set up the trip themselves, book it through a **corporate travel manager** (*a person employed by a company to arrange travel for its employees*), or arrange it by using the services of a travel agent (more about them soon).

Leisure travel can be further subdivided in several ways. Many people today opt to travel through a travel package. In a **travel package** *several travel components are "bundled" together and sold as one product.*

For instance, a person might buy an **escorted tour**, for which transportation, sightseeing, some (or all) meals, lodging, and the services of a tour manager are all prearranged. On such an escorted tour, the person will be traveling with dozens of others who bought the same package. Other examples of travel packages are **independent tours** (in which many of the travel components are prearranged but the buyer travels independently of a group or a tour manager), cruises (where the cruise fare includes transportation, meals, the stateroom, and so on), and **all-inclusive resorts** (which include lodging, food, entertainment, and many activities for one price). You'll learn about each of these types of packages in far greater detail in later chapters.

> **insider info**
>
> A packaged trip to Hawaii or the Caribbean that includes air, hotel, transfers between the airport and the hotel, and perhaps a one-day car rental sometimes costs less than what an airline would charge for the flight alone.

Most leisure travelers, however, travel on their own, not through a package. They set up their own trips or enlist the help of a **travel agent**, *a professional who analyzes a traveler's needs and then prices, recommends, arranges, and sells one or more components of that person's trip.* (Travel agents are also called *travel counselors.*) A common form of travel—in fact, the most prevalent—is **VFR travel**, or "**V**isiting **F**riends and **R**elatives."

Typically, family members travel together, say, in the family car, to visit people they know and perhaps even stay at those people's homes. This sort of travel should be familiar to you. Almost everyone has taken a VFR trip at one time or another. In fact, VFR represents about 75 percent of all leisure travel. For some people, it's the *only* form of travel they'll consider.

> **insider info**
>
> The best discounts, or "perks," given to travel professionals are from the lodging, cruise, and tour industries.

Work or Pleasure?

Corporate and leisure travel can and often do overlap. When visiting an interesting city, a business traveler might choose to extend the trip a day or two to see some of the city's attractions. (An **attraction** is *anything that leisure travelers find interesting*, such as a famous building, museum, or theme park. It "attracts" visitors.) In fact, studies show that about 20 to 25 percent of all business travelers take time off during a work-related trip to engage in some leisure activities.

Conversely, someone taking a cruise—clearly a leisure trip—might bring along some work-related documents to read while at sea or decide to check and respond to business e-mail in the ship's Internet center or, where Wi-Fi is available, on their laptops or smartphones. The bottom line: business and leisure travel frequently intermix these days.

Other Travel Terminology

So now you know a bit about what travel means, but other travel-related terms crop up all the time. Here are three common ones:

- **Transportation:** This refers to moving not just people but also *things*, such as cargo. (Cargo is an important revenue source for most passenger airlines.) In addition to the airlines, other transportation providers that are considered partially or fully in the travel industry include motorcoach operators; railroads; ferry services; car rental companies; taxi, shuttle, and limousine services; and possibly even the cruise industry. Some transportation companies, such as trucking firms, cargo ship companies, and express shipping services such as FedEx, have little to do with the travel business as we're defining it.

- **Hospitality:** The hospitality industry is usually accepted as encompassing the lodging and food services (food and beverage) industries. Sometimes the definition of hospitality is expanded to include theme and amusement parks; entertainment businesses (when they target vacationers); meeting, sports, entertainment, and convention venues; attractions; and cruise companies.

- **Tourism:** This may be the fuzziest term of all. Some experts equate travel with transportation and classify all *nontransportational* businesses (such as attractions) as part of the tourism industry. Others argue for a more all-encompassing definition: that tourism describes the entire travel industry. Still others believe that tourism describes only those organizations that promote travel to a certain destination. Another possibility: that tourism is a synonym for leisure travel. The word *tourism*, after all, comes from the word *tourist*, which clearly implies that pleasure—not business—is the motive for travel. A common, easy solution to this ambiguity is to call the whole business "travel and tourism," with no clear-cut distinction between the two terms, and leave it at that.

A unique form of lodging: overwater bungalows.

Sectors of the Travel Industry

In just a few pages, you've already read about many major subdivisions of the travel business, such as cruising, lodging, and touring. What follows is a list of the important sectors of travel and tourism, with thumbnail descriptions of each. Remember,

insider info

Foreign airlines spend two to three times more on in-flight food than U.S. airlines do.

Technology and Travel

Have you ever bought travel on a Web site? By now, most people have. In fact, by some criteria, travel has become the number-one selling category on the Internet. This is especially true for flights, car rentals, and lodging. One reason: travel is an "intangible"—it's not something you can touch, like a car, a house, or a TV set. So buying travel "virtually" seems quite normal, whereas you'd certainly hesitate about buying a car, a house, or a TV set online without seeing and experiencing it first.

From a travel company's point of view, technology is critical too. It enables travel professionals to easily and swiftly research, price, and book travel. In some cases, this is done through a **GDS** (**G**lobal **D**istribution **S**ystem, which you'll learn more about later), and in other situations, through the Internet itself. Other technologies used by the travel industry include back-office systems such as accounting; customer relationship management systems (CRM), which help analyze customer data and buying patterns; social media; and, of course, e-mail.

Expect to see references to technology throughout this textbook, as well as an extended analysis in Chapter 11 of its importance and effect on travel purchases.

you'll learn far more about many of these sectors in future chapters. Again, expect some overlap:

- **The air transportation industry:** This segment includes airlines of all sizes and sorts (such as *American Airlines*, *Alaska Airlines*, *Southwest Airlines*, and *JetBlue*), as well as the industries that directly support them, such as airline catering services (companies that provide in-flight meals), governmental organizations (such as the Federal Aviation Administration [FAA]), and airports. Airports are sometimes listed as a separate industry group because they, in turn, encompass so many services including security staff, gift shops and retail stores, dining venues, air traffic controllers, shuttle services, aircraft maintenance companies, and airline caterers.

- **Lodging companies:** The lodging industry is huge. It embraces a much broader spectrum of lodging types than you probably know, including hotels, motels, condominiums, timeshares, lodges, all-suite hotels, and campgrounds. Among the more familiar brands are *Marriott*, *Hilton*, *Hyatt*, *Days Inn*, *Motel 6*, and *Sheraton*. Lodging, as you've learned, is part of the larger hospitality sector.

- **Travel agencies:** Travel agencies are businesses that help the public with their travel plans and needs. Some agencies are small, whereas others are part of vast networks such as *American Express* and the *American Automobile Association (AAA)*, or **consortia**, *alliances of semi-independent agencies that work together to leverage buying clout and share common resources.*

Most travel agencies operate offices that consumers can visit or call. A few, such as *Expedia*, *Orbitz*, and *Travelocity*, are "virtual" agencies that sell through Internet Web sites. They have no offices open to the public and largely rely on their computer-based self-service approach to sell travel. They *do* employ travel agents, however, to handle sales situations in which customers feel a strong need to talk to someone (such as when selecting cruises and tours).

Travel agencies can target their sales primarily to leisure travelers, to business travelers, or to both. And travel agents can work out of traditional "brick-and-mortar" locations (for example, in a mall) or, increasingly, out of their homes.

A new-generation jumbo jet about to take off.

© Naiyyer/www.Shutterstock.com

- **Corporate travel services:** Just about every big corporation or government entity must use travel to achieve its goals. To do this, these organizations must have either an in-house travel management department or an outside travel agency to handle the many hotel, air, and other travel-related services their personnel may require.

- **Cruise lines:** Constituting one of the fastest growing segments in travel, cruise companies such as *Carnival, Royal Caribbean, Norwegian,* and *Holland America* take millions of passengers yearly to just about every place that's accessible by water. As with the airlines, all sorts of support services (such as port facilities, local tour operators, and food providers) make cruising possible.

- **Motorcoach operators:** These companies own and operate buses. Some provide scheduled city-to-city service. (The largest is *Greyhound.*) Others, such as *Coach USA,* mostly charter their vehicles to groups and tour companies. (To **charter** means to *lease or rent.*) Some motorcoach operators do both: they charter *and* operate regular service. City sightseeing companies also operate their own fleets of buses, as do, of course, local public transit systems.

- **Tour operators:** Tours are one of the most common forms of packaged travel. Some tour companies operate only *local tours* (for example, *Gray Line*), whereas others offer *independent tour packages* (for example, *Pleasant Holidays*), and still others sell *escorted tours* (for example, *Trafalgar*). You'll learn about their differences later.

Some companies rely exclusively on motorcoaches, whereas others fuse several modes of transportation (air, rail, sea, and/or motorcoach) into one seamless package. These packages can be designed to appeal to the general public or to serve the needs of specialized groups, such as **ecotourists** (*travelers who are interested in the natural environment and its preservation*), culture seekers, or religious pilgrims.

A specialized form of travel is the **incentive trip**, *a vacation provided by a company as a reward to certain employees for achieving exceptional, preidentified goals* (for example, salespeople at a car dealership who sell more than 60 cars per year).

- **Food services:** Because most restaurants, fast-food outlets, and other dining venues cater primarily to locals, food services appears to be something apart from the

At sea, on a cruise.

© Losevsky Pavel/www.Shutterstock.com

travel industry. But travelers need to eat. Many food providers—such as airport restaurants, hotel dining and catering facilities, convention centers, roadside restaurants, and themed dining venues—derive much, and in some cases almost all, of their profits from travelers.

- **Car rentals:** Sometimes located on or near airport property, sometimes in city or suburban locations, the car rental facilities of such companies as *Hertz*, *Avis*, *Budget*, *Enterprise*, and *National* give both business and leisure travelers the freedom to go where and when they want without having to rely on public transportation or by being part of a multiday tour. Car rentals are often included in independent tour packages too.

- **Rail travel:** Once the dominant form of transit, rail travel—especially in Europe and Asia—still represents an important part of the transportation industry. Some rail services are public (such as *VIA Rail Canada* and, in the United States, *Amtrak*), but others are privately operated. Sometimes also considered part of rail travel are subways, streetcars, and San Francisco's legendary cable cars, all of which can serve a traveler's transportation needs.

- **Meetings and conventions:** This huge sector of the travel industry facilitates the event functions of all sizes for businesses, organizations, and societies. It encompasses not only meetings and conventions but also trade shows, expositions, conferences, and World's Fairs. There is a strong connection between this industry and the lodging, food, and beverage sectors—that's why it's sometimes classified under hospitality.

- **Sports and entertainment management:** Is a baseball game at Boston's Fenway Park or a Lady Gaga concert part of the travel business? Some would say no. Yet such events have an appeal well beyond locals because so many people travel from afar to attend. Moreover, when a sports team or entertainment entourage moves from city to city, transportation and lodging issues are extremely important.

- **Attractions:** As you've learned, attractions are what vacationers go to see. Some are so famous that they have become icons for a place: the Eiffel Tower (Paris), the Golden Gate Bridge (San Francisco), the Great Wall (China), and the Pyramids (Egypt). Certain attractions are governmentally operated (for example, the Washington Monument), and others are privately run (like the Empire State Building).

- **Theme parks:** A theme park is a sort of "super" attraction, the updated inheritor of the old amusement park concept. Most of these businesses feature themed areas (for example, Disneyland's Tomorrowland and Frontierland sections). The Orlando area has the highest concentration of theme parks anywhere, including four major parks within *Walt Disney World*, two at *Universal Orlando*, and one at *Sea World*. Smaller parks or larger ones without any theming still, in some cases, do call themselves amusement parks.

- **Stores and shops:** Some stores rely quite a bit on tourism for profitability. Some examples: souvenir shops, factory outlet malls, and duty-free stores. Certain companies, like Magellan's, sell travel-related products both through traditional and online stores.

- **Parks and recreation programs:** Usually these programs don't immediately come to mind when you think of travel. Yet some of the greatest travel facilities and attractions are operated by local, state, or national governments. The wildlife parks of Africa, the national parks of the United States, certain attractions like the Statue of Liberty—all of these fall within the mission of governmental parks and recreation organizations.

- **Governmental regulatory agencies:** Travel was once highly regulated by governmental organizations. It is less so today. Nonetheless, things such as aircraft and motorcoach maintenance, air traffic, airport operations and security, cruise line policies, lodging safety and pricing regulations, and casino gaming are still overseen by government entities.

- **Destination marketing organizations:** DMOs, as the travel industry calls them, are *organizations whose purpose is to promote and facilitate travel to and within their districts, cities, regions, states/provinces, nations, or even continents.* Usually they are operated by a combination of private member such as hotels and attractions and public funding. National and regional DMOs are usually called **tourist offices** or **tourist bureaus**; city DMOs are often labeled **convention and visitors bureaus**.

- **Research companies:** Just about every travel industry segment you've just read about—and organizations and companies within these segments—rely on

Analyze This

Demographics pertain to *easily measurable factors,* such as age, income, gender, marital status, and the like. **Psychographics** deal with *factors that are more difficult to assess,* such as attitudes, preferences, and beliefs. The description "a 25-year-old woman who lives in London" yields three demographic factors: age, gender, and location. If we add that she considers ecology as a prime motivation for travel, then we have added a psychographic feature to her profile. Both demographics and psychographics are integral to figuring out what customers need and want.

Telling Terms

demographic and psychographic information about their customers, both actual and potential, to create their marketing strategy. Some have their own in-house research departments. Others contract with companies whose purpose is to carefully and cleverly analyze the consumer marketplace and, sometimes, recommend actions to be taken to adjust to those findings and increase business.

- **Insurance companies:** Travel is subject to many unpredictable factors. This is why certain corporations such as *Access America*, *UATP*, and *Travel Guard* specialize in protecting travelers from unanticipated incidents such as lost luggage, missed airline connections, illnesses, and accidents.

- **Financial companies:** Certain banks, credit card companies, accounting firms, and financial software providers have close relationships with travel-related businesses. Traveler's check issuers act as suppliers to the travel industry too.

- **Technology providers:** Reservations systems; database developers; online training, delivery, and management businesses; software and Web site designers; cost-control software developers; and others who provide technological solutions specific to travel businesses have become essential for industry success.

- **Trade associations:** Most industries have organizations that represent their interests, provide a forum for information exchange, furnish training opportunities, and perhaps do research. The travel business is no exception. Among its largest associations in the United States are the following:

  - American Hotel & Lodging Association (AH&LA)
  - American Society of Travel Agents (ASTA)
  - Cruise Lines International Association (CLIA)
  - Meeting Professionals International (MPI)
  - National Business Travel Association (NBTA)
  - National Tour Association (NTA)
  - Society of Incentive Travel Executives (SITE)
  - U.S. Travel Association
  - United States Tour Operators Association (USTOA)

- **Travel publications:** Have you ever dreamed of being a travel writer or photographer? Many people do. This industry sector is divided into two general categories. *Consumer publications* target the traveling public. *Trade publications* address the readership of travel professionals. Travel publications can be print-based (such as books, magazines, and newspaper travel sections) or electronically based (such as e-zines and online informational resources). Many informational resources that were once print-based are now Web-based, offering swift access to timely information and opinions. They, too, require technology experts to do things right.

insider info

Many credit cards provide automatic travel insurance when the card is used to buy a trip.

Careers

Career Opportunities in Travel

Most chapters in *Access* feature a sidebar on career opportunities for the sector examined in that chapter. Here are some general observations about the travel business, some of which expand on material in the Preface:

- **Your choices will be nearly endless.** Touring, lodging, hospitality services, air travel, cruising, destination promotion, airport operations, theme parks—all of these sectors and more provide hundreds of thousands of jobs, each unique, potentially rewarding, and offering great growth opportunities.

- **You can make a difference.** Travel, especially leisure travel, helps people learn about other cultures, grow in their understanding of the world, and fulfill their dreams. It has a more measurable effect, too, providing vital economic support to thousands of places and creating enormous economic success.

In many ways, tourism has become a critical force for world peace. Few industries can claim that.

- **You can get ahead fast.** If you have talent, energy, and a good work ethic, promotions will probably come swiftly to you. The travel industry provides a wide-open path for career advancement, especially in those sectors that are growing rapidly and for employees who are committed to hard work. And if you're an entrepreneur, you'll find plenty of opportunities in travel for achievement and success.

- **It's fun!** Travel and tourism is exciting, gratifying, and immensely enjoyable. As with any job, though, the demands can be challenging, but these are often offset by the simple fact that travel and tourism is one of the most wonderful industries around.

- **Professional services:** A number of occupational groups specialize in travel-related issues and services. Among them are attorneys, accountants, advertising agencies, public relations firms, travel writers and photographers, physicians who specialize in travel-related medicine, training consultants, speakers, and travel instructors.

How Travel Is Sold

Yes, travel is a complex industry, one far larger than you ever imagined. (Now you know why it's the world's biggest business.) Yet somehow all of these diverse organizations and companies work together to deliver an efficient, profitable, interdependent, and satisfying travel experience. To fully comprehend how it all works, though, you need to understand three key players: *consumers*, *suppliers*, and *intermediaries*.

- **Consumers:** That's you. You "consume" or use the travel product. Even if you're already in the travel business, you still are a consumer because you travel too, and buy services from other travel sectors. Different sectors of the travel business refer to you in different ways. Hotels, cruise lines, and theme park workers call you a *guest*. Travel agents refer to you as a *client*. Airlines, tour companies, motorcoach operators, rail service providers, and, sometimes, cruise lines, will label you a *passenger* (often abbreviated as *pax*). DMOs call you a *visitor*. The word *customer* is a possibility in any sector, although it tends to be used more when simple transactional buying and selling is taking place.

- **Suppliers:** Suppliers are *companies that create, own, and provide the travel products being sold*. Clear-cut examples of suppliers are airlines, lodging companies, car rental firms, rail companies, motorcoach operators, and travel insurance companies. Strictly speaking, attractions, theme parks, and food service providers are also suppliers. Because their services are often bought on-site (that is, when the traveler gets there), the travel industry seems a bit reluctant to label them as suppliers.

- **Intermediaries:** These are *companies that act as go-betweens, linking suppliers with the traveling public*. The most obvious example is travel agencies. Usually they neither create nor own the product they sell, nor do they actually *provide* the travel experience. In marketing terms, they *distribute* these products. That's why travel agencies are often also called *retailers*. They sell travel directly to consumers on behalf of suppliers. Unlike suppliers, travel agencies make their money through sales commissions from suppliers and/or by charging their service fees to their clients.

Tour operators represent a more ambiguous situation. They can be classified as intermediaries because they rarely own the motorcoaches, hotels, airlines, or other products they use and sell. However, because the *package* they provide is, in a sense, assembled and created by them, and because they sell these packages directly to the public and/or through travel agencies, they are often labeled suppliers. Cruise lines, like tour operators, also package many components together, such as air, insurance, hotel stays before and/or after the cruise, transfers, and *tours at ports* (called **shore excursions**). But they own their ships and sell most of their cruises through travel agencies, making them more like suppliers than intermediaries.

This all may seem complicated, but study Figure 1–1 carefully. It clarifies the situation and sets up an analysis of the distribution system that follows.

Distributing the Travel Product

How do travel products flow from suppliers to consumers? There are two main possibilities:

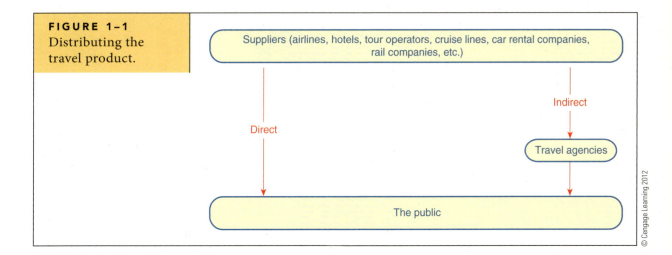

FIGURE 1–1
Distributing the travel product.

Suppliers (airlines, hotels, tour operators, cruise lines, car rental companies, rail companies, etc.)

Indirect

Direct

Travel agencies

The public

© Cengage Learning 2012

- **The supplier sells directly to the public.** For example, if you want to buy an airline ticket, you can call the airline via a toll-free line, book through the airline's Web site, or even purchase a flight at the airline's airport ticket counter. Many consumers seem comfortable buying simple travel products such as air, car rentals, and lodging directly from suppliers.

- **The supplier sells indirectly to the public, through intermediaries.** Most cruise lines and tour operators prefer to sell through travel agencies because consumers need a lot of guidance before deciding if they want a cruise or a tour, and which brand would be right for them. This counseling process typically occupies a great deal of time, and cruise and tour companies would have to maintain huge reservations staffs to deal with all of the questions. It's generally better to have travel agents handle the process instead.

  Even an online agency like Travelocity has a sales staff to handle customer questions. If you're on their site and doing a lot of research on, say, cruises, a pop-up will ask if you'd like to speak to or online chat with one of their "cruise experts."

  This works for consumers too. They would rather buy comple[...] as tours and cruises with the guidance and counseling—hopefu[...] that a travel agent can provide them with.

  Note that a purely either-or sales situation—either selling directly to [...] indirectly through travel agents—is rare. Most suppliers do both. The re[...] consumers never use travel agents; they'd rather buy direct. Other consum[...] always buy through travel agents; the expertise and time savings that [...] represents are worth it to them, even when purchasing such simple commo[...] flights, car rentals, and lodging.

Document ot

Commodity or Experience?

The way people buy travel (and how it's sold) is determined by the public's perception of each product—whether it's viewed as a commodity or an experience. A **commodity** is *a product that's simple, similar to other products in its sector, and is usually bought based on price and logistic factors alone.* A classic example is an airline ticket. When you buy one, you try to get the best itinerary (for example, a nonstop flight) and the best price. The airline you choose usually doesn't matter, unless you're concerned with such things as a frequent-flyer mileage program. For the most part, airlines are basically alike. This applies to car rentals too. Many consumers seem willing to buy commodities in a self-service style, by phone or on the Internet, without help from, say, a travel agent.

An **experience**, however, is quite different. It's usually *a complex product, and suppliers in that sector provide very different types of vacations.*

A *Norwegian Cruise Line* cruise is unlike one on *Windstar*. An *Abercrombie & Kent* tour (for older, upscale travelers) is nothing like a *Contiki* tour (designed for people younger than 35). Price and logistics (for example, the itinerary) may be important to you, but the "personality" of the supplier—and whether it matches yours—is even more critical to your decision. That's why consumers usually buy tours and cruises with the help of travel agents; it's hard to know which experiential product is right for them.

What about lodging? Each chain—even each hotel—has a different profile, so lodging should be treated as an experience. Yet, for some reason, consumers often purchase lodging as if it's a commodity. A common industry joke about the way consumers think about a hotel is, "When the lights are out, it doesn't matter where you're sleeping."

Why People Travel

Perhaps it's now appropriate to consider a larger question, Why do people travel at all? Travel can be stressful. In fact, the word *travel* comes from the French word *travail*, which means "work." Why would people want to *work* at enjoying themselves, and want to spend their discretionary money to achieve it? **Discretionary money** is *money that's left over after paying for the necessities of life such as food, shelter, and clothing.*

An activity at the end of this chapter will help you explore this question. But to prepare you for that exploration of traveler motives, it's critical that you understand this point: each individual's personality determines what he or she likes to do while traveling—and what he or she doesn't like to do. Some people prefer to visit museums, others to party, and still others to shop. Some are very sensitive to ecological and cultural issues, whereas others aren't at all. It all depends on the person. And the most illuminating way to understand this concept is through something called Plog's Continuum.

Plog's Continuum

Researcher Stanley Plog has identified three types of travelers: Dependables, Venturers, and Centrics.

Seasonality

THIS & that

When people travel is as important to travel businesses as *how* or *why* they travel. As you can probably guess, the flow of travelers isn't constant or even. For example, most leisure travelers who visit Venice, Italy, do so in the summer, when the weather there is best and many people get their vacation time. This is called **high season**. Not many tourists visit in winter, though, when it's rainy and flooding is common. This is called **low season**. Spring and fall are in-between times, when tourism is neither high nor low. This is labeled **shoulder season**. Prices, of course, parallel seasonality. Lodging, for example, in low season is available at bargain rates, whereas during high season, discounts are difficult to find.

- **Dependables** are cautious people. They prefer predictable, routine lives and avoid unusual things or challenging situations. When they travel, they favor safe, familiar destinations such as Orlando. A trip to Hawaii, Australia, or London would be an adventure for them. They sometimes visit the same place over and over. VFR travel very much appeals to them too. The only way they might consider visiting more exotic places would be on an escorted tour or a cruise, where they're "cocooned" from what they consider strange and foreign.

- **Venturers** are bolder people. They like different and challenging things and love to travel to unusual, exotic places. To them, safe, predictable places are, for the most part, boring. Their idea of a great trip would be to hike through Nepal, explore ancient Mayan ruins, or safari through Kenya. They usually prefer independent travel but will consider a cruise or a tour when it's the most efficient way to sample a place or when they're traveling to destinations such as Russia, Kenya, or China, which are so exotic that it would be difficult or even a bit dangerous to visit on their own.

- **Centrics** occupy a psychological middle ground between Dependables and Venturers. Most travelers fall into this category. They like a little adventure in their lives but not too much. They'd enjoy Hawaii, but Tahiti and Fiji would also attract them, as would the less typically visited nations of Europe such as Portugal or Romania. Exotic but well-known cities such as Rio, Cairo, or Tokyo appeal to them as well.

insider info

When the dollar's value is strong compared to other currencies, American travel to foreign lands (or "outbound" tourism) increases. Foreign destinations become a relative bargain. When the dollar is weaker, however, the United States becomes more attractive to foreigners (or "inbound" tourism) for their vacation.

A good example of a safari experience.

© Steffen Foerster Photography/www.Shutterstock.com

Where's the Third World?

After World War II, many politicians and journalists began to categorize the world into three groupings: *Third World* countries with little industrialized development, like those of Africa, South America, and parts of Asia; *Second World* industrialized communist countries, like the Soviet Union and those of Eastern Europe; and *First World* industrialized, noncommunist countries, like the United States and those in Western Europe. Though "Third World" continues to be used, the terms *developing* and *nonindustrialized* have largely replaced it. "Second World" is rarely used because so few communist countries now exist.

insider info
The best deals at tropical locations usually occur in October and May.

Of course, there are no distinct breaks between each of these personality types. Each blends into the other in a "continuum," as Plog calls it, with most people in the middle (Figure 1–2) and the fewest people at the extremes.

One final point: as you read the previous section, did you make any value judgments? Did you decide that Venturers are the best travelers or Dependables the most sensible ones? A lesson you must keep in mind is this: there's no right or wrong way to travel, no right or wrong personality type, just different kinds of people who like different kinds of things. Only by being truly nonjudgmental can you ever expect to succeed in the travel business.

FIGURE 1–2
The Plog Continuum.

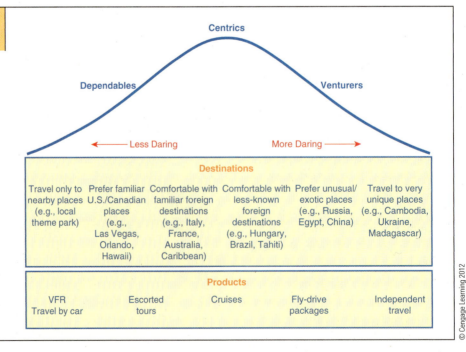

© Cengage Learning 2012

Review Questions

1. Define *travel* and explain the two major kinds of travel that exist.

2. List at least 10 sectors of the travel industry and describe each in one sentence.

3. Describe how travel product sales typically flow from suppliers to consumers.

4. Explain what Dependables, Venturers, and Centrics are and what types of travel each favors.

5. What is seasonality and how does it affect prices?

NAME   DATE

It's All About You Questions

1. What are the two things you read in Chapter 1 that surprised you the most?

2. What's the one insight you discovered in this chapter that you might be able to use on your next vacation?

NAME   DATE

Activity 1: Why and Who?

Many motives inspire people to travel. List the first 10 you can think of. I've given you one to get you started.

1. *To sightsee*

2.

3.

4.

5.

6.

7.

8.

9.

10.

Now circle the *two* motives you listed that are the most important to *you* when you travel. Finally, do you consider yourself to be a Dependable, a Venturer, or a Centric? Explain which label you chose for yourself, and why:

NAME   DATE

Activity 2: Your Future, Maybe

The fact that you're studying this textbook indicates you're certainly giving some thought to a career in travel and tourism. Following is a list of potential entry-level positions in the travel and tourism industry. Based on the limited knowledge you have now, rate your interest in each of these potential jobs, and then explain *why* you arrived at your assessment.

3 = Very interested   2 = Maybe interested   1 = Not interested

Job	Amount of Interest	Why?
1. Airport ticket counter representative for an airline		
2. Hotel front-desk person		
3. Travel agent working at a large agency		
4. Travel agent working out of your home		
5. City sightseeing tour guide		
6. Front-desk person on a cruise ship		
7. Front-desk person at a car rental office		
8. Onboard service person on a train		
9. Apprentice chef at a large theme restaurant		
10. Motorcoach driver on multi-day, multicity tours		
Other possibilities that you're interested in		

NAME   DATE

Gale Hospitality, Tourism and Leisure Database Assignment

The following assignment requires access to the Gale Hospitality, Tourism and Leisure Database. Check with your instructor to see if you have access to this database.

Find the article *Extreme Honeymoon, Anyone?* in the Gale Hospitality, Tourism & Leisure Collection.

Where would people who are interested in this sort of honeymoon place on the Plog Continuum? Why?

Do you know anyone who would actually want to do this? If yes, describe him or her.

2

Ribbons in the Sky: The Air Transportation Industry

KEY TERMS

- Aviation
- Bulkhead
- Bulkhead row
- Bumped
- Business class
- Carrier
- Charter flight
- Circle flight itinerary
- Civil aviation
- Coach class
- Code-sharing
- Commercial flight
- Commuter airline
- Commuter jet
- Configuration
- Connecting flight
- Direct flight
- Domestic hub
- Domestic service
- Exit row
- First class
- Flight attendants
- Flight record
- Fractional ownership
- Gate agent
- Gateway
- Hub
- Interline agreement
- International hub
- International service
- Legacy airline
- Load factor
- Mechanical
- Military aviation
- Minimum connecting time
- Narrow-body jet
- Nonstop flight
- No-show
- One-way flight itinerary
- Open-jaw flight itinerary
- Oversold flight
- Pitch
- Privately owned jet
- Red-eye flight
- Regional jet
- Round-trip flight itinerary
- Scheduled service
- Segment
- Sleeper seat
- Transcon service
- Wide-body jet
- Yield management

After studying this chapter, you'll be able to:

- Define airline industry terminology

- Explain how the various types of aircraft used in commercial aviation differ

- Categorize airline types

Photo courtesy of Dave Hilfman

Dave Hilfman

CURRENT POSITION/TITLE:

Sr. Vice President Worldwide Sales, United Airlines

SHORT DESCRIPTION OF WHAT YOUR RESPONSIBILITIES ARE:

I direct the efforts of a team of more than 800 sales professionals who manage our worldwide corporate relationships, revenues, and sales programs.

EDUCATION:

BA Finance, University of South Florida

FIRST JOB IN TRAVEL/HOSPITALITY INDUSTRY:

Eastern Airlines Campus Sales Rep

FIRST PAID JOB (IF DIFFERENT FROM ABOVE):

Pulling out the tassels from the tops of corn plants for Pioneer Seed Corn

THING I WISH I DIDN'T HAVE TO DO:

E-mail

SOMEONE WHO INSPIRES ME:

My 8-year-old son

BEST CAREER MEMORY I HAVE:

Helping Continental Airlines turn around from "Worst to First" in the U.S. Department of Transportation ratings

STRANGEST OR FUNNIEST CAREER-RELATED THING I'VE EVER EXPERIENCED:

Getting Gordon Bethune, Continental's legendary CEO, to speak at a travel agency convention dressed up as Captain Kirk

We've all had this moment: You look up and see a white, narrow ribbon of cloud tracing itself high across the sky. A jet, you think. No big deal. Yet until recent times, no one could have seen such a thing. Even now, when you really think about it, it's rather astonishing. Right now, as you read this, tens of thousands of people are sitting in narrow tubes of metal, flying along at more than 500 miles per hour, perhaps watching a movie, or eating, or sleeping, six or seven miles above the earth—as if it were a perfectly normal thing to do.

We take the air transportation industry for granted, as well as the many suppliers that make it possible. Supporting air travel is an intricate network of airports, air traffic control centers, food services, maintenance departments, airport hotels, shuttle vans, industry associations, aircraft manufacturers, and security teams, as well as salespeople, service people, Web sites, and travel agencies, which enable you to obtain a flight in the first place. Indeed, just about every segment of the travel, tourism, and hospitality industries, in some way, supports or depends on air travel. Let's take a look at how it all works.

The Aviation System

Aviation is the broad term used to describe the *industry that builds and flies aircraft*. It is usually subdivided into **military aviation** (*aircraft flown by a nation's air force and other branches of its military*) and the one we're concerned with, **civil aviation**,

A Boeing 747 wide-body cargo plane.

© Christopher Parypa/www.Shutterstock.com

the *industry that flies the public from place to place.* Also part of the civil aviation system are chartered, cargo, and private aircraft that belong to individuals or companies and use some of the same airports and routes that commercial flights do.

Civil aviation, in turn, can be divided into domestic service and international service. For **domestic service**, *a flight must start and end within the borders of the same country.* With **international service**, *the flight starts in one country and ends in another.* A flight from Houston to Chicago is domestic. So, too, is one from Vancouver, Canada, to Toronto, Canada. But a flight from Houston to Toronto would be international because it starts in the United States and ends in Canada.

Controlling the Skies—and More

As you can imagine, keeping order in such a complex transportation web—in the sky, no less—is no easy task. A network of regulatory bodies brings organization to the system, as well as to ticketing issues:

- **The Federal Aviation Administration** (FAA) is in charge of air traffic control operations, licenses pilots, inspects aircraft, and oversees maintenance.

- **The Air Transport Association** (ATA), an airline trade association, standardizes and regulates ticketing.

- **The Airlines Reporting Corporation** (ARC), also owned by the airlines, controls the *distribution* of tickets. (The equivalent of ARC in Canada is the Bank Settlement Plan, or BSP.)

- **The Department of Transportation** (DOT), a division of the U.S. government, creates and applies policies that regulate not just air travel but most forms of transportation.

- **The International Air Transport Association** (IATA), an association made up of most of the world's airlines, sets standards for civil aviation.

- **The International Airlines Travel Agent Network** (IATAN), a subsidiary of IATA, links airlines with travel agencies and other air travel distributors. One of its most important duties is to set standards to determine who is a legitimate seller of travel and therefore is eligible for industry benefits (from all suppliers, not just the airlines).

- **The Transportation Security Administration** (TSA) is a government entity responsible for security at airports in the United States. Its agents staff security checkpoints, check luggage, and do whatever is necessary to keep air travelers safe. At some airports, they may be assisted by local police and personnel from private security firms.

Airline Service and Routes

Aircraft can't simply fly wherever and whenever they want. Chaos would result. Governments, airports, and even the economic environment help shape what routes

insider info
If you categorized FedEx as an airline and judged its size by number of aircraft, FedEx would be one of the largest airlines . . . in the world.

are taken and what schedules are observed. This book won't go into detail about how this all comes to pass. You should understand, though, how it works from an airline's and the public's points of view.

When you think about flying, either for business or for vacation travel, you're generally dealing with something called scheduled service. **Scheduled service** is *air transportation that operates regularly at set, advertised times, no matter how many people are booked on the flight.* With scheduled service, a passenger buys a ticket for a specific flight that's scheduled on a daily basis (usually) and that flies at the same time each day between the same two cities. (Some flights might not be scheduled to operate every day of the week.) Each flight is identified by its airline's code and flight number (for example, DL 102 means Delta Airlines flight number 102).

Of course, the airline might decide to alter the regularly scheduled departure time to adjust to changing needs. For example, an airline could decide that its Flight 522, which usually departs at 7:52 a.m., should begin leaving at 7:48 a.m. instead. Another scenario: On a certain day, the flight—because of bad weather or mechanical problems (but not because there are too few passengers)—might not depart at its scheduled time. It may be delayed or even canceled for that day. That doesn't change the fact, though, that it constitutes scheduled service. Factors beyond the control of the airline caused the change.

Scheduled service isn't the only way for the public to fly. Another option is called a **charter flight**, *occasional flights flown by charter airlines.* Such companies usually sell seats, to or through tour operators, to mass-market vacation destinations such as Hawaii or the Caribbean. (Sometimes the airline is *owned* by the tour operator.)

A Southwest Airlines Boeing 737.

© Christopher Parypa/www.Shutterstock.com

You Can't Get There From Here

For the most part, airlines are allowed to fly only within their national borders or from their own countries to others, but not between airports in other countries. American Airlines, for example, can fly from Dallas to Miami. It can also fly from Dallas to Paris (it must receive landing rights for Paris, of course).

But it cannot provide passenger service within France between Paris and Lyons, or even from Paris to Rome, Italy. A foreign airline cannot fly passengers between two U.S. cities either. There are exceptions, but not many, and the rules are "stretched" a bit through code-sharing agreements.

They may fly only two or three days a week, but at scheduled times. Still, the occasional nature of their flights, that they're not usually advertised and sold the way scheduled flights are, and the theoretical possibility that the flight could be canceled if there aren't enough passengers exclude them from the scheduled airline category.

Charter flights are usually less expensive than scheduled flights, are almost always nonstop, and can be canceled (with a refund to passengers) for any reason. In industry jargon, a charter airline may be called a *direct air carrier*; the entity that charters the plane (for example, the tour operator or athletic team) is called a *public charter operator*.

Another rapidly growing alternative is the **privately owned jet**. In some cases, business travelers (usually senior executives) fly on a corporate jet that their company owns. Corporate jets are usually smaller than the ones commercial airlines fly. In another scenario, an individual or a company may buy **fractional ownership** in an aircraft. The plane has multiple owners who have a set amount of flight hours they can use. This is somewhat similar to timeshares in the lodging industry, which you'll learn about in Chapter 4. Many companies have discovered that private jets or fractional ownership are less expensive than frequently buying first- or business-class seats for their executives.

Flight Types and Routes

insider info

Luggage is least likely to be lost on a nonstop flight; it's most likely to be lost on connecting flights between two different airlines.

In the public's mind—and perhaps in yours—there's great confusion as to flight types and what each means. Let's clarify it all (Figure 2–1).

- On a **nonstop flight** *the traveler goes from Point A to Point B on the same aircraft*, with no stop in between. That flight will have one flight number. If American Airlines Flight 118 goes from LAX airport in Los Angeles to New York City's JFK airport with no stop in between, that's a nonstop flight.

- On a **direct flight** *the traveler goes from Point A to Point B on the same aircraft but that aircraft stops at an airport in between*. That flight will have one flight

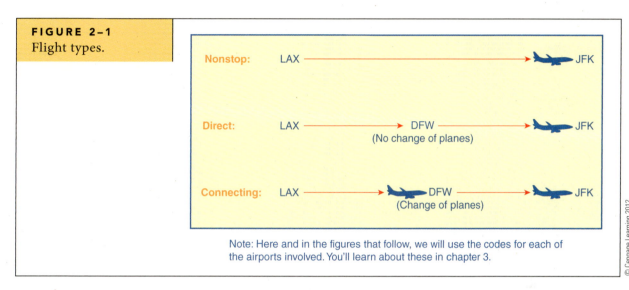

FIGURE 2–1
Flight types.

Nonstop: LAX ————————————————————→ ✈ JFK

Direct: LAX ————————→ DFW ———————→ ✈ JFK
                    (No change of planes)

Connecting: LAX ———————→ ✈ DFW ———————→ ✈ JFK
                    (Change of planes)

Note: Here and in the figures that follow, we will use the codes for each of the airports involved. You'll learn about these in chapter 3.

© Cengage Learning 2012

number, though, just like a nonstop flight. If American Airlines Flight 1158 goes from Los Angeles to Dallas and then the same aircraft continues on from Dallas to New York City with no change in flight number, that's a direct flight. Direct flights are also sometimes called *continuing* or *one-stop flights* (or however many stops are involved).

Why doesn't the plane just keep going to New York without stopping in Dallas? Perhaps because the aircraft is small and needs refueling before going on. It also may be because the airline wants some flexibility. Some people will stay on the plane all the way to New York, but others will get off in Dallas—this may be their final destination—or will connect to another flight, say, to New Orleans. And some passengers will pick up Flight 1158 in Dallas to get to New York. Their journey may be starting in Dallas, or they may have flown in from, say, Oklahoma City and are now connecting to Flight 1158 to get to New York. Which leads us to the third type of flight.

- On a **connecting flight** *the traveler, to get to his or her destination, must change planes once, twice, or even more times.* Each flight will have a different flight number. In the travel industry, each flight is called a **segment** of the passenger's trip. Occasionally, an airline will use the word *direct*, rather than *connecting*, to describe an itinerary composed of two connecting flights.

You may encounter other odd, surprising variations to the generally accepted flight type terminology. For instance, you may think you have a direct flight (with one flight number), but when you get to the intermediate airport, you'll have to get off your plane and onto another; you might even get on a plane from another airline! (More about why later.) Or you may think you're on a nonstop flight, yet the aircraft lands at another airport before continuing on, so you're really on a direct flight. Don't assume that the differences among nonstop, direct, and connecting flights are always clear-cut.

insider info

If you must take connecting flights in the winter, it's better—if you have a choice—to connect at southern airports than at northern ones because the northern ones may be affected by snow.

FIGURE 2–2
Itineraries.

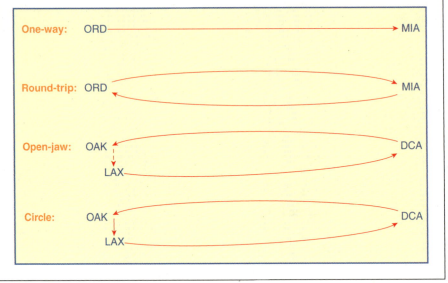

© Cengage Learning 2012

Another way to look at flights—from the traveler's ticketing point of view—is which itinerary route the passenger is following (Figure 2–2):

- A **one-way flight itinerary** means that *the traveler just goes from Point A to Point B*, and that's it. Let's say you're moving from Chicago to Miami. You'd only need a one-way ticket from Chicago to Miami. Or perhaps you're a student from Houston who'll be studying at Oxford University in England. Then you'll only need a one-way ticket from Houston to London. (Yes, you'll come back in nine months, but airlines often restrict the length of time a return ticket will be valid.) And don't forget: your one-way itinerary may involve a nonstop flight, a direct flight, or connecting flights. Oddly, a one-way ticket to a destination is sometimes more expensive than a round-trip ticket to the same place.

- A **round-trip flight itinerary** is the most common. The *traveler flies from Point A to Point B, stays awhile, and then returns from Point B to A*. Again, it can be nonstop, direct, or connecting.

- An **open-jaw flight itinerary** is one where the *traveler flies from Point A to Point B, then travels by ground transportation (such as car rental or by rail) from Point B to C, then returns by air transportation from Point C to A*. If you were to fly from Washington, D.C., to Oakland, California, stay there a while, then drive down the coast of California and fly from Los Angeles back across the country to Washington, D.C., that would be an open-jaw itinerary. Another possibility: In the previous scenario, you might take United Airlines for your **transcon service** (*a flight that crosses the continent*), but use a Southwest Airlines flight (ticketed separately) between Oakland and LAX because it would be less expensive that way. Since United's **flight record** (*the information in its computer about a passenger's trip*) doesn't show the Southwest flight, it will treat the trip as if it's an open-jaw itinerary.

- A **circle flight itinerary** is one where the *traveler has two or more extended stopovers and returns to the originating city.* Let's say you did set up all of your flights in the previous scenario in one flight record (that is, leave from Washington for Oakland, stay in Oakland, then fly to L.A., stay a while, then return to Washington). That would be a circle itinerary.

Hubs and Spokes

Before the 1970s, most passengers flew either direct or nonstop. But as airlines (or **carriers**, as they're sometimes called) began to analyze air-booking patterns, they realized it would be more efficient and economical to make the majority of their flights flow through a few key airports. These airports would become **hubs** for a vast system of "spoke" flights (see Figure 2–3).

For example, each day hundreds of United Airlines flights converge in Chicago; American Airlines flights in Dallas; and Delta Airlines flights in Atlanta. These cities are each airline's hubs. **Domestic hubs** handle mostly domestic flights, whereas **international hubs** feature many flights to other countries.

This hub-and-spoke system may not be ideal for customers, however. Whereas United might have had eight nonstop flights between New York and Los Angeles back in the 1960s, it may now have only five, but offer a dozen possible connecting options through its Chicago hub.

With connections, the hassles and possibility of something going wrong increases. What if the second flight is canceled? Suppose your first flight is delayed and you miss your next one? Each airport has official **minimum connecting times**, *the minimum amount of time needed to transfer from one flight to a connecting one.* But those times assume no problems with, say, late flights. (An airline *may* hold some flight departures to enable passengers on a delayed flight to make their connections,

FIGURE 2–3
The hub-and-spoke system, with Chicago O'Hare as the hub.

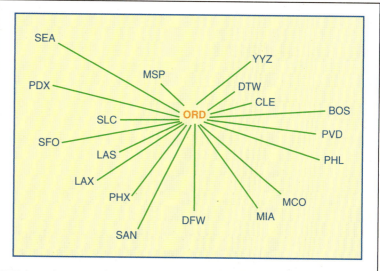

© Cengage Learning 2012

Major Airline Hubs for Domestic and Domestic/International Flights

Atlanta (Delta)

Baltimore (Southwest)

Charlotte, North Carolina (US Airways)

Chicago Midway (Southwest)

Chicago O'Hare (American, United)

Cincinnati (Delta)

Cleveland (United)

Dallas (American, Delta)

Denver (United)

Detroit (Delta)

Houston (United)

Los Angeles (American, United)

Miami (American)

Minneapolis (Delta)

Montreal (Air Canada)

New York City (American, Delta, United)

Newark (United)

Philadelphia (US Airways)

Phoenix (Southwest, US Airways)

Pittsburgh (US Airways)

St. Louis (American)

Salt Lake City (Delta)

San Francisco (United)

Seattle (Alaska)

Toronto (Air Canada)

Vancouver (Air Canada)

Washington, D.C. (United)

so long as the delayed flight isn't extremely late.) In addition, with a connection, the possibility of lost luggage is increased.

The hub-and-spoke system isn't always traveler-friendly, but it benefits the airlines and, in theory, leads to efficiencies that result in lower fares.

Aircraft

Most aircraft can be divided into two broad categories: those powered by *jet engines* and those driven by *propellers*, or *props*. Prop planes are smaller, go relatively slowly (about 300 mph), and travel short distances. Jet aircraft fly faster (520 to 560 mph or so), can go much longer distances, and tend to be larger (although, increasingly, small jet planes are replacing prop ones). There's also something called a *jet prop*, which combines features of both prop and jet engines. Jet prop planes tend to be larger and a little faster than regular prop aircraft.

Jets come in two variations: **narrow-body jet** and **wide-body jet** (also called "jumbo jets"). To understand the difference, it's essential to examine something called *configuration*.

THIS & that

Narrow Versus Wide

The most common models of jets in use worldwide today are listed here. Regional, short-route jets that seat fewer than 100 passengers have been omitted.

Wide-Body Jets

- Boeing 747
- Boeing 767
- Boeing 777
- Boeing 787
- Airbus A300 / 310
- Airbus A330
- Airbus A340
- Airbus A350
- Airbus A380
- McDonnell-Douglas DC-10

Narrow-Body Jets

- Boeing Super 80
- Boeing 717
- Boeing 727
- Boeing 737
- Boeing 757
- McDonnell-Douglas DC-9
- McDonnell-Douglas MD-80 / 90
- Airbus A318
- Airbus A319
- Airbus A320
- Airbus A321

In turn, each airliner type may have a *series number* after its model number. So a Boeing 737-800 is newer, with more up-to-date features, than a Boeing 737-300 *unless* the Boeing 737-300 has been refurbished. Because aircraft are built to last for decades, airlines often install a new interior to freshen up an older aircraft.

© Vetal/www.Shutterstock.com

Interior of a narrow-body jet.

Configuration refers to *the way seating is arranged within the aircraft* (Figure 2–4). For example, a plane's coach section might have three seats on its left side (labeled ABC), an aisle, and then three seats on the right side (labeled DEF), with 24 rows. Its first-class cabin might have two seats on its left side (AB), an aisle, and two seats on the right (CD or DF). (You'll learn more about first class and coach later.)

A jet with one aisle, like the one just described, is called a narrow-body jet. In a few cases, a plane may have two seats per row on one side of the aisle and three on the other, but three-and-three is a more common configuration. A narrow-body jet usually carries fewer than 200 passengers. If it's even smaller (for example, one seat on one side, two seats on the other), it may be called a **regional jet** or a **commuter jet**. Such "mini-jets" carry fewer than 100 people.

FIGURE 2–4
Seating charts for a Boeing 737 jet (L) and a wide-body Airbus A310 (R).

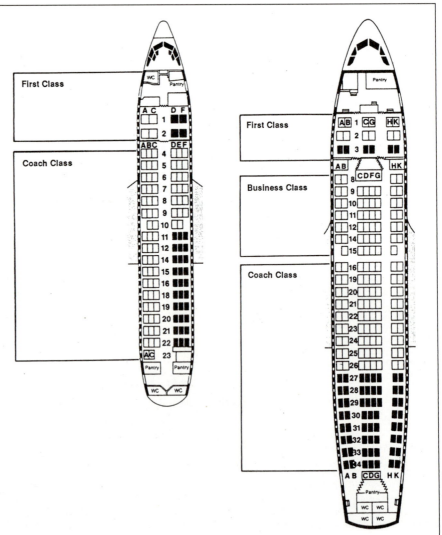

Unusual Aircraft

Although most aircraft are of the jet or prop variety, other travel-related possibilities exist. Helicopters and small planes (including some that land on water) provide sightseeing over dramatic places such as the Grand Canyon, Alaska's glaciers, or Hawaii's volcanoes. Hot-air balloons are an offbeat way to experience, say, France's countryside from above. And blimps carry tourists over some visually striking cities.

A wide-body jet, because of its greater size, has two aisles. A possible coach cabin configuration is AB-CDEF-GH that is, two seats, an aisle, four seats, another aisle, and two seats). Such planes can carry well over 200 passengers. The Boeing 747 even has a second, shorter upper deck, usually with an AB-CD first-class or business-class layout, and the Airbus A380 has two full-length decks. Most full-size aircraft are built either by Boeing or Airbus. Regional jets and prop planes are built by many manufacturers throughout the world.

Pitch, Width, and Recline

If someone refers to the "pitch" of seating, wouldn't you assume that it had to do with how far a seat reclines? That would be logical, but wrong. **Pitch** is *the distance between a point on one seat and the same point on the seat in the row in front of or behind it*. This is also sometimes called *legroom*.

For the majority of their seats, most airlines (and charter ones especially) provide the smallest amount of pitch possible without causing too great a degree of discomfort for an average-size person. The reason: reduced pitch permits more rows on the aircraft, which yields more revenue. A few airlines offer more generous pitch (33 or 34 inches instead of the average 31 to 32) as a way to set themselves apart from other carriers and attract those for whom roominess is a high priority. The theory: a higher **load factor** (*the percentage of seats filled with people*) will offset the lost revenue from those extra rows. It's not uncommon for an airline to create and promote greater legroom, then quietly return to tighter pitch later.

Seat width also affects comfort. The average seat on an aircraft is a mere 17 to 18 inches wide, with some as narrow as 16.5!

A third comfort element is recline. Some airlines set seats to recline only about 10 percent, others by as much as 45 percent or more, or even full recline, creating a bed-like situation (Figure 2–5). Of course, all this depends on which class you're in.

insider info

Wide-body aircraft are more likely to have better pitch, seat width, recline, food service, and video entertainment than narrow-body planes. The reason: these aircraft are often used on long-haul international or transcon flights.

insider info

Exit-row seats usually have much better pitch, but sometimes don't recline. Always ask. These seats are usually assigned at the airport only.

insider info

Mathematically, window and aisle seats (the most desirable) are more common on wide-body planes (because of their two aisles). Conversely, narrow-body aircraft have a higher proportion of the undesirable middle seats.

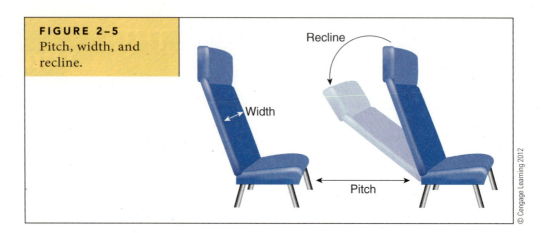

FIGURE 2–5
Pitch, width, and recline.

Recline

Width

Pitch

© Cengage Learning 2012

Classes of Service

Earlier you learned that service refers to the routes an airline offers (for example, Delta Airlines offers service between Cincinnati, Ohio, and Providence, Rhode Island). The word *service* can also apply to the *class of service* that an aircraft's configuration offers.

Most aircraft have two classes of service: first and coach. **First class** is in the *compartment at the front of the plane*. It usually features, among other things, wider seats, greater pitch, more recline, more elaborate meals, complimentary alcoholic beverages, and free movies.

Coach class (sometimes called *economy class*) is *the more standard level of service* that has been described up to now. It features narrower seats, less pitch and recline (rarely more than 30 percent), simple meals or snacks (sometimes with no menu choice), or even no food service at all, except perhaps for a bag of pretzels and a soft drink. Alcoholic beverages cost extra in coach, as do movies, although some airlines offer free movies in coach or sell headsets that passengers can keep for use on future flights. Some airlines offer something called *premium coach* or *premium economy*, which provide more pitch between coach seats, usually toward the front of the coach compartment. Usually, *separating the coach- and first-class compartments is a wall* called a **bulkhead**. The row of coach seats immediately behind this partition is called the **bulkhead row**.

On longer flights, especially international ones, an aircraft might have *three* classes of service: first class, business class, and coach. Usually sandwiched between first and coach, **business class** represents *a class of service that's almost as good as that found in the first class*. Pitch may be 40 inches in the business class compartment, whereas, in first class, it's more than 50. Recline in business-class may be 40 to 60 percent, whereas in first class recline is 60 percent or more. The seats may even fully convert to beds. (This type of seat is called a **sleeper seat**.) The first-class traveler may even be provided with free pajamas!

Flight attendants have more responsibilities than ever.

In some cases, an airline may have, as its two classes, business and coach, with no first class. Here, the front-of-the-aircraft compartment will have seating and food that's somewhat better than coach. (This is especially common in Europe.) In other cases, business class may be almost as impressive as what would have been first class. Almost always, business- and first-class seating features fewer seats per row than in coach because these seats are wider.

Seating Assignments

How are seats assigned? In most cases, when making a flight reservation, a passenger can reserve a specific seat in advance, either by phone with a travel agent or an airline reservationist, or on the Internet. Passengers can also reserve a seat when they check in at the airport: at the check-in counter, at a self-service kiosk, or at the gate. The **exit rows** (*the rows where the emergency exits are located*) are usually assigned at airport check-in because they require able-bodied passengers to help open the exterior door in an emergency. Only airport personnel can make sure that the people sitting in exit-row seats aren't, say, children or physically challenged passengers.

Most airlines, however, keep some seats under "airport control." Passengers can't book these seats in advance. So if you discover that there are no seats left for prebooking, you must wait until you get to the airport to obtain your assigned seat. In a few cases, seats that were prebooked may reenter the inventory because of cancellations or other changes. So just because you can't get a seat assignment today doesn't mean you won't be able to tomorrow. Also, some airlines do not permit preassigned seats for deeply discounted promotional fares. Other

insider info

Bulkhead seats often have more legroom, and (usually) no one can recline the seat in front of you to further reduce your space. The downside: there's usually no under-seat space in front of you to stow your carry-on luggage. It has to go in the overhead bin, at least during takeoffs and landings.

THIS & that

Overbooking

If the demand for a certain flight is great, an airline will allow bookings to exceed the number of seats available on that flight. When that happens, the flight is said to be **oversold** or overbooked.

How can the airlines do this without causing big problems? They maintain sophisticated computer programs that, based on past patterns, help them predict how many people on a certain flight might be **no-shows** (*people with reservations who don't show up for the flight*). For example, a business traveler may need to stay at a meeting longer than planned and have to take his or her chances on catching a later flight.

Also, airlines have rules stating that passengers must check in for their flight no later than 20 to 30 minutes before the departure time, depending on the airline. Once that time passes, the **gate agent** (*the airline employee who works at the gate where passengers board the plane*) will release any unclaimed seats to those passengers who have arrived but have yet to receive their seat assignments. Gate agents will also sometimes ask for volunteers to release their seats and take a later flight. These volunteers usually receive a voucher worth a few hundred dollars toward a future trip on that carrier. The reward may escalate even further—a free flight, an upgrade to first- or business-class, or even cash—if there aren't enough takers initially or if it is clear, early on, that the flight is significantly overbooked.

If there still aren't enough seats available, the last arriving passengers may be **bumped** (*not allowed to board the plane*) and will have to take a later flight. If the passenger arrived before the 20- to 30-minute cutoff limit, he or she will be eligible for a government-required involuntary denied boarding compensation, in the form of several hundred dollars. Overbooking policies are in constant flux and vary from country to country.

carriers don't allow preassigned seating at all. For example, Southwest Airlines simply lets passengers take any seat they want as they board. Passengers board the plane based on a priority numbering system that is assigned when they check in. On some airlines, passengers can pay extra to board the plane before other passengers.

The Airlines

Most travelers have a love-hate relationship with the airlines. We love them for getting us to places swiftly and safely. We become annoyed, though, when they cram us into small spaces, serve us mediocre (or no) food, and make us wait, and wait, and wait.

There's no denying, though, that the airlines are major cogs in the mechanisms of travel. Some of them are so powerful that they've become among the most recognizable brands of all. Let's divide the airlines into four categories: major U.S. airlines, secondary airlines, low-fare airlines, and regional airlines.

The Major North American Airlines

These are the airlines—all of them huge companies—that provide service to a substantial number of North American cities, as well as to many international ones. Here they are, with their airline codes (more about codes later):

- Aeromexico (AM)
- Air Canada (AC)
- American Airlines (AA)
- Delta Air Lines (DL)
- United Airlines (UA)
- US Airways (US)

Because these carriers have been around a long time, they're sometimes called **legacy airlines**. Note that this list is current at press time. Mergers and bankruptcies are common to the airline business.

Other countries have major airlines too, with considerable service within their national borders, as well as to other countries (including those in North America). Here are some of the biggest ones, with their codes:

- Air France (AF)
- Air New Zealand (NZ)
- British Airways (BA)
- Japan Airlines, or JAL (JL)
- KLM-Royal Dutch Airlines (KL)
- Lufthansa (LH)
- Qantas Airways (QF)
- SAS Scandinavian Airlines (SK)
- Singapore Airlines (SQ)
- Virgin Atlantic (VS)

An airline that offers only service within a country is called a domestic carrier, one that offers service among multiple countries is called an international or foreign carrier.

Many carriers have formed worldwide alliances that enable them to work more efficiently with one another. Among them: *oneworld* (which includes AA, BA, and QF, among others) and *Star Alliance* (consisting of UA, LH, AC, and others). Each alliance partner may share the following services with the others: common ticketing, reciprocal frequent-flyer mileage, connecting boarding passes, coordinated baggage transfer, departures from the same terminal, and coordinated connections to minimize waiting time.

insider info

Over the past few decades, the following major airlines have disappeared or merged with other airlines:

- Continental (merged with United)
- Eastern (bankruptcy)
- Northwest (merged with Delta)
- Pan Am (bankruptcy)
- TWA (absorbed by American)

Secondary Airlines

Several airlines aren't as huge as the majors but do offer considerable service. For example, Alaska Airlines (AS) has many flights up and down the western coasts of the United States, Canada, and Mexico, and Hawaiian Airlines (HA) offers service among the islands of Hawaii, as well as to and from the U.S. mainland.

Low-Fare Airlines

Everyone has heard of Southwest Airlines (WN). Once an airline that flew only between cities in Texas, Southwest is now a company that rivals the majors in both size and route network. But it achieved its impressive growth by pursuing a different business model from that of its mega-competitors. Dozens of similar U.S. airlines, like *JetBlue Airlines* (B6) and *Frontier* (F9), as well as some carriers in other countries, have imitated the Southwest formula.

What are the practices that have made low-fare (and sometimes "low-frills") airlines a success? Well, for starters, they offer fares that are often lower—sometimes much lower—than the majors. In fact, whenever a low-fare airline begins offering service to a city, the major airlines are forced to compete with equally low fares there. Low-fare airlines also offer *highly simplified rate structures* compared to the major airlines. (More about rates soon.) Among their other strategies are the following:

- **They tend to target leisure travelers**, because these people are the most price-sensitive.

- **They establish their hubs at secondary airports** that the majors tend to use sparingly. Such airports, because they're smaller, offer easier parking, shorter

Not all air travel is by jet.

Careers

Careers in the Air Transportation Industry

Here are the most typical jobs in the air transportation industry:

- Senior executives, directors, and managers
- Reservationists
- Ticketing
- Customer service representatives
- Dispatchers
- Accountants
- District sales representatives
- Maintenance personnel
- Air traffic controllers
- Pilots
- Clerical support
- Crew schedulers
- Airport ground crew
- Human resources/training specialists
- Security/safety personnel (TSA and private)
- Sky marshals
- Baggage handlers

waiting time, less flight congestion (thus fewer delays), and other advantages that result from their modest size. For example, Southwest has, among its hubs, Providence, Rhode Island. Many travelers find the Providence airport to be a pleasant alternative to Boston's, which is usually quite congested.

- **They offer fewer nonstop long flights**. If you want to cross the country on a low-fare airline, you're more likely to make connections.

- **Many of them offer no meals or movies** on their flights. Imitating these low-cost carriers, the major airlines now seldom offer meal service on flights of three hours or less.

- In most cases, **they offer only coach seating**, sometimes with no advanced seat assignments allowed.

- **They tend to use only one or two aircraft models** in their fleet. This simplifies their maintenance procedures and parts inventories.

- Their fares generally have **fewer rules and restrictions.**

- Some **don't appear on travel agent and Internet air ticket booking sites**. You must go to that airline's Web site.

- **The tickets of a low-cost airline usually aren't accepted by other airlines**. Let's say United must cancel a flight. It *may* place its passengers on an American flight instead, with American accepting the value of the United ticket and exchanging it for one of its own. But this won't happen with a Southwest ticket. If a Southwest flight is canceled, its passengers need to wait for the next Southwest flight.

What separates low-fare airlines from secondary ones? These days, not much. Legacy carriers often adopt pricing and policies that are more typical of the low-fare airlines. Some airlines, like Virgin America (VX), are considered low-fare airlines but actually have more in common with legacy carriers.

Regional Airlines

These carriers, also called **commuter airlines**, serve a limited section of the country and are often affiliated with a major airline (for example, *American Eagle* provides short, regional flights out of American Airlines' hubs. In fact, it carries the same airline code: AA). Regional airlines tend to use small jets and prop planes for their service. Among other significant commuter airlines are *Comair, Skywest, Mesa, Horizon*, and *Expressjet*.

Telling Terms

Here are some commonly used terms in air travel that go beyond those defined in the main body of the text:

- **Commercial flight:** A flight whose seats have been sold by an airline to the general public. Commercial flights are not military or private flights.

- **Code-sharing:** When an airline uses the code of another carrier for a scheduled flight. For example, UA 3506 may also be LH 445. (The aircraft may be either a United or Lufthansa one.) Used among partner airlines (often within their "alliances"), code-shares make each airline appear to offer greater service than it actually does.

- **Red-eye flight:** An overnight flight. Called "red-eye" because the passengers are trying to sleep—usually unsuccessfully—on the plane.

- **Interline agreement:** A formal agreement between two airlines. Often both are code-sharing partners, with easy baggage transfer and acceptance of each other's documents (such as tickets).

- **Gateway:** A city and/or airport that serves an airline as its departure/arrival point for international travel. For example, Air Jamaica might have 16 cities with nonstop travel to Jamaica. These are its gateways.

- **Yield management:** A computer-assisted process that, by assessing supply and demand, enables airlines to arrive at pricing that yields maximum load factors and revenue. (Yield management is also used by the lodging industry and other industry segments.)

- **Flight attendants:** Airline personnel who see to the safety, comfort, and needs of passengers on a plane. Formerly called *stewards* and *stewardesses*.

- **Mechanical:** When a flight is canceled because of a problem with the aircraft (for example, the door does not close properly), as opposed to a flight canceled for extreme weather conditions.

Review Questions

1. Explain the differences between:

    a. domestic and international service

    b. scheduled and charter service

    c. a one-way flight and a round-trip flight

    d. a narrow-body aircraft and a wide-body aircraft

    e. pitch and recline

    f. first, business, and coach classes

2. Describe how the following flights differ: nonstop, direct, and connecting.

3. What are the three major kinds of flight itineraries?

4. Which airlines use the following as hubs? Give your answers as airline codes: Chicago, Atlanta, Denver, Toronto, Houston, Minneapolis, Dallas.

5. How do the following affect air travel: class; overbooking; the type of airline, such as major versus commuter?

NAME   DATE

It's All About You Questions

1. Which seat do you prefer on a flight: window or aisle, toward the front or toward the back? Why?

2. What was the worst flight you ever had? What made it awful? Or have you never had a bad flight?

3. While on a flight, what do you generally do?

Activity 1: What's It Like?

Interview someone you know who does a lot of business traveling. What do they like about it? What don't they like? Describe their responses to the following questions:

1. What do you like most about business travel?

2. What don't you like about it?

3. How has business travel changed since 9/11?

NAME   DATE

Activity 2: Flying the Net

Here's your chance to compare three Web sites that consumers regularly use to book flights. Visit the Web sites and answer the following questions for each one:

Expedia (http://www.expedia.com)

1. What do you feel is its greatest strength?

2. What do you think is its greatest weakness?

3. What do you feel is its most unique feature?

Travelocity (http://www.travelocity.com)

1. What do you feel is its greatest strength?

2. What do you think is its greatest weakness?

3. What do you feel is its most unique feature?

Orbitz (http://www.orbitz.com)

1. What do you feel is its greatest strength?

2. What do you think is its greatest weakness?

3. What do you feel is its most unique feature?

Gale Hospitality, Tourism and Leisure Database Assignment

The following assignment requires access to the Gale Hospitality, Tourism and Leisure Database. Check with your instructor to see if you have access to this database.

Find the article *The Airline Dictionary (Marc My Words)* on the Gale Hospitality, Tourism & Leisure Collection.

- Which five of the items listed did you find the most amusing? How would you explain the humor in each to someone who had never flown in an airliner?

- Which five items did you *not* understand? Try to figure out what each refers to by skimming the next chapter or any other resources available to you.

3

Taking to the Skies: Airports, Airfares, and Airline Tickets

KEY TERMS

- Airport management
- Change fee
- Computer Reservation System
- Confirmed reservation
- Consolidator
- Customs
- Electronic ticket
- Fixed-base operators
- Gate check
- Global Distribution System
- Immigration
- Jetway
- Passenger Name Record
- Promotional fare
- Rate desk
- Record locator number
- Revenue ticket
- Service animals
- Skycap
- Standby passenger
- Unaccompanied minors
- Unrestricted fare
- Waitlist

After studying this chapter, you'll be able to:

- Describe what factors affect airfares
- Decipher the codes of major airports
- Describe airport procedures

Photo courtesy of Helen Brixey and JCPenney Portrait Studio

Helen Brixey

CURRENT POSITION/TITLE:

Training Design Specialist at American Express Company – Consumer Travel Network

EDUCATION:

Standish Travel School

FIRST JOB IN TRAVEL/HOSPITALITY INDUSTRY:

Reservations Agent for Eastern Airlines in Boston

FIRST PAID JOB (IF DIFFERENT FROM ABOVE):

Cashier – Star Market

FAVORITE PART OF WHAT I DO:

Being able to use my creativity and imagination to design training courses that help make our Travel Counselors extraordinary.

THING I WISH I DIDN'T HAVE TO DO:

My monthly expense report.

SOMEONE WHO INSPIRES ME:

My parents – they are great role models.

BEST CAREER MEMORY I HAVE:

When I worked for Eastern Airlines, I had the chance to fly in the cockpit jumpseat on an A300 jet between Boston and La Guardia. It was a truly amazing, once-in-a-lifetime experience.

STRANGEST OR FUNNIEST CAREER-RELATED THING I'VE EVER EXPERIENCED:

Attending a team-building event with my American Express colleagues, I learned how to drive a racecar at the Skip Barber Racing School.

FAVORITE QUOTE:

Don't be part of the problem; be part of the solution.

SOMETHING ALMOST NO ONE KNOWS ABOUT ME:

As a teenager, I was a classically trained ballet dancer and always thought that would be my career.

f the Wright Brothers were to somehow fast-forward to our time, they would be in shock. Instead of remote fields of dust, grass, and tar, they'd find that tiny airstrips had become vast airports, each with its own fire and police departments, dozens of food services, stores, and shops of all kinds, covering many square miles, with a workforce in the thousands, surrounded by dozens of hotels, car rental lots, and parking facilities. Even more astonishing to them would be the fact that the largest airports handle hundreds of flights each day.

The Airport Experience

What do today's major airports feature? To find out, let's follow the typical passenger arriving for a flight. First, the traveler parks at a lot or structure, perhaps owned by the airport, perhaps independent. The other possibility is that he arrives in a taxi, bus, shuttle, subway, or train, or maybe a friend drops him off.

At *curbside*, he's able to give his luggage to a **skycap** (*a luggage handler at curbside*) and avoid waiting in line at the check-in counter within the airport. (The skycap expects a tip.) But no, instead he decides to go inside the *terminal* and wait in the regular line. Too bad he's not in first or business class. These often have their own check-in lines, which usually are shorter. After about a 15-minute wait, a *customer service representative* calls him over. The traveler thought about going in the automated, do-it-yourself check-in line—such self-service kiosks are now common—but he likes that personal touch. The service rep asks to see his photo ID, prints him a *boarding pass* (or has him do it on a kiosk at the check-in counter), asks the passenger to take his checked luggage to a security screener (or takes it from the passenger and sends it off to the screener), and directs him toward the *gate* from which his flight will depart.

The passenger strolls off and, because he has 90 minutes before his flight departs, decides to buy a bagel at a store in the terminal. He then heads to security, where he must show his boarding pass and photo ID, have his small carry-on bag scanned through an x-ray machine, and pass through a metal detector or imaging device. He may be pulled aside for a more detailed security check, including having a wandlike device passed over him or a physical pat-down to detect anything illegal, such as a weapon. The contents of his carry-on bag may be examined too. (See Figure 3–1 for a sample airport floor plan.)

The security check is over, so he continues on. He passes a bookstore and buys a newspaper. This airport has stores and food services both before and after the security screening. He gets to the gate, sits down (no need to check in again at the gate), and waits for boarding to commence, usually 30 to 45 minutes before flight departure. The passengers are asked to board by row numbers, starting from the back of the plane. He's in the second group called (rows 42 to 30), again shows his boarding pass, and gets onto the jet, where he settles into his assigned window seat.

insider info
Some car rental lots are a short walk from an airport terminal; others require a shuttle bus to get to them.

insider info
At some airports, a first- or business-class ticket may permit you to use a special, shorter security line.

insider info
For most flights you can preprint your boarding pass at the airline's Web site, usually within 24 hours of your departure. If you have no luggage to check, you can then bypass the airline check-in counter, go through the security check, and proceed to your departure gate. Many airlines now allow passengers to "load their boarding passes" onto their mobile phones.

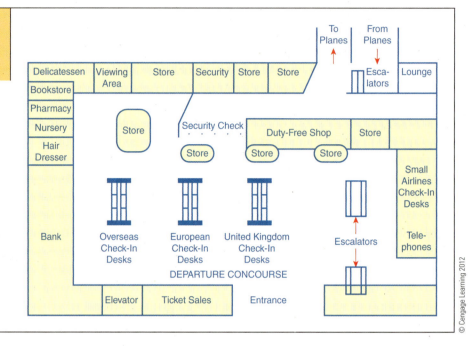

FIGURE 3–1
Floor plan of an airport's departures area.

© Cengage Learning 2012

After an uneventful flight, he exits the plane as he entered it: along a **jetway** corridor, *a moveable device that connects the aircraft to the terminal*. He follows the signs to *baggage claim*. His luggage comes off the *baggage carousel* after a modest 10-minute wait.

If our imaginary passenger had been on an international flight, his arrival would have been a bit more complicated (Figure 3–2). He would have had to show his passport and gone through **Immigration** and **Customs**. (Immigration deals with *people-related factors* such as citizenship, purpose of the trip, and so on. Customs deals with *things* such as items purchased abroad.)

For simplicity's sake, we've left out several steps, details, and complexities in our little scenario. Compare it with your own experiences at the airport to "fill in the blanks" of the typical flight experience.

Airport and Aviation Management

It's hard to conceive of how huge, complex, and interdependent the network of airport and aviation-related businesses is. Let's divide it into four groups: airport management, fixed-base operators, airport ancillary services, and government organizations.

- **Airport management** *concerns itself with making the operations of an airport efficient, safe, and profitable* (or at least break even). It must serve the needs—sometimes conflicting—of travelers, tenants (the airlines and airport shops),

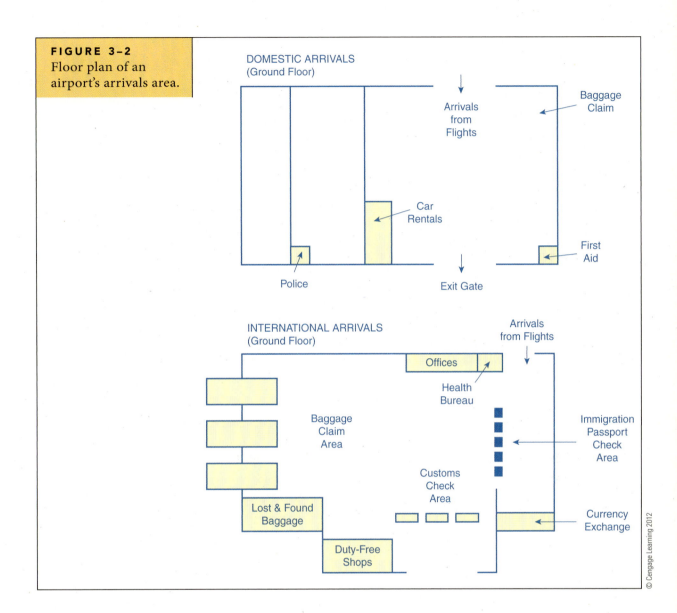

FIGURE 3–2
Floor plan of an
airport's arrivals area.

government entities, and the airport's nearby community. Most of the time, airports belong to a municipal government, but occasionally they're operated as private businesses. Among the duties of airport management personnel are administration, operations, marketing, finances, maintenance, interterminal transportation, safety, security, policing, firefighting, and noise abatement.

- **Fixed-base operators** (FBOs) are *companies that provide ground services and support to the aviation industry*. These businesses provide aircraft inspection, repair, and maintenance (for airlines that do not have their own maintenance programs at the airport), pilot training, aircraft sales and rentals, de-icing services, and aircraft cabin cleaning services. Their trade association is the National Air Transportation Association (NATA).

Do You Know the Code?

For ticketing and air traffic control purposes, each of the world's airports and cities has a three-letter code assigned to it. Cities with only one airport usually have the same code for both the city and the airport. A city with multiple airports has both a city code *and* a code for each airport that serves it. So, for example, the code for New York City is NYC; its three major airports are La Guardia (LGA), Kennedy (JFK), and Newark Liberty (EWR).

For some airports, the code's source is obvious, but in other cases, it's obscure. LGA is clearly derived from La Guardia. Kennedy is a little more subtle: JFK is named for president John Fitzgerald Kennedy. Newark Liberty's source is unknown to most people: EWR are three letters in Newark.

Here's a code list for North America's biggest airports:

• Acapulco, Mexico	ACA	• Milwaukee, Wisconsin	MKE
• Atlanta, Georgia	ATL	• Minneapolis, Minnesota	MSP
• Baltimore, Maryland	BWI	• Montego Bay, Jamaica	MBJ
• Bermuda	BDA	• Montreal, Quebec, Canada	YUL
• Boston, Massachusetts	BOS	• Nassau, Bahamas	NAS
• Calgary, Alberta, Canada	YYC	• New Orleans, Louisiana	MSY
• Cancun, Mexico	CUN	• Oakland, California	OAK
• Chicago, Illinois (O'Hare)	ORD	• Orlando, Florida	MCO
• Cincinnati, Ohio	CVG	• Ottawa, Ontario, Canada	YOW
• Charlotte, North Carolina	CLT	• Philadelphia, Pennsylvania	PHL
• Cleveland, Ohio	CLE	• Phoenix, Arizona	PHX
• Dallas, Texas	DFW	• Pittsburgh, Pennsylvania	PIT
• Denver, Colorado	DEN	• Salt Lake City, Utah	SLC
• Detroit, Michigan	DTW	• San Diego, California	SAN
• Fort Lauderdale, Florida	FLL	• San Francisco, California	SFO
• Honolulu, Hawaii	HNL	• San Juan, Puerto Rico	SJU
• Houston (Bush Intercontinental), Texas	IAH	• Seattle, Washington	SEA
• Kansas City, Missouri	MCI	• St. Louis, Missouri	STL
• Las Vegas, Nevada	LAS	• Tampa, Florida	TPA
• Los Angeles, California	LAX	• Toronto, Ontario, Canada (Pearson)	YYZ
• Memphis, Tennessee	MEM	• Vancouver, British Columbia, Canada	YVR
• Mexico City, Mexico	MEX	• Washington, D.C. (Dulles)	IAD
• Miami, Florida	MIA	• Washington, D.C. (Reagan National)	DCA

- **Airport ancillary services** consist of just about every other airport-related supplier you can think of. Some are based on-site at the airport (such as airline caterers, stores, restaurants, and private security firms); others are based partially or completely off-site (such as taxis, shuttle and limo services, airport hotels, car rental firms, and bus companies).

Modern airports, like the Dubai Airport shown here, often feature dramatic architecture.

- **Government organizations** can be the cities or counties that own the airports (including their police). However, the government entity that has the most crucial presence at airports is the FAA. The FAA monitors the air travel system to ensure safety and manages the airspace above the United States (primarily through their air traffic control facilities). Another subsidiary of the Department of Transportation is the TSA, which helps keep airports and flights safe.

This system describes how airport and aviation management operates in the United States. Most major nations have very similar systems to that in place in the United States.

Airfares

Navigating your way through an airport and exploring its many businesses is easy compared to finding your way through the thicket of airfares that face a would-be traveler, even for a simple trip. For example, on any given flight, odds are that one passenger may have paid $300, the person sitting next to him $700, and the person next to her $1,200. In fact, it's theoretically possible that every single person on the flight has paid a different fare.

To help clarify things, let's look at some of the factors that influence what you pay for a flight:

- **If you're traveling on a full-coach fare.** Coach fares that aren't eligible for any discounts (and that could cost nearly as much as a business- or first-class fare) are usually **unrestricted fares**, meaning that you *can make changes to* *your itinerary without incurring a penalty. Fares that have been discounted* are usually called **promotional fares**. These types of fares almost always apply to coach only, though occasionally airlines discount first- or business-class fares. (See the This & That box "Great Fare, But There's a Catch" for more information on promotional fare restrictions.)

- **How far in advance you buy the ticket.** Generally, the farther in advance you buy, the less you pay. Tickets purchased less than, say, seven days before the flight will be charged at full fare. (An exception: a few last-minute seats may be available at a deep discount on the airline's Web site.) Just making a reservation, by the way, doesn't lock in the price. The price becomes guaranteed only when the ticket is actually purchased. What if the price goes *down* after you bought it? You *may* be able to change your ticket, but in most cases the airline will apply a **change fee** (*a fee to change the reservation*) that costs more than the difference in price. Also, some airlines will issue a credit for the difference—to be applied to a future flight—rather than refund any money.

- **What class of service you bought.** Coach almost always costs less than premium coach, premium coach less than business, and business less than first. Remember, though, that the difference between full-fare coach and business or first may not be that much.

- **Whom you bought it from, or how.** The majority of all airline tickets are bought through travel agencies, both brick-and-mortar and online. However, because most airlines no longer pay travel agencies a commission for the sale, agencies usually add a service fee to the cost of the ticket. Because travel agents are generally more adept than consumers at finding the best fares available, buying a ticket from an agency, even with the service fee tacked on, may save the traveler money. Buying through a cruise line or tour operator may result in a special airfare too.

Some airlines offer low, Internet-only fares on their Web sites. The idea is that because no employee directly aids the process, the cost to the airline

What Will They Do Next?

Hard to believe, but some airlines have actually considered installing pay toilets on aircraft, charging passengers by weight, and offering standing-room seating (the passenger would strap into a bulkhead-supported semi-seated position). Among the things airlines now charge extra for: checked luggage, meals, blankets, pillows, coach seats toward the front of the aircraft, non-middle seats, credit card purchases, video entertainment, advance seat assignments, extra legroom, overhead luggage space, and printing boarding passes (even if you print out the pass on your home computer). These fees usually apply only to coach passengers.

of providing the ticket in this self-service way is much lower. However, if you purchase a deeply discounted ticket, you sometimes may not be eligible for frequent-flyer miles or may not be able to get your seat assignment in advance.

If an airline is having trouble selling seats, it sometimes sells them through **consolidators**, *companies that specialize in unsold air inventory*. Consolidators are the equivalent of outlet stores that sell shirts or other goods that the manufacturer is having difficulty moving. International flights are more commonly sold through consolidators than are domestic ones.

- **What add-on taxes and fees there are.** Fuel surcharges, segment taxes, departure taxes, airport taxes, security fees, and service fees—all these and more may be tacked on to the base fare.

- **If there's a "fare war" going on.** Occasionally, airlines discover that their product may not be selling as well as they would like. One airline then drops its fares, either on all or on selected flights. The other carriers will quickly jump in and match these prices. A "war" of promotional fares has begun.

- **Which airports are involved.** You would think that flights into or out of airports in the same vicinity would cost the same. Not true. A flight from Dallas to Ft. Lauderdale might cost a lot less than one to Miami, just a few dozen miles from Ft Lauderdale. It all depends on supply, demand, and competition.

- **Which routes are involved.** A flight of 2,000 miles should cost more than one of 1,000 miles, right? Not necessarily. It's sometimes far more expensive, for example, to fly from Seattle to Chicago than from Seattle to Washington, D.C., which is a thousand miles farther than Chicago. Again, it has to do with supply, demand, and competition.

- **What time you're flying.** Maybe the 10 a.m. flight from San Francisco to Atlanta is nearly sold out (so the prices on the few remaining seats are costly), but the 7 a.m. flight or even the 12:30 a.m. red-eye flight will be a lot less expensive because fewer people are booked on those flights.

- **Which airline is involved.** Low-fare airlines usually offer better deals than do their competitors, especially on last-minute flights. However, some of these airlines, like Ireland's *Ryanair*, charge extra fees for many services that other airlines include in their fares.

- **How many passengers are traveling.** Airlines sometimes offer "two-for-one" sales or similar promotions. A large group (usually 15 or more) sometimes can negotiate a reduced per-person rate or one free ticket.

- **If an international flight is involved.** International flights, like domestic ones, are often calculated based on routes. But in some cases, especially when multiple stops are involved, fares are based on *mileage*. Computations can become so complicated that airlines maintain **rate desks**, *staffed by people who specialize in international fares, to help calculate the cost of the ticket.*

You Have a Point . . .

Virtually every airline has a frequent-flyer loyalty program. Members of these programs receive points, usually one point per mile flown on a **revenue ticket,** that is, *a ticket that's paid for.* Free tickets and certain specially priced promotional tickets don't yield frequent-flyer points or miles. Points aren't accrued only from flying: you can get points from staying at a partner hotel or renting from a partner car rental agency, for example. You can even have a credit card that yields one point per dollar charged on anything, not just travel-related products.

Once you reach certain thresholds (for example, 25,000 miles for a domestic coach ticket, 60,000 miles for an international one), you can "buy" an award ticket (get a free flight) with your points. If you're just short of the mileage you need, you may be able to purchase miles, at two to three cents per mile. One caveat: only a certain number of seats on each flight are eligible for lowest mileage awards. When those seats are gone, you can usually book a seat for twice as many miles (for example, 50,000 miles for a domestic ticket).You also may be able to

purchase a coach ticket and use your miles to upgrade to business or first class. Often, though, deeply discounted coach fares don't qualify for upgrades, or you must pay a fee in addition to your miles.

Ironically, mileage plans were conceived of as loyalty programs, which would cause consumers to limit their purchases to one airline. What actually happened: travelers built up points on multiple airlines, with only some brand loyalty driving their buying decisions.

Points do expire if they're not used after a certain amount of time or if the customer doesn't accrue more points within, say, 18 months.

If consumers decided to cash in all their mileage points at once, it would probably destroy the airline industry. There are *billions* of miles "banked" in frequent-flyer accounts that have yet to be used and have not yet expired. Every now and then, airlines approach their governments to make frequent-flyer rules more flexible (such as having points expire quickly). The airlines usually are turned down—in part, perhaps, because lawmakers fly a lot and rack up huge amounts of points.

- **Whom you work for.** It's quite common for the airlines to offer special, prenegotiated *contract fares* to large companies.

- **If you belong to a special group.** Called "status fares," these have become increasingly rare. Some examples (depending on the airline) are *senior fares* (aged 65 and over), *youth passes* (aged 21 and under), *children's fares* (aged 11 and under), *infant fares* (aged 2 and under), *bereavement fares* (passengers traveling because of a death in the family), and *military fares* (for service personnel and their families). Similar to these are special fares for people attending a conference. (Unlike most other status fares, these conference rates are still commonly offered.)

- **If you're a travel professional.** Airline employees usually fly free or almost free on their own airline and get as much as 90 percent off on other carriers. Travel agents usually receive 75 percent off full fares, but they must have a special card issued by IATAN that's given only to travel agents who meet certain IATAN criteria and who sell enough airline tickets to warrant this discount.

Great Fare, But There's a Catch

THIS & that

At certain times of the year, airlines sometimes wish to spark sales on certain routes, to compete with another airline or for any of a dozen other reasons. In other words, *they put on a sale*. Many of the situations described in these pages involve promotional fares such as this. But there's a catch. Many, in fact. They're called *restrictions*. Almost all promotional fares have them. Here are some possible examples:

- You must stay over a Saturday night. Much less common than it used to be, this practice helps filter out business travelers, who usually want to return home on weekends and are less price-sensitive than leisure travelers, who are paying for their trips out of their own pockets (not those of their employers) and generally include weekend days in their vacation.

- You must reserve and pay for your ticket a certain number of days in advance of the flight.

- You may stay at your destination no longer than 30 days.

- Your travel must start by a certain date and finish by another date.

- There's a $100 fee to make any changes to your flight itinerary, or the entire ticket's value is lost if you don't take the flight.

- You must fly on only one airline for your entire trip.

- Your itinerary must be round-trip.

- Your ticket is nonrefundable.

- You must be a certain astrological sign. (Just kidding.)

By the way, the airlines give each fare a special code. Typical codes are Y for coach, C for business class, and F for first class. A series of numbers and/or letters may be attached to this code to further define the specific fare that applies. For example, K14NR represents a discounted coach fare that was purchased at least 14 days in advance and is nonrefundable.

Fares and Ticketing

You have no doubt concluded the obvious: airfares are complicated. Fortunately, computers help make the task manageable. Consumers are able to sift through a multitude of fares on the Internet (or, more accurately, use the operating software resources of a site that manages it for them) and usually can find an acceptable route, time, and deal.

If you ever go to work for an airline or a travel agency, you'll probably take courses that will make you far more proficient than a layperson. You'll learn how to do your bookings using the Internet or an industry system called the **Computer Reservation System** (**CRS**) or **Global Distribution System** (**GDS**). A CRS/GDS system allows you to book not only airline tickets but also hotels, tours, cruises, car rentals, and many other travel products.

Shopping has become important to the airport experience.

You should know at least a few commonly used terms relating to reservations and ticketing:

- *The reservation system's record of a booking* is called the **Passenger Name Record** (**PNR**). This computer file lists the client's name, flight number, travel times, travel dates, airline used, ticket cost, and a **record locator number**, which consists of *six numbers and/or letters that identify the reservation.* This is also sometimes called the *confirmation number* or the *reservation number.* Other optional information can be entered into the PNR as well.

- Tickets are rarely printed on paper or cardstock, as they were in the past. Although this option is sometimes available (usually at an extra cost), most tickets today are **electronic tickets**, or *e-tickets,* which *exist only as a computer record*, much like a hotel or car rental reservation. When passengers arrive at the airport, they give their name or record locator number. A boarding pass is then printed for them, either at the check-in counter, through a self-service kiosk, or by the skycap. Most airlines allow passengers to check in for their flight and print their boarding passes from their home computers before leaving for the airport.

- *Once a reservation is entered into the airline's computer system*, it's said to be a **confirmed reservation**. If it cannot be entered because the desired flight is fully booked, the traveler can ask to be placed on the **waitlist**, in case a seat becomes available. If cancellations on the desired flight do occur, the person may *clear the waitlist* and be offered a confirmed reservation by phone or e-mail. Generally, waitlisted passengers take a reserved confirmation on an alternate flight in case they don't clear the waitlist. Your position on the waitlist is based on *when* you were put on it and, more important, what kind of fare you paid. A person who bought a full-fare ticket of $1,300 will probably clear the waitlist before someone with a $300 promotional ticket, even if the person with the $300 ticket was waitlisted much earlier.

Who Sells Airline Tickets?

By now you should have figured out who sells airline tickets; in other words, how the product is distributed. Let's summarize it all here. The prime suppliers of airline tickets, of course, are the airlines themselves, but—surprising to most people—airlines are not the major *distributors*: travel agencies are. Eventually, this may change. Because most airlines no longer pay commissions to travel agencies for selling their product, agencies find it difficult to make a profit selling flights—and some price-sensitive consumers resent paying the extra service fees that most agencies must charge to make a profit on selling airline tickets. It should be noted, though, that airlines do rather confidentially continue to provide commissions or tickets at reduced cost to mega-agency chains, including online ones, and to large individual agencies that do considerable business with them.

How do the airlines distribute tickets? Tickets are distributed through toll-free reservation numbers, the Internet, and at airport ticket counters. Other distributors

Baggage claim at a major airport.

© Jonathan Feinstein/www.Shutterstock.com

Careers

Careers Relating to Airports, Airfares, and Air Tickets

Here are the most typical jobs relating to airports, airfares, and air tickets:

- Senior executives, directors, and managers
- Reservationists
- Ticketing/gate agents
- Customer service representatives
- Dispatchers
- Accountants
- District sales representatives
- Flight attendants
- Maintenance personnel
- Air traffic controllers
- Shuttle drivers

- Pilots
- Clerical support
- Rate desk agents
- Crew schedulers
- Airport ground crew
- Human resources/training specialists
- Security/safety personnel (TSA and private)
- Sky marshals
- Baggage handlers
- Dining and store personnel

of airline tickets include consolidators, tour operators, rail companies, and cruise lines. Sometimes tickets sold by such intermediaries carry special restrictions: they don't allow advance seat assignment, for example, or yield no frequent-flyer miles.

More This and That

Here are some miscellaneous things you need to know about air travel:

- Smoking is permitted on only a few airlines, mostly foreign ones.

- *Jet lag* is the psychological and physiological discomfort caused by flying long distances over multiple time zones. The body's "internal clock" becomes confused and causes the traveler to feel tired at odd times during the day (or to remain awake late at night). Usually the effect is more pronounced when traveling from west to east.

- *Jet streams* are bands of high-level wind that flow from west to east. This is why flights going from west to east take less time than those going from east to west. Jet streams are often featured on TV weather maps.

- A waitlisted person can choose to go to the airport and be listed as a **standby passenger** for a certain flight. If there are enough no-shows, the standby passenger may get on his or her desired flight. (Some airlines do not accept standby passengers.) Another scenario: a passenger gets to the airport early (or late); he can be a standby passenger for a flight other than the one on which he has a reservation. In some cases, customers with nonrefundable tickets are not allowed to stand by for alternate flights. Some airlines charge passengers a standby fee.

- Most passengers in first or business class are flying free on mileage awards, are airline employees, or have upgraded from coach—with miles, for a fee, or because of high frequent-flyer status.

- Though they may still offer pretzels and soft drinks at no charge, most airlines no longer serve free meals on flights. This has created an opportunity for airport food vendors, who sell packaged meals for passengers to take onboard. Many airlines do *sell* packaged meals or snacks during the flight. Free meals, however, continue to be part of the flight experience for passengers in first class, business class, and in coach on long, international flights.

- Many airlines and airports will make special arrangements for people with physical disabilities, **unaccompanied minors** (*children flying alone*), pets, **service animals** (*animals that provide a service to a person,* for example, seeing-eye dogs), and people with special meal requirements (for example, vegetarian or kosher meals).

- Shipping cargo is a significant source of added revenue for many airlines. In addition to passenger luggage, carriers usually transport all sorts of commercial

insider info

The earlier in the day the flight is, the more likely it will depart on time.

Rules and More Rules

All sorts of rules—some governmental, some airline-generated—apply to certain unusual situations. For example, as you learned in Chapter 2, if a passenger with a confirmed reservation checks in at least 20 to 30 minutes before the flight but cannot be accommodated (is bumped), then government regulations require that the airline get that passenger to his or her destination within an hour of the originally scheduled time (on its own plane or another airline's). If the airline fails to do so, it must award the passenger *denied boarding compensation*, usually several hundred dollars. However, if the traveler does not get to the destination on time (or at all) because of weather, security alerts, airport problems, or other similar factors beyond the airline's control, the airline has no obligation to pay denied boarding compensation. It will try, however, to get passengers to their destinations in a reasonable time and may even pay for overnight accommodations, if necessary.

shipments in the hold of their passenger aircraft. Many all-cargo and overnight delivery services (for example, FedEx) have fleets of aircraft that arrive and depart from most of the world's major airports. Most airlines charge a fee to coach passengers for luggage they check, and rules for carry-on luggage size is strictly regulated.

- What if baggage is lost? The airline will endeavor to find the luggage. If it can't, it has to compensate the passenger, with the amount due varying from situation to situation. Lost luggage also may be covered by the passenger's insurance or credit card benefits. By the way, baggage is seldom permanently lost. It is usually found and delivered to the passenger within a day or two.

- What if the luggage is damaged? The airline may pay to fix it or even replace it, but the key word is *may*. It is not required to do so.

- CRS/GDSs and airline Web sites show on-time percentages, information about which flights are usually on time and which ones are typically late.

- Club lounges are special "private" areas at an airport terminal, usually operated by one airline or a group of airlines, which offer more comfortable seating, snacks, beverages, business facilities, even shower facilities for long-distance travelers who are connecting and have enough "layover" time. To be admitted to such a lounge if you're on a domestic flight, you must buy a membership (usually about $500 per year) or a one-day pass (usually $50). If you're flying business or first class on an international flight, you are usually automatically

Passengers with carry-on luggage.

admitted, even without membership. Some airlines permit their frequent flyers to use airline miles to purchase a club membership. A few premium credit cards include club membership as one of their benefits.

- Most airlines have rules for checked luggage. Generally, a passenger can check one or, more often, two standard suitcases for a fee, but rules about weight and dimensions may come into play. Sometimes the airlines enforce these rules, sometimes they don't. When they do, an *additional* fee may be charged for oversized or overweight baggage. One invariable: each piece of luggage must have an ID tag on the outside, with the passenger's name and address.

- Most airlines permit two carry-ons: one that fits under the seat in front of you and one that goes in the overhead bin. (Sometimes you're allowed one carry-on and one "personal item," such as a purse, briefcase, or laptop computer.) If the plane is expected to run close to or at full passenger capacity, gate agents can limit this to one carry-on only and have you *check in the second piece at the gate* (called a **gate check**).

- Most hotels near airports and all car rental companies at the airport provide free shuttle service to and from their locations, if needed. To get to more distant city locations, travelers need to take taxis, shuttles, buses, or, in some cases, rail or subway lines.

THIS & that

The Perfect Airport

There's no such thing as a perfect airport, but some are definitely better than others. What makes one airport better than another? Here are some criteria:

- Easy access into and out of the airport (road or rail)
- Convenient parking, both on-site and off-site
- Good traffic flow to and within the airport
- Easy movement between terminals and among gates (moving sidewalks, monorails, etc.)
- A hotel on-site and more near the airport
- Plenty of dining and shopping outlets
- Swift moving lines at security
- Clear public address systems

- Check-in kiosks at multiple locations
- Plenty of luggage carts—preferably at no cost
- Dependable Wi-Fi service
- Plenty of seating at gates
- Clear and convenient signage
- Terminals that feel spacious and are well lit
- Friendly and helpful staff
- Good safety protocols
- Swift luggage delivery to the claim area

Review Questions

1. Define each of the following: skycap; boarding pass; gate; jetway; carousel; immigration; customs.

2. What are the airport codes for the following airports: Los Angeles; Miami; Chicago (O'Hare); Orlando; Washington, D.C. (Dulles); Detroit; Baltimore; Minneapolis?

3. List at least 10 factors that affect airfares.

4. What do airlines do if each of the following occurs?

   a. Your luggage is lost.

   b. Your luggage arrives damaged.

   c. You arrive at the gate 45 minutes before departure but the plane you're scheduled to fly on is already full.

   d. You're a vegetarian.

5. Define the following: club lounge, jet lag, PNR, e-ticket, CRS/GDS, revenue ticket, promotional fare, consolidator.

It's All About You Questions

Look over the "Perfect Airport" This & That. What three features do you appreciate most when you go to an airport? Why? Would you add anything to this list?

Activity 1: What's Your Priority?

Everyone has a different priority as to what is most important. If you were to fly on a red-eye next week from your city to Paris, France, what would you consider most valuable? Some potential factors are on the left. Rate them from 1 (not at all important) to 5 (extremely important) in the right-hand column.

Factors	Your rating of these factors
Pitch between seats	
Recline of seat	
Good on-time performance of your flight	
Nonstop flight, rather than a direct or connecting one	
Price of ticket	
Type of aircraft used	
The possibility that you can upgrade with your mileage	
Whether there will be in-flight movies	
Pleasant experience on a previous flight you had with that airline	

Now explain in one paragraph how you came to your decisions rating the factors.

Activity 2: Getting to Africa

Using the Internet, or any source available to you, figure out the best routes that could get you from the airport nearest your city to Cape Town, South Africa. Try to set up the fewest connections possible, even a nonstop flight if you can find one. Leave your airport on January 23 and return from Cape Town on February 17. Be sure to include (a) the cities involved in the trip, (b) the airlines and flight numbers involved, and (c) the departure and arrival times. Try to keep the itinerary on one or two airlines only. Here is a fictitious example.

Outbound itinerary:
1. Lufthansa Flight #261: Depart Los Angeles, January 23, 2:45 p.m.; arrive Frankfurt, January 23, 10:30 a.m.

2. Lufthansa Flight #535: Depart Frankfurt, January 23, 10:15 p.m.; arrive Cape Town, January 24, 9:30 a.m.

Return itinerary:
1. Lufthansa Flight #579: Depart Cape Town, February 16, 7:50 p.m.; arrive Frankfurt, February 17, 5:10 a.m.

2. Lufthansa Flight #456: Depart Frankfurt, February 17, 10:00 a.m.; arrive Los Angeles, February 17, 12:30 p.m.

A. Outbound:

B. Return:

•   Which Web site(s) or other resources did you use to complete this activity?

•   What criteria did you use to decide on the *best* route?

•   What was the hardest thing about this activity?

•   What was the most interesting thing you learned?

Gale Hospitality, Tourism and Leisure Database Assignment

The following assignment requires access to the Gale Hospitality, Tourism and Leisure Database. Check with your instructor to see if you have access to this database.

Find the article *New Ideas in Retail: Innovation Key to Revenue Generation* in the Gale Hospitality, Tourism & Leisure Collection. *Retail concessions* is the term used for stores, food venues, and similar facilities at airport terminals. Dr. Patricia Ryan suggests that airport officials should decide which retailers should have space at their airports, that they should "take the time to sit and watch customers."

- What would *you* typically buy—and not buy—at an airport? Why?

- Later in the article, a debate over "street pricing" occurs, but the term *street pricing* is not defined. What do you think it means? Which side would you take in the discussion? Why?

4

Homes Away from Home: The Hospitality Industry

KEY TERMS

- Adjoining room
- All-inclusive resort
- All-suite hotel
- Amenities
- American Plan
- Bed-and-breakfast
- Bermuda Plan
- Business hotel
- Casino resort
- Concept
- Concierge
- Concierge level
- Connecting room
- Continental Plan
- Convention and meeting hotel
- Converted hotel
- Corporate rate
- Day rate
- European Plan
- Folio
- Food services
- Hotel
- Hotel occupancy
- Hotel representative firm
- Inventory
- Junior suite
- Mega-resort
- Modified American Plan
- Property
- Rack rate
- Resort hotel
- Room service
- Run-of-the-house rate
- Ski resort
- Spa resort
- Themed resort
- Walking the guest

After studying this chapter, you'll be able to:

- Classify the many kinds of lodging

- Define key terms used in the lodging industry

- Explain the many factors that determine the cost of lodging

- Describe how lodging is sold

- Explain how the food services industry relates to hospitality, travel, and tourism

Photo courtesy of Julius W. Robinson

Julius W. Robinson

CURRENT POSITION/TITLE:

Vice President Operations, Fairfield Inn & Suites by Marriott

SHORT DESCRIPTION OF WHAT YOUR RESPONSIBILITIES ARE:

Lead operations and growth for one of Marriott's largest and fastest-growing brands

EDUCATION:

BA, Rutgers University; MBA, Smith Business School, University of Maryland

FIRST JOB IN TRAVEL/HOSPITALITY INDUSTRY:

Reservations Sales Agent

FIRST PAID JOB (IF DIFFERENT FROM ABOVE):

Hardware Department Associate, local store

FAVORITE PART OF WHAT I DO:

Engaging our guests, associates, and franchise partners daily to exceed expectations

THING I WISH I DIDN'T HAVE TO DO:

Making cuts to staff

SOMEONE WHO INSPIRES ME:

My father, now retired

BEST CAREER MEMORY I HAVE:

As Vice President of Global Sales, congratulating my team for winning Global Sales Team of the Year

STRANGEST OR FUNNIEST CAREER-RELATED THING I'VE EVER EXPERIENCED:

Joining the paparazzi on the red carpet at the Oscars

FAVORITE QUOTE:

"Measure twice, cut once."

SOMETHING ALMOST NO ONE KNOWS ABOUT ME:

I don't eat my Brussels sprouts.

Think of your home. Wouldn't it be nice if you didn't have to make your bed each morning, if someone else did it for you? And that someone would clean your bathroom daily, replacing used towels with fresh, fluffy ones. Your room would have a wide-screen high-definition TV, with cable service, of course, and air conditioning too. And suppose you wanted breakfast in bed? With a simple phone call, someone would prepare it for you and bring it to your bedroom within 30 minutes.

Unless you're extremely wealthy, the scenario you just read will remain a fantasy, except when you're staying at a hotel. Hotels treat guests like royalty, providing the kinds of service and amenities that we're highly unlikely to experience in our everyday lives. When well maintained and operated, a hotel becomes a splendid, comforting, and dreamlike home away from home for its guests.

In a way, the food services industry—which is often included, along with lodging, in the hospitality sector—also provides a home away from home. Better: it provides a kitchen and dining room away from home, where other people cook the food, serve the meal, and even clean the dishes for you.

Kinds of Accommodations

A hotel seems like an easy thing to define, doesn't it? But think again. There are so many kinds of hotels that to pin down one single definition is a challenge. In fact, most industry professionals prefer two synonyms to the word *hotel*: *lodging* and *accommodations*. These words embrace a broader spectrum of possibilities, and, as you'll see, you need that kind of flexibility to accommodate the diverse kinds of lodging that exist. Note also that people within the travel industry often refer to specific lodging facilities as **properties** (as in "Disney has many great properties in Orlando"), and they refer to their customers as *guests*. Finally, lodging is often considered a part of the larger hospitality industry, which, as you've learned, also covers dining services and theme parks.

Hotels

Let's start with lodging categories that *do* fit within the "hotel" concept. And let's define a **hotel** this way: *a structure that provides sleeping accommodations to travelers and that usually features dining facilities and daily housekeeping service*. So which categories fit within this definition? Let's look at three of the most important types of hotels: resort, business, and all-suite.

Resort Hotels

Resort hotels *cater primarily to leisure travelers*. They're generally found in four environments: at beaches, near ski areas, in the desert, and near (or even in) theme parks and attractions. They usually have facilities for recreational activities, such as a swimming pool, tennis courts, perhaps a golf course, and one or two dining facilities. When *a resort hotel is especially large, with very many facilities and activities covering acres of land*, it's called a **mega-resort**.

A resort that charges one price that includes most or all of the costs of staying there (lodging, some or all meals, activities) is called an **all-inclusive resort**. A **spa resort** *provides extensive facilities for massages, facials, fitness activities, and healthy dining.* A **ski resort** *provides a site and facilities to serve the needs of winter sports enthusiasts.* A **casino resort** *features extensive gaming opportunities in a destination where gambling is legal* (for example, Las Vegas or Native American tribal lands such as those in southeastern Connecticut). Casino hotels are a huge growth area in the lodging industry.

A **themed resort** *has a strong identity, often tied to some other place and time.* The *Venetian* hotel in Las Vegas, for example, re-creates its legendary namesake city (complete with canals and gondolas), and *Disney's Animal Kingdom Lodge* is surrounded by African-style savannahs (in Orlando, Florida!), complete with giraffes, zebras, and other exotic creatures that guests can watch from the lodge's rooms.

Themed lodging properties often are so famous that they're attractions unto themselves. So, too, are **converted hotel**s. In certain situations, old castles, monasteries, or even commercial buildings are reconfigured to accommodate tourists. For example, the *Camino Real* hotel in Oaxaca, Mexico, is a former nunnery; the *Cairo Marriott* has an elegant former palace at its core; and the *London Marriott County Hall* was converted from a portion of a former government office building.

A themed hotel: the Venetian in Las Vegas.

© Gary Paul Lewis/www.Shutterstock.com

Business Hotels

Business, or corporate, **hotels** *target the needs of business travelers*. They generally feature a business center (where guests can send faxes, print documents, make photocopies, arrange package deliveries, and so forth), a small store, and guestrooms with spacious desks, multiple telephones (as well as several phone lines), and sometimes even printer/fax machines and computer terminals. Usually, at least one dining facility is on-site, as well as perhaps a pool and health club (often small). Although these hotels serve the fitness and recreational needs of business travelers, they also are appealing to leisure travelers who might stay at such a property as well (especially on weekends, when rates at business hotels usually are much lower than during the week).

Business hotels tend to be located in city centers, near "business parks" (clusters of buildings housing various companies), and at airports. Such airport hotels are used primarily by business travelers:

- For overnight layovers between two flights that don't connect on the same day

- For times when they have an early morning meeting and need to fly in the night before

- For meetings in which travelers from distant places converge at one geographically central hotel. For example, if a company has major facilities in Denver, Minneapolis, New York, and Tampa, it may decide to fly key employees from all of those locations to Chicago's O'Hare airport for a meeting at the Hilton there.

Another type of business-related lodging is the **convention and meeting hotel**. These hotels have numerous meeting rooms and large ballrooms that can host groups of any size. Convention hotels usually are situated in city centers, in rural locations (where distractions are minimal), or next to (sometimes even connected to) a city's convention center. A large convention center will probably have several hotels within a short distance. They accommodate leisure travelers and tour groups too, although these aren't their prime target market.

All-Suite Hotels

All-suite hotels (*where all accommodations are suites instead of conventional rooms*) have become increasingly popular in the travel marketplace. But first, what's a suite? Traditionally, suites are accommodations with at least two rooms (for example, a bedroom and a living room, with a wall between them). They may also feature kitchen elements. In recent times, hotels began offering *large, oversized rooms* that they also call suites or **junior suites**. These have "separate" sleeping and living areas, although only a curtain, railing, or other barrier may separate the two spaces. In some cases, there's no barrier at all; the suite is just a very big room.

All-suite lodging may be either leisure- or business-oriented, or a mix of the two. Vacationers, especially families, like them because they feature plenty of space.

insider info

Some of the more unusual kinds of lodging: a farm silo, a lighthouse, a decommissioned prison, a cave, a cluster of hammocks high in the trees, and a hotel made entirely of ice.

insider info

Single business travelers often learn to request a room with two double beds instead of one king- or queen-sized bed. The reasons: the room may be larger and the second bed can be used for "staging" business materials and clothes.

insider info

Your best chance of getting upgraded is to arrive very late, when perhaps the only rooms available are suites. It's a dangerous ploy, though: maybe only the *worst* rooms are left—or none at all.

Here are some commonly used lodging industry terms that go beyond what are defined in the main body of the text:

- **Amenities**: In-room or bathroom extras, such as shampoo, a hair dryer, an iron/ironing board, or mouthwash. Amenities also may refer to a hotel's facilities such as a health club, swimming pool, and business center; or a service, such as Wi-Fi, that allows guests to connect wirelessly to the Internet.

- **Rack rate**: A hotel's official, published rate. Travelers usually don't pay the rack rate, however. (A rack rate is like the "suggested retail price.")

- **Folio**: The hotel bill.

- **Inventory**: The number of rooms a hotel has available for occupancy.

- **Day rate**: The cost of renting a room for the day, rather than for overnight. It is used by travelers who need to check out very late or need to rest between flights with long connecting times.

- **Concierge**: A person, usually stationed near the hotel front desk, who helps guests with special requests, such as obtaining theater tickets, booking restaurant reservations, providing transfer services, and giving sightseeing advice. *Concierge* also sometimes refers to a private floor (or floors) with enhanced guestrooms and facilities.

- **Run-of-the-house rate** (**ROH**): A rate guaranteeing that the guest will receive the best room available at check-in. Suites and concierge-level rooms are usually excluded. It may also refer to a flat rate offered to a group, with the understanding that any rooms in the hotel may be assigned to the group members.

- **Room service**: The service that provides in-room dining.

- **Connecting** versus **adjoining rooms**: Connecting rooms are two guestrooms with a door between them that can be opened. Adjoining rooms are guestrooms that are near or next to one another but that do not have a door between them. (These two terms are often confused with each other.)

insider info

Where does the term *rack rate* come from? Before computers, hotels had large wooden racks behind the front desk. Each rack had small open compartments, in room number order. Each compartment contained a little plastic tab that described the room (for example, one or two beds) and listed its official "rack" rate.

Corporate travelers favor them because they provide room for work in a more home-like environment. Some brands that feature all-suite lodging are *Embassy Suites*, *Homewood Suites*, and *SpringHill Suites*.

Remember, too, that you can find suites of all sizes and shapes, not just at all-suite properties but in regular resort and business hotels too. In these cases, suites represent only a small percentage of the accommodations available. The rest are conventional, standard-sized guestrooms.

Other Kinds of Lodging

Certain kinds of properties vary so much from the traditional concept of a hotel that they merit their own categories. Here are 10 alternate types of lodging:

A classic motel-like design.

1. **Motels**: Since the 1920s, motels (also called *motor hotels* or *motor inns*) have been a mainstay of the industry. The idea is to offer inexpensive lodging that's easily accessible to the motoring public. Motels are usually only a few stories high. They often permit access to guestrooms through exterior doors that open onto a parking area, allowing guests to park near their rooms. Motels usually don't have full dining facilities or provide staff to assist with luggage. They're often on or near major highways and roads.

2. **Limited-service lodging**: A hybrid of a hotel and motel, these modestly sized and economically priced properties generally have rooms that open onto an interior hallway rather than to the outside like in a motel. Rooms are simple, with dining usually consisting of continental breakfast only. Limited-service properties, however, tend to be situated near popularly priced restaurants, fast-food outlets, and shopping centers. They may lack pools or exercise facilities. Some examples are *Days Inn* and *Hampton Inn*.

3. **Extended-stay lodging**: Not very well known to the traveling public (but familiar to business travelers), these properties appeal to those who need lodging for a week or more. Accommodations tend to be spacious and often resemble small apartments with kitchenettes. A pool, an exercise facility, and a self-service laundry are common. Some of these properties offer daily housekeeping service, whereas others provide it only once or twice a week. Extended-stay properties attract businesspeople on lengthy business trips, those relocating to a new city, and families. They feature a more home- or apartment-like ambience than do all-suite hotels. Examples are *Residence Inn* and *TownePlace Suites*.

insider info

Connecting rooms are especially popular with families.

4. **Condominiums (condos)**: These apartment-like facilities resemble extended-stay properties. The big difference is that instead of a company owning the lodging, individuals own each unit and also pay fees for upkeep, security, landscaping, and maintenance. But when the condo owners aren't in residence (which could be most of the year), they rent out their units to travelers. Condos are most typically found at beach and ski destinations. Some provide housekeeping service, but others don't.

5. **Timeshares**: Here's another sort of apartment-like lodging that is similar to condos. However, owners don't purchase individual units, they own a *certain amount of yearly time* at the property or even at a whole network of such properties. The timeshare industry often goes by the name *vacation ownership*. A variation of a timeshare is a *club*. A company agrees to use lodging at the club (or chain of clubs) on a regular basis. The commitment usually requires payment of a membership fee and/or deposit for the agreed-upon room nights. Unlike timeshares, clubs provide full-service amenities. They are value-priced and are commonly situated in costly cities, such as New York City.

6. **Bed-and-breakfasts (B&Bs)**: These home-like properties (often they *are* homes that have been converted) charge guests to stay in a bedroom (sometimes with shared bath facilities) and offer full breakfast in a communal dining room area or in the guestroom.

7. **Lodges:** These properties are usually in rural, nature-dominated settings (such as at national parks) or in exotic places (for example, the African wilderness). They can be anything from spartan to luxurious.

Guest at an ice hotel.

© Claude Beaubien/www.Shutterstock.com

8. **Campgrounds**: Once these facilities were where hardy tourists pitched tents. Today they usually refer to facilities where those who travel in recreational vehicles (RVs) stay.

9. **Hostels**: Frequented by students and those on a very tight budget, these dormitory-like accommodations or converted hotels usually offer low-cost lodging in major cities. Some hostels require guests to bring their own linens or to perform small chores in exchange for cheap lodging.

10. **Dude ranches**: A unique form of lodging, these facilities convey a theme of the American West. Usually located in resort areas, they feature horseback riding, cattle roundups, outdoor barbecues, and other cowboy-type activities.

Who Owns Lodging Facilities?

Almost as diversified as categories of accommodations is the issue of ownership. Here are some possibilities:

- The property may be *wholly owned* by a parent chain corporation such as Hyatt, Hilton, Marriott, or Fairmont. Most people believe that if a hotel has a brand name, it is owned by the parent chain, but that is not always true, as you are about to see.

- A property may be only a *franchise* of a chain. Just as the McDonald's Corporation doesn't own all McDonald's restaurants across the world, Holiday Inn, for instance, doesn't own all of the Holiday Inns. In such franchise situations, an outside person or company (a *franchisee*) owns the property.

  The franchisee pays a royalty, a percentage of room sales, an advertising fee, and other miscellaneous costs to the chain, and must adhere to at least the minimum lodging standards that the chain sets. In turn, the chain provides a recognizable brand name, advertising, various business-related systems (for example, an accounting system), and certain supplies. Most important, the property is available for booking through the chain's central reservations system.

- A property may have only a *management contract* with the chain. The chain provides executives to run the hotel, and that's about it. In some cases, the property will also use the chain's brand name and reservations system. There are even some odd situations where the management of one chain (say, Marriott) oversees a property owned or franchised by another chain (for example, Hilton).

- A property may be *totally independent*, with no chain affiliations. These are usually hotels that are so famous for example, the *Hotel Bel-Air* in Los Angeles or the *Ritz* in London) that they don't need to operate under a brand name. In other cases, they are so small that they don't have the resources or see the need for brand affiliations.

However, independent hotels usually *do* need access to some sort of global reservations system. As a result, they affiliate with organizations called **hotel representative firms**. For a fee, these companies provide Web- and telephone-based services through which potential guests can book their reservations for independent hotels. One such company is *Utell Hotels & Resorts*. Others specialize in specific kinds of properties: *Leading Hotels of the World* is a rep firm that accepts only very distinguished properties (sometimes some branded ones like *Ritz-Carlton* too). And *Relais et Chateaux* represents many converted castles and inns.

All sorts of variations on these types are possible. Most major chains, in fact, count wholly owned, franchised, and managed properties all within their brand's offerings. They may even represent condos and timeshares.

Brands and Brand Families

The variety of chains that provide lodging worldwide is astonishing. In some cases, these brands represent a distinct value level: Four Seasons hotels, for instance, are almost always very upscale and pricey, whereas Motel 6 properties are basic and inexpensive. Some brands accommodate a broader range of price, "personality," and

Lodging Levels

Many hotels in North America belong to chains, and each chain tries to maintain a certain quality level among all its properties. Though there can be *great* variation within a chain (especially Radisson, Hilton, Sheraton, and Holiday Inn), here is what level each chain generally represents:

Luxury	High End	Mid-Range	Budget
Four Seasons	Crowne Plaza	Clarion	Baymont
Peninsula	Fairmont	Delta	Best Western
Regent	Hyatt Regency	Doubletree	Comfort Inns
Ritz-Carlton	Inter-Continental	Embassy Suites	Days Inn
	Le Meridien	Hilton	Econo Lodge
	Marriott	Holiday Inn	Hampton Inns
	Omni	Hyatt	Howard Johnson
	Renaissance	Radisson	La Quinta
	Sheraton Resorts	Ramada	Quality Inn
	Sofitel	Sheraton	Red Roof
	Westin		Rodeway Inn
			Travelodge

How Does It Rate?

THIS & that

Ever hear the phrase *five-star hotel*? Of course you have. But who awards those stars? The answer is, it depends. In certain countries, such as France and Mexico, the government rates lodging. In most nations, including the United States, private organizations or publications do the ratings. *AAA, Michelin*, and *Forbes* provide excellent and reliable assessments of hotels. So do consumer guidebooks such as those of *Fodor*, *Frommer*, and *Zagat*. Many Web "opinion" sites feature ratings and commentaries from the general public. But be cautious. (See Chapter 11 to see why.) Finally, two highly reliable travel industry resources rate hotels: *The Hotel & Travel Index* (the *HTI*) uses a 10-level rating system, and *The Star Service Online* is a remarkable reference work that provides highly specific analyses and ratings of more than ten thousand properties worldwide.

quality levels, often indicated by a sort of subtitle: *Park Hyatts*, for instance, are usually more upscale and business-oriented than regular Hyatts. And a few brands, such as *Aston* and *Outrigger* in Hawaii, offer everything from budget to luxurious properties.

Moreover, certain large companies oversee multiple brands. A company called *Wyndham* counts *Wyndham Hotels & Resorts, Ramada*, and *Travelodge* as part of its family of products. Marriott has more than a dozen brands in its portfolio, some with Marriott in the name (such as *Courtyard by Marriott*), and others with totally distinct names (such as *Ritz-Carlton* and *Renaissance*).

insider info

The brand of a hotel can swiftly change. For example, one popular Ft. Lauderdale, Florida, property has changed hands three times in five years: from a Marriott, to an independent hotel, to a Hilton.

A hotel's decor can be traditional . . .

© olly/www.Shutterstock.com

. . . or contemporary.

insider info

Very new hotels are often great bargains. The property is not yet well known, and managers are trying to pump up occupancy rates.

Another interesting development has been to group several brands from one family in a geographic cluster. For instance, Marriott might position a Fairfield Inn, a Courtyard by Marriott, and a Renaissance Hotel—which are all part of the same "family"—in proximity to each other. The advantage is that the different brands can share supplies, facilities, maybe even staff, and all sorts of other resources.

What Rooms Cost

What determines the price of lodging? Dozens of variables come into play when pricing a room. Among these factors are the following:

- **The quality of the property.** Generally the more luxurious it is, the more it will cost.

- **The facilities it offers.** Hotels with a large health club, expansive public areas, multiple dining rooms, and an adjoining golf course will probably be more pricey than those with few facilities.

- **The service level it provides.** Properties with a high staff-to-guest ratio (for example, 300 staff members for a 450-room hotel) generally charge more.

- **The prime market it serves.** Hotels that target business travelers usually cost more than leisure-oriented properties because with corporate travelers, their company is paying. With leisure travel, the vacationer is paying—it's coming directly out of his or her pocket. That guest is more price-sensitive than a corporate traveler. On the other hand, businesses can lessen the impact of these rates by negotiating a special **corporate rate** with the hotel for volume business.

- **Where it is located.** The better the location, the higher the price. Accommodations directly on Hawaii's Waikiki Beach are more expensive than those situated three or four blocks back from the ocean. A hotel in toney Beverly Hills charges more than one in a blue-collar town such as nearby Culver City. And a big-city downtown hotel is almost always more expensive than one in a smaller city or in the suburbs.

- **The season when the accommodations are needed.** As with many travel products, hotel rooms cost more in high or peak season, low season yields the best rates, and shoulder season offers in-between values. As you learned in Chapter 1, seasonality differs from place to place.

- **If it has a casino.** Most casino hotels cost less than equivalent accommodations elsewhere. Gaming is such a powerful profit center that such hotels don't have to make a large amount of money from rooms.

- **When the accommodations are booked.** Many hotels today adjust their rates according to when rooms are booked. Let's say a hotel has 500 rooms. The first 100 will sell at, say, $180, the next 100 will sell at $250, and so on. Rates also may be adjusted through a yield management system, similar to that deployed by airlines and described in Chapter 2.

- **Whether the hotel or chain is offering a special promotion.** Hotels and entire brands sometimes decide that their bookings are so "soft" that something should be done to stimulate demand. They then publicize and offer a special promotional rate.

- **If it's a prepaid, nonrefundable rate.** A hotel may offer a lower rate than it would normally charge if guests agree to pay the entire cost of their stay at the time of booking. Guests must realize that to get this lower rate they are waiving their right to change the reserved dates or to apply the cost to another stay.

- **If it's a landmark.** Certain hotels, because of their noted history or architecture, can charge a premium rate. For example, in the late nineteenth and early twentieth centuries, the Canadian Pacific Railway built a series of striking, castle-like hotels across Canada. These properties are now part of the upscale Fairmont Hotels & Resorts chain.

- **Whether anything spectacular or unusual is going on.** Is a convention monopolizing a city's hotels? Is some special event like the Super Bowl taking place? If so, hotel space will be hard to secure. And, as in most cases where demand exceeds supply, prices go up (except for the convention delegates, as you'll see).

- **If the guest is part of a conference.** Because of the volume purchase of room nights, hotels usually extend a reduced conference rate to attendees.

insider info

Some destinations experience *two* high seasons. Hawaii—where the weather is pleasant year-round—sees increased occupancy from January to March, when people in cold climes want a break from chilly weather, and again in the summer, when families with kids on summer vacation are most likely to travel.

insider info

Hotels are usually refurbished every five to seven years. But beach or ski resorts usually require refurbishing every three to five years due to the wear and tear that beachgoers and skiers cause.

- **Which day of the week it is.** Some lodging types have predictable weekly patterns. For instance, airport and business hotels tend to offer their best rates on weekends, when corporate travelers are more likely to be home, not on the road. Conversely, resort hotels tend to lower their rates midweek, especially if they depend on people who drive to their destination (for example, Palm Springs, Las Vegas, and Disneyland Paris).

- **How inclusive the property is.** As you've learned, the more that's included in the price, the more a room will cost. The number of meals included especially helps determine the price.

- **How long the guest's stay will be.** Some hotels give a lower rate to guests whose stay is uncommonly long. This stay can be as short as five days, but a week to a month or more is typical for such an extended stay.

- **The number of people in the room.** Rates sometimes vary according to how many people occupy the room. Sometimes a *single-occupancy* room may cost a little less than a *double-occupancy* one. *Triple* or *quad occupancy* usually increases the price.

- **If there's a resort fee.** Some resorts add a mandatory daily extra fee for use of its facilities (whether the guest uses them or not.) As with airline fees, it's a way to make the rate seem lower.

- **If the guest is using frequent-stay or -flyer points.** Like airlines, hotel chains award points to guests who participate in their *frequent-stay* loyalty programs. Some award points toward airline mileage programs too. Guests can eventually redeem points for reduced-cost or free lodging. Because many hotels also partner with airlines, frequent flyers may receive offers for free or reduced-price nights.

- **How the lodging is purchased.** Like airlines, hotel chains may offer special reduced rates to travelers who book on the Internet. Also like airlines, better rates can sometimes be obtained through consolidators.

These are just some of the many possible factors that can affect room prices. Here are other ways to obtain special rates: membership in an association (for example, AAA), profession (for example, clergy status, travel professionals), government status (for example, military), or age (for example, seniors rate).

Rates also vary *within* a hotel. A room with an ocean view will cost more than one that overlooks the parking lot. Many hotels also feature a **concierge,** or club, **level** of *guestrooms that features better amenities* (for example, a bathrobe for the guest's use) and, often, a complimentary continental breakfast and evening hors d'oeuvres. Concierge-level rooms usually cost 20 to 50 percent more than standard rooms. Larger rooms and suites (those in a conventional hotel, not an all-suite one) usually cost more than a standard guestroom as well.

Finally, hotels may tack on extra fees, such as energy surcharges, as well as the government lodging taxes that almost always apply. Depending on its location, taxes and fees can sometimes increase a hotel room's cost by 20 percent or more.

Telling Terms

Are Meals Included?

Here are the major meal plans that hotels offer, with their usual abbreviations:

- **American Plan (AP)**: A room rate that includes three meals daily.

- **Bermuda Plan (BP)**: A room rate that includes a full breakfast daily. In Britain this is called a bed-and-breakfast rate.

- **Continental Plan (CP)**: A room rate that includes a daily continental breakfast (such as rolls, toast, muffins, pastries, and various beverages).

- **European Plan (EP)**: A room rate that doesn't include any meals.

- **Modified American Plan (MAP)**: A room rate that includes two meals (usually breakfast and dinner) daily in the room rate. Common during high season in Mexico.

Note also that all-inclusive properties (which often are booked per week, and not per day, and per person, not per room) include all meals, and more (for example, sports and entertainment) in their price.

How Lodging Is Sold

About 60 percent of all lodging is sold by hotels and their chains directly to leisure and business travelers. Another 25 percent is sold by conventional and online travel agencies. Some of the remaining 15 percent is sold to tour operators and cruise lines, who then fold the room costs into their packages. The rest is bought by meeting planners, consolidators, and "intermediaries" who select properties and negotiate lodging rates on behalf of corporations and meeting planners.

That a comparatively low percentage of lodging is sold through travel agents is surprising considering that agents sell the majority of most other travel products. One reason is that the public, in general, believes that all lodging at a certain price point is basically the same (which isn't really true). They see lodging as a commodity. Believing that a hotel is a hotel, people feel they can do their own research and bookings based on price and a few other easy-to-research factors such as location and facilities.

Also, hotel stays often occur during a driving trip, and the public seldom feels the need for a travel agent when a motoring journey is involved. Travelers may even wait until they get to a motel with a *vacancy* sign to set up their lodging.

In turn, travel agents often feel overwhelmed by the public's expectation that agents should be familiar with the tens of thousands of hotels worldwide. That perception is just as misleading as the public's belief that all hotels are alike. With the right research tools, feedback from their clients, personal experience, and good judgment, skilled travel agents can help find the accommodations that will best meet their clients' needs.

insider info

The American Plan is more common in Europe, and the European Plan is more typical in the United States. Why? In the early twentieth century, Americans who visited Europe preferred to dine in their hotel, whereas Europeans visiting the United States liked to try out local restaurants.

insider info

Some hotels automatically charge guests when they take something out of a mini-bar, even if they put it back. (The mini-bar has sensors that detect the selection.)

Hotel Booking Procedures

Guests (or their travel agents) can book accommodations by phone (either to a reservations center or to the hotel directly), on a Web site (either the hotel's or a general travel Web site), by fax, through e-mail, or even by regular mail. After giving the necessary information, the person booking the reservation is typically asked to *guarantee the reservation,* either with a credit card number or with an actual deposit paid by check, credit card, or money order. The room will be held, in theory, no matter what time of day the customer arrives.

Why the words "in theory"? Hotels use yield management programs (explained in Chapter 2) to try to predict **hotel occupancy** (*the percentage of rooms occupied*) based on the patterns seen in previous years. They usually identify a certain "no-show" rate of people who fail, for whatever reason, to arrive at the hotel or who cancel at the last minute. To adjust for this, hotels, like airlines, often overbook, based on the predicted no-show rate. If that prediction is off, a guest arriving late in the evening may not be able to stay at the hotel because all rooms are already occupied. The guest is then transferred to another hotel; the original hotel pays for the room (even if it's more than its own rate) and, if necessary, a taxi to get there. In lodging language, this is called **walking the guest**, because hotel personnel used to literally walk the guest to another hotel.

Careers

Careers in Lodging

The lodging industry is huge, with millions of job positions worldwide. Here are some of them:

- Senior executives, directors, and managers
- Reservationists
- Front-desk staff
- Food and beverage staff
- Concierges
- Business center staff
- Maintenance staff

- Bell captain/staff
- Human resources/training specialists
- Audio-visual coordinators
- Groups/meetings coordinators
- Safety/security specialists
- Sales representatives
- Housekeepers
- Accountants/auditors

Let's get back to the reservation process. Once the room is guaranteed, the guest is given a confirmation number, either directly or through his or her travel agency. Most lodging companies have a cancellation policy, which is stated at the time of the reservation (for example, "You can cancel 48 hours in advance without penalty"). A client who fails to arrive or who cancels after the cutoff time (say, only 12 hours in advance) will probably be charged for the first night, even if the hotel sells out all its rooms that night—including the one reserved for the no-show. If a credit card number was used to guarantee the reservation, the card account will be charged. If a deposit was used to guarantee the reservation, the hotel will keep the deposit.

Many variations exist: stricter cancellation policies, for example, or guarantees without a credit card number or deposit. At some resorts, the deposit is the room cost of the whole stay, not just one night. But the process described characterizes most hotel bookings today.

More This and That

Here are some additional insights into the lodging industry:

- Hotels draw profits from sources other than travelers. Weddings, anniversaries, Bar and Bat Mitzvahs, meetings, and locals who patronize its restaurants and lounges all contribute to a hotel's bottom line.

- Hotels were the first to adopt fully interactive television. In addition to broadcast and cable stations, guests can rent movies on-demand and even review their hotel bill and check out, all via video.

- The world's best hotels provide in-room stationery with the guest's name embossed on it and have staff who memorize each guest's name.

- A major problem in trans-Pacific travel: guests who arrive on the wrong day because someone (the traveler, reservationist, or travel agent) failed to adjust correctly for the international date line. When you cross the date line, it becomes the next day (if you're traveling westbound) or the day before (if you're traveling eastbound).

- Almost all hotels today have selected rooms that are fully accessible to people with physical disabilities.

- Internet access has become a major priority for guests. Among the possibilities: Wi-Fi, in-room broadband, interactive TV, a business center, or an Internet cafe. Of course, simpler, highly accessible technologies now in development may soon make the availability of such services less critical to guests.

- Some common "special needs" that guests request are a nonsmoking room, a special kind of pillow (foam or feather), a quiet room (away from elevators and vending machine), and early check-in.

- Rooms typically are ready for occupancy at about 4 P.M. If guests arrive before then and a room is ready, they may be able to check in and go to their room. If

insider info
Many veteran travelers swear that calling a hotel directly rather than the chain's toll-free number often yields better rates. Increasingly, though, chains have created computer reservations systems that make that approach impossible.

insider info
Guests should always get a printed copy of the hotel's confirmation and bring it with them. If a reservation is lost (and it happens), the guests will have written proof. If they can't get a copy of the confirmation, they should at least have the confirmation number.

no rooms are ready, the guests will probably be able to check in, but that's all. The desk clerk will give them an estimate as to when the room will be ready (or will contact them on their cell phone when it is). The guests may either wait at the hotel or check their luggage at the bell desk and spend time sightseeing, shopping, or whatever else they feel like doing until the room is ready.

- Hotels sometimes give inferior rooms and/or no frequent-stay program points to guests who purchase their lodging through a hotel consolidator or online agency.

- Hotels located close to airports usually provide free transfer shuttle service. For longer distances, the guest usually has to pay for taxi or shuttle service from a private company.

- Larger hotels often provide 24-hour room service. At others, room service typically extends from 6 A.M. to 10 P.M. or so.

- Luxury hotels not only provide housekeeping service but also an early evening turndown service, when used towels are replaced and the bed is prepared for the guest (the bedspread or duvet is taken off or folded back and a chocolate or mint may be placed on the pillow).

- Many large resort hotels, especially those in Las Vegas, adjoin or own large shopping areas.

insider info

If a traveler is scheduled to arrive early in the morning, it might be worth it to book a day room for the first day of arrival at a hotel or even make a reservation for the night before. You can also notify the hotel of an early arrival—but a room's availability will depend on occupancy the night before.

Food Services

Along with lodging, food services represent a huge and vital part of the hospitality sector. Food service providers not only serve the everyday needs of the neighborhood locals, they also cross paths with travel and tourism all the time. Meals represent a significant aspect of the travel experience and often shape one's satisfaction with a trip. In some cases, it is *the* reason some people travel.

Moreover, the food services industry provides a growing wealth of career opportunities. In fact, it is estimated that this industry provides 4 percent of all jobs in America.

Many well-known brands in travel and tourism began in food services. Some examples are *Marriott International* (which began as an A&W Root Beer stand), *Howard Johnson* (which started as an ice cream shop), and *Knott's Berry Farm* (a Southern California theme park that was initially famous for serving chicken dinners and boysenberry pies).

What follows is a review of the food services industry, with special emphasis on how it intersects with the travel and tourism industries.

Key Terms

As with other huge industries, the food services sector uses many terms—some familiar, some not—to describe what it does. Let's start with **food services**, *the industry that provides dining and food to people, usually outside their own home* *environment.* By this definition, restaurants, buffets, hotel room service, and even a food court in a mall would qualify, but supermarkets would not. One type of food service that lies somewhere at our definition's edge is home-delivery food providers such as *Domino's Pizza.* (That's why our definition features the word *usually.*)

A common term applied by marketers to food services is **concept,** which refers to *those food service elements that, together, address the needs and expectations of customers.* Among these elements are the following:

- **Location.** As with real estate, food providers must carefully select the right location for the concept they are trying to achieve. The huge and highly successful *Hard Rock Cafe* that adjoins Orlando's Universal Studios would probably go out of business if, instead, it were located on a seldom-traveled road in Arkansas. A restaurant with a view of Niagara Falls would need to have plenty of space and large windows to achieve an optimum effect for guests. A *Denny's* at a highway rest area will find dining patterns that are different from a city-center location. In each case, location dictates the approach.

- **Size of facility.** How is the size of a dining facility described? Usually by the number of its seats. Again, location drives the concept. A coffee shop near a limited-service hotel will be smaller than a dinner theater in Branson, Missouri, which can accommodate busloads of tourists.

- **Hours of operation.** Customer needs dictate when a food service will operate. Luxury or big resort hotels, for example, are expected to provide 24-hour room service, as are major airport hotels, where travelers arrive at all hours. On the

A centuries-old hotel in Venice, Italy.

other hand, a museum cafeteria is open only during that museum's operating hours (and usually only during limited hours, based on visitors' patterns).

- **Theme.** Remember our discussion of theming? As with hotels, theming has become a popular path toward food service success. Some examples are the *Rainforest Cafe,* which makes you feel as if you're in a jungle; *Planet Hollywood,* which displays movie memorabilia; and *Hard Rock Cafe,* whose ambience is dictated by rock music. Theme restaurants especially rely on tourists for their success because they are, in effect, destinations unto themselves and are frequently placed at or near tourist destinations.

Types of Service

The food services sector is often subdivided and classified according to the forms of service each category provides. Here are the service types that are most significant to travel and tourism:

- **Table service.** Also known as sit-down service, this is the type of food service we know best. Usually a greeter seats you, a server takes your order from a menu, and then food and beverage are delivered to your table. Before leaving, you pay your server or a cashier. Many mass-market coffee shop chains also offer the option of counter service, where the diner can sit on a stool at the counter and be served directly and swiftly.

  Table-service restaurants can provide anything from an upscale, fine-dining experience to an extremely casual, budget approach. Virtually every segment of the travel industry uses traditional table-service restaurants.

- **Banquet table service.** This form of service comes in three versions. In the first, everyone is served the same meal, at the same time. The second version features several choices, but again, all meals are served at the same time. Both of these approaches are common at conventions and hotel meetings. The third variation is found on many cruise ships: guests select from a menu and are served at about the same time, at what the cruise business calls a seating. (More about this in Chapter 7.)

  The one thing all three have in common is that the price of the event (the conference, the cruise) includes the cost of such meals. The diner does not pay a bill.

- **Cafeteria service.** Guests pick up a tray, select their food (which is dished up—either in advance or at the diner's request—by service people), place their choices on the tray, pay for their selections at a cashier, and take the food themselves to a table. In the travel industry, attractions, airports, and theme parks often use cafeterias.

- **Buffet service.** This is very similar to cafeteria service, except that it's even more self-serve. Perhaps only one or two employees dish up the food. Sometimes none do. A critical difference from cafeteria service is that one price, paid in advance, covers everything (rather than paying per food item selected). Hotels find breakfast buffets to be extremely popular and some, especially casino hotels, feature lavish buffets for breakfast, lunch, and dinner. Cruise ships typically have a buffet on their Lido decks (a high-up deck that also features a pool). Motorcoach tours frequently stop at buffet restaurants, like those of the *Hometown Buffet* chain.

- **Room service.** Guests order their meals from a special in-room menu, and the meal is brought to their guestroom, usually within 30 to 45 minutes. A service charge and perhaps gratuity are, in most cases, automatically added to the bill, which appears on the guests' folio and is paid when they check out.

- **Fast-food service.** You surely recognize this: you walk up to a counter or drive through and order your Big Mac, Chalupa, or Whopper. Similar to traditional fast-food outlets are coffeehouses, such as *Starbucks*, and even *Dunkin' Donuts*, which provide a limited menu of food choices. Most fast-food facilities have an open-seating area. Family or road travelers often use fast-food outlets to save time and money. Occasionally, escorted tour groups use them too, and these facilities have become popular in airport terminals as well.

- **Fast casual service.** Guests order food at a counter, like they do at a fast-food restaurant, but usually the food is of a higher quality and the atmosphere is nicer.

insider info

In the largest hotels, beverages are distributed to various beverage outlets by pipes, from a central source.

Careers

Careers in the Food Services Industry

Here are some of the jobs that the food services industry provides:

- Senior executives, directors, and managers
- Accountants/controllers
- Busboys
- Chefs/cooks
- Bartenders
- Cashiers
- Food servers (waiters/waitresses)
- Food and beverage managers
- Clerical support
- Human resources/training specialists
- Maintenance personnel
- Kitchen staff
- Maitre d's/hosts/hostesses (greeters)
- Pastry chefs
- Purchasers
- Receptionists
- Sommeliers (wine stewards)
- Sous chefs (assistant chefs)

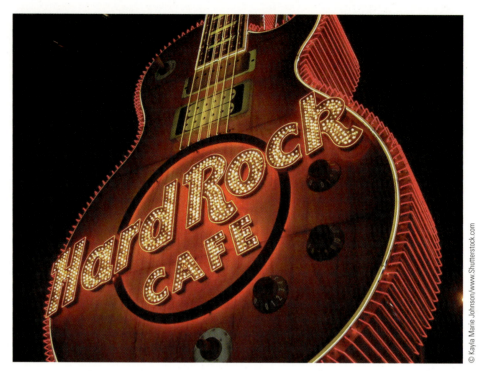

The Hard Rock Cafe was one of the first themed restaurants.

- **Delivery service.** Food is prepared and then delivered, usually to the customer's home. However, hotels are increasingly using delivery services to provide an alternative to in-house room service. Limited-service hotels often rely entirely on delivery service because they have no full kitchen on-site.

More This and That

Here are some bits of miscellaneous information you should know:

- Ownership of food outlets is similar to what you find in the lodging industry. The facility may be independently owned, part of a chain, or franchised. As with hotels, a large company may control many different food service chains or franchise brands.

- Other segments of food services affect travel and tourism. *Food courts*, with multiple fast-food outlets and common seating (like those at malls) can serve shoppers on vacation. Some large hotels or hotel clusters feature food courts too. *Vending machines*—providing everything from snacks and beverages to full-course dinners—are located at just about every travel venue. *Mini-bars* in hotel rooms are, in essence, a variation of vending machines. And *airline and rail catering companies* constitute a huge business. As airlines cut back on meals, some of these catering companies (and others) are expanding into different business models (such as *selling* meals to passengers *before* they board a flight).

- Menu planning is an art that requires not only skill and inspiration but also a clear, insightful understanding of what the typical customer wants in a dining experience.

- Visitors to foreign countries make their dining choices very much according to their comfort level. Dependables (remember them from Chapter 1?) prefer food familiar to their own country, no matter where they're traveling. Venturers *prefer* trying the cuisine of the locals wherever they go.

- Entertainment venues and bars that serve drinks to patrons are also technically part of food services. In fact, they often have limited food menus.

- Food services are critical to a cruise's success. In fact, many experts categorize cruising as part of the hospitality industry. You'll learn lots more about cruising in Chapter 7.

insider info

Mexican food has become the number-one ethnic cuisine in America, surpassing Chinese and Italian food.

Telling Terms

Here's a list of "insider" terms that people in the food industry use that the average person—even someone who eats out a lot—probably wouldn't know:

- **Back-of-the-house**: "Behind-the-scenes" area of food services (for example, the kitchen) accessible only to staff, not the public. (Used similarly in the lodging industry.)

- **First in, first out (FIFO)**: Rotating and storing system in which older food items are used before newer ones. Affected also by how *perishable* the food is (how long it remains safely edible).

- **Flowchart**: Diagram that depicts the order in which a menu item is prepared, beginning with the ingredients and ending with service to the customer.

- **Front-of-the-house**: Opposite of back-of-the-house!

- **No-show**: A customer with a reservation at a restaurant who fails to show up or cancel. (Also used in the lodging industry.)

- **"BOGO"**: Buy one, get one free offer.

- **Day-part**: The time period when a certain set of menu items is served for example, a lunch menu).

- **Dual-branding**: When two or more brand-name operators are located in the same retail location (such as Pizza Hut and Taco Bell). Common in airports.

- **LTO**: Limited-time offer.

- **Paid-outs**: Money taken from the register to purchase something with cash.

- **Stair-stepping**: Scheduling according to typical customer flow.

- **Table turns**: How many times a table is used to serve a new customer over a period of time (for example, three times an evening).

Review Questions

1. Identify the three major types of hotels.

2. Explain what characterizes each of the following types of lodging: motels, limited-service lodging, extended-stay lodging, condos, timeshares.

3. What are the possible variations of hotel ownership?

4. Cite 10 factors that affect the cost of a room.

5. What are three ways lodging can be sold?

6. Describe four concepts in food services.

7. What is the difference between table service and banquet service? Between cafeteria service and buffet service?

It's All About You Questions

1. Describe what you think makes for great lodging. List at least five factors.

2. What is your favorite table-service restaurant? Give at least three reasons.

3. What is the most surprising thing you learned in this chapter?

NAME	DATE

Activity 1: Coming to a Hotel Near You

Visit a lodging property near you, either on your own or as part of a class group hotel inspection. Then answer the following questions:

• Name/location of the property: _____

• How would you characterize this property? Check the one or two boxes that *most* apply:

☐ Resort	☐ Spa	☐ Casino
☐ Business hotel	☐ Convention/meeting hotel	☐ Limited-service property
☐ Condominium	☐ Bed & breakfast	☐ Campground
☐ Mega-resort	☐ All-inclusive	☐ Themed
☐ Airport hotel	☐ All-suite property	☐ Extended-stay property
☐ Timeshare	☐ Lodge	☐ Hostel

• Does the property have any of the following?

	Yes	How many?	No	Comments
1. More than one dining facility?	☐	_____	☐	
2. Meeting room(s)?	☐	_____	☐	
3. Ballroom(s)?	☐	_____	☐	
4. Business center?	☐	_____	☐	
5. Pool area?	☐	_____	☐	
6. Exercise facility?	☐	_____	☐	
7. Concierge desk?	☐	_____	☐	

• Any other comments?

NAME   DATE

Activity 2: And on Our Tour Menu Today . . .

This is an exercise in evaluating restaurants and their suitability for hosting tour groups. Select six sit-down restaurants. The first three (A, B, C) should be within a half-mile of your school or training classroom; they need not be ideally suited for tours. The second three (D, E, F) should be restaurants within 10 miles of your school that you feel would be most appropriate for tours. Use the following chart to rate each restaurant, with 3 being the highest rating in each category and 0 the lowest.

3 = Excellent   2 = Very good   1 = Fair   0 = Poor

Restaurant		Location	Variety of Food	Price	Amount of Space	View	Ambience	Total Score
A	Name:							
	Address:							
B	Name:							
	Address:							
C	Name:							
	Address:							
D	Name:							
	Address:							
E	Name:							
	Address:							
F	Name:							
	Address:							

Source: From *Conducting Tours* (p. 158), by Marc Mancini 2001, Clifton Park, NY: Delmar Cengage Learning. Copyright 2001 by Delmar Cengage Learning. Reprinted with permission.

Gale Hospitality, Tourism and Leisure Database Assignment

The following assignment requires access to the Gale Hospitality, Tourism and Leisure Database. Check with your instructor to see if you have access to this database.

Find the article *The Greening of Hotels* in the Gale Hospitality, Tourism & Leisure Collection.

Come up with five specific "green" practices that the author cites and that you feel are the most creative, original, and impactful. Be prepared to say why. Each of your five selections must be from a different hotel chain.

5

Dealing with Dreams: The Travel Agency Industry

KEY TERMS

- Approval code
- Consortium
- Corporate travel manager
- Cross-selling
- Debit memo
- FIT
- Group space
- Host agency
- Override
- Preferred supplier
- Queue
- Space available
- Tariffs
- Upselling

After studying this chapter, you'll be able to:

- Explain why consumers use travel agents

- Describe the different kinds of travel agencies and agents

- Contrast the skills of a leisure agent with one who deals primarily with business travelers

- List the sources that agents use to obtain information

Paula Mitchell Manning

CURRENT POSITION/TITLE:

Travel consultant/co-owner of a two-person, home-based travel agency; director, local chapter of OSSN (Outside Sales Support Network)

SHORT DESCRIPTION OF WHAT YOUR RESPONSIBILITIES ARE:

Create interesting and unique travel experiences for individuals and groups, as well as event planning

EDUCATION:

Herkimer County Community College; California State University Los Angeles

FIRST JOB IN TRAVEL/HOSPITALITY INDUSTRY:

Reservation Sales Agent, Northwest Airlines

FIRST PAID JOB (IF DIFFERENT FROM ABOVE):

Crew Member at McDonald's

FAVORITE PART OF WHAT I DO:

Designing a vacation that makes my client say, "Wow!"

THING I WISH I DIDN'T HAVE TO DO:

Bookkeeping, but it is essential to success in this business

BEST CAREER MEMORY I HAVE:

When I received my first Trendsetter Award from *TravelAge West Magazine*—at the Beverly Hills Four Seasons, no less

SOMETHING ALMOST NO ONE KNOWS ABOUT ME:

I wanted to be a dancer.

Here's a saying that's been around for a long time, "To function well in today's world, you need a good doctor, a good lawyer, and a good travel agent." The first keeps you healthy, the second helps you navigate the law, and the third helps make your dreams come true.

You may question the value and role a travel agent plays today in transforming your travel dreams into reality. As you learned in Chapter 2, the airlines have aggressively deflected the sale of their tickets away from travel agents and toward their Web sites. That has been very bad news for travel agencies because, for many, air sales have constituted a critical source of their profitability. Airlines—which once paid anywhere from 8 percent to 11 percent of a ticket's value to the travel agency that sold it—now, in most cases, pay agents nothing. In turn, most travel agencies, in order to make a profit, have to tack a service fee onto every ticket sale, putting them at a price disadvantage and making many consumers decide to just do it themselves, without the help of a pro.

Yet the travel agency industry hasn't collapsed at all. In fact, many agencies are doing quite well. They've done it by rethinking their role in the travel planning process and reshaping how they bring value to their clients. And nonairline supplier groups, such as hotels and car rental companies, continue to pay them commissions. As a result, most experts are convinced that travel agents will continue to play a pivotal role in helping people travel.

insider info

Airlines still quietly give commissions to agencies that sell a large number of their tickets.

A Travel Agent's Value

There are many reasons why it is a good idea for consumers to book through a travel agent. The following sections list some of those reasons.

A Travel Agent Is More Skilled at Finding the Best Travel Solution

The average person spends only a handful of hours each year planning and booking travel. Travel agents do this sort of thing all day, every week, all year. They are professionals who know what they're doing. They can decipher jargon, spot hidden drawbacks, discover opportunities, and be marvelously resourceful.

insider info

About 70 percent of all home-based travel agents have sold travel for at least five years.

A Travel Agent Can Find the Best Deal

Most people feel that the Internet can easily help them discover the best price on, say, a flight or a hotel stay. Yet travel agents can find lower airfares than consumers can most of the time. Furthermore, agents are better at spotting genuine *values*.

For example, a layperson might discover online that a certain hotel in Philadelphia has rooms available at $159 per night, whereas other nearby lodging is priced at $169 to $189. This looks like a bargain. But does the layperson know that the hotel offering $159 rooms hasn't been renovated in seven years, is at the edge of a seedy neighborhood, charges more for parking, and has rather small rooms? A good travel agent will know these things, or at least how to find out. That $159 price may be a bargain, but what a traveler gets for it is a poor value compared to its competitors.

Travel agents understand air ticket pricing much better than most—and the many restrictions that may come with that "cheap" fare. They can often find better connections or alternate airports that the average person would never think of. Finally, they have access to hotel, car, cruise, and tour rates that the public, and even some of their competitors, don't.

A Travel Agent Saves Time and Trouble

Most of us today lead highly busy lives. It often makes plenty of sense to pay a professional to do certain tasks for you. Perhaps you could mend a hem, polish a pair of shoes, and even do your own plumbing if you wanted to, but do you have the time, and would you do it well? The same applies to planning and booking travel. You can take time to do it yourself, or let a pro take over for you.

Telling Terms

This book regularly uses the term *travel agents* because that is how the public generally knows them. (Consider all the supplier ads that finish with "See your travel agent.") But because travel agents today go well beyond being "agents" for suppliers, they sometimes refer to themselves as *travel counselors, travel consultants, travel advisors,* or *travel planners.*

Here are some "telling terms" used in the travel agency environment:

- **FIT:** Any trip assembled by an agent from scratch rather than a package. (By the way, these days no one agrees on what those letters stand for, except that the letter "I" refers to "independent.")

- **Approval code:** A number issued by a credit card company that indicates its authorization of a credit card transaction.

- **Debit memo:** A request for payment, usually from an airline, when the airline believes a travel agent or agency made an error on a fare and provided too little money to the airline for that ticket.

- **Queues (pronounced "cues"):** A feature of a CRS/GDS to remind the agent of an important action to be taken or message to be delivered.

- **Tariffs:** The official rules, regulations, and fares of airlines.

A travel agent knows destinations better.

A Travel Agent Is Accountable

If something goes wrong with a trip you bought through an online agency, who can you call to get help? Although some online agencies have help lines, they're notoriously understaffed. A good conventional travel agency will do all it can to solve your problem.

A Travel Agent Knows Suppliers Better

Ask a typical person how many cruise lines there are and they might say five or six. Actually, there are dozens, each different. And what about tour operators? There are thousands. How to choose? That's where the travel agent comes in. A really good one can analyze a client's needs, sift through all the supplier choices, and recommend the perfect match of personality and product.

That travel agents know suppliers well and that such knowledge is clearly valuable is reflected in the high trust the public places in their recommendations of subtly complex, experience-like products such as tours, cruises, and complicated itineraries. In fact, more than 80 percent of people on tours or cruises bought their vacations through travel agents. After all, would you want to invest thousands of dollars on a multiday cruise or a tour that might be totally wrong for you?

A Travel Agent Knows Destinations Better

Most people today have hazy ideas about where places are and what's there when they get there. Travel agents almost always have a much better sense of geography than their clients do. Also, some agents are specialists in certain destinations, products, or categories of travel. For instance, an agent may be an expert on southern France, another on Caribbean resorts, and a third on prime ecological destinations.

A Travel Agent Is Largely Impartial

Most consumers don't trust advertising. An ad or commercial can make any cruise line appear good, any hotel look great, any airline seem wonderful. A travel agent, with insider knowledge and experience, can cut through the hype and recommend the best product for a client's needs. But do they? Today, most travel agencies have **preferred suppliers** who they favor in their recommendations and who, in turn, provide them and their agencies with *better or extra commissions* (called **overrides**), *access to special inventory* (otherwise known as "**group space**"), and perhaps free or low-cost travel.

Is this practice bad for the buying public? In most cases, no. First, travel agencies usually have preferred relationships with multiple suppliers in each travel sector: perhaps five or six cruise lines, six or more tour operators, two or three airlines, a family of hotel brands, and one or two car rental companies. Moreover, these suppliers are presumably chosen for an agency's portfolio of preferred products because they have demonstrated a high degree of reliability, value, service, and overall excellence.

As a result, the agency is able to solve almost any client's needs using its preferred suppliers. If an agent can't find the right product from a preferred, though, he or she may very well book a nonpreferred. Many agents are so fiercely dedicated to providing the best trip for their customers that they're quite prepared to recommend a nonpreferred if that's what the client needs or insists on.

> **insider info**
> Most suppliers (except airlines) pay agencies 10 percent commission for bookings. Cruise lines and tour operators pay between 10 and 16 percent, depending on the volume that agency does with the supplier.

> **insider info**
> About 75 percent of all travel agents are women.

Kinds of Travel Agencies

Not long ago, most travel agencies followed a common prototype: small, family-owned, serving a neighborhood or small region, and selling just about every form of travel. That has changed. Four patterns now dominate the agency landscape: (1) conventional, full-service agencies, (2) online agencies, (3) specialized agencies, and (4) home-based agencies.

Conventional, Full-Service Agencies

These agencies sell it all: air, lodging, car rentals, rail travel, cruises, tours, and most other forms of travel packages. Customers can book travel and receive advice by phone, via e-mail, or by visiting the agency in person. Conventional agencies tend to sell mostly to people in their own geographic community. Their neighborhood presence often makes them a comfortable choice for locals.

What Are Your Credentials?

Occasionally you'll see a series of degree-like letters after a travel agent's name, or you'll read that he or she is a "specialist." What does this mean? First, in most countries, travel agents don't need a license, credential, or certificate to do their jobs. It's left to travel agencies to determine whether a potential agent has the knowledge, experience, and skills to help customers with their travel needs. However, many travel agents feel, rightly, that ongoing training is necessary to keep their skills sharp. They also like the thought of having their hard work and knowledge validated. And they realize that such validation will make their clients aware of their qualifications and, by extension, make them worthy of their clients' trust.

Four types of programs address the training needs of the travel agency community:

- *Professional organizations* such as the *Cruise Lines International Association* (CLIA) and the *Travel Institute* blend self-study print materials, Web-based programs, live seminars, videos, and testing to create comprehensive certification programs.

- *Destination marketing organizations (DMOs)* offer programs that are specific to their destinations. As with professional organizations, various media are combined to deliver the training, with a test to gauge the agent's achievement. The agent then becomes a specialist in that destination.

- *Suppliers* likewise provide specialist programs to bring agents up to speed on their products. Again, various media can be used, sometimes with a proficiency test administered at the end.

- *Travel schools*—either private or public—offer comprehensive courses of study that lead to a certificate or degree. Travel agencies usually feel that graduates of travel schools are better trained, motivated, and informed than typical novice job applicants. Also, travel agents sometimes take classes at travel schools to upgrade their knowledge.

Full-service agencies can, in turn, be subdivided according to how they operate:

- They may be *wholly owned or operated* by a large agency chain, such as *AAA* or by a smaller regional or local chain. Large chains usually have a thousand or more locations and are called *mega-agency* chains. "Regional chains" count several hundred locations and "local chains" a half-dozen or more.

- Travel agencies may be *franchises* that are owned by individuals or families but are affiliated with a large brand, such as *American Express* or *Travel Leaders*, to whom the owners pay an annual franchise fee and/or percentage of profits.

- Travel agencies may be affiliated with a **consortium**, a group of agencies that work together to obtain and develop marketing tools, accounting systems, training programs, and higher commissions from select, preferred suppliers. Among the biggest are *Ensemble Travel, Travelsavers*, and *Signature Travel Network*.

Agencies that belong to a consortium keep their local identities and have no brand recognition among the public. So if Robinson Travel affiliates with Signature, it will still be called Robinson Travel. If it affiliates with American Express, it will advertise as an American Express agency. In many cases, each agency also has an ownership interest in its consortium.

- Travel agencies may simply be *independent*, with no affiliations whatsoever. These are often called "mom-and-pop" agencies.

Online Agencies

Online agencies operate almost exclusively through their Web sites. The best-known, most prominent brands are *Travelocity, Expedia, Orbitz,* and *Priceline.* These agencies concentrate on selling travel commodities such as air, lodging, and car rentals. They do also sell experiential products such as cruises and tours, sometimes in conjunction with a toll-free phone number that enables customers to speak to, or "online chat" with, a travel agent who works for the online agency and can explain the products and offer advice. A great marketing strength is that online agencies are not bound by geography. They can sell to people anywhere in the world.

It bears mentioning that most conventional travel agencies maintain Web presences, where would-be customers can find out about the agency and the deals that it may be offering. In many cases, the public can also book online with such an agency. Agencies that sell conventionally as well as on the Web are called "brick-and-click" agencies.

What Should an Agency Be?

THIS & that

In today's travel agency environment, it's often difficult for owners to decide whether to be a franchise of a mega-agency chain, join a consortium, or remain independent. Each type has its advantages and disadvantages. Being part of a mega-agency brings the instant credibility that its well-known brand furnishes. It provides buying clout with suppliers. And brand chains make available promotional, technical, and training support. Of the three choices, however, affiliating with a mega-agency is usually the costliest option.

An agency can choose to remain independent. This do-it-yourself approach is certainly economical, but a lack of purchasing leverage with suppliers is a critical shortcoming. This is why mom-and-pop agencies have become much less common than they once were.

Consortia represent a compromise option. Supplier leverage, ready-made technical systems, and guidance, as well as some training opportunities, are all pluses, as are the lower price for affiliation and the ability of the agency to keep its local identity.

Specialized Agencies

Many agencies, especially independent and consortium-affiliated ones, have discovered that they can be most competitive and profitable by narrowing their focus to a particular kind of customer. For example, an agency may be a *corporate* one, specializing in the needs of a business's employees. It may be a *cruise-only* agency, with cruising as the core product it offers. Or it may specialize in *student travel*, as does the *STA Travel* chain.

Another business model is that a full-service agency may have several *specialties*, such as ski travel, upscale vacations, trips for people with physical disabilities, or travel to family destinations such as Orlando.

In some cases, an agency may be so focused on its specialty that it doesn't need to be a full-service business. For example, a cruise-only agency may sell air, but only from consolidators or from the cruise lines' own inventory. It therefore doesn't need to satisfy the complicated rules that govern an agency "appointed" by the airlines (see This & That, "Appointed Agencies").

Home-Based Agencies

Like many businesspeople, agency owners, managers, and employees have discovered that—in the "electronic village" we now live in—you can work from just about anywhere, including your home. The rules for being an appointed travel seller have been made easier to accommodate this change. There are several types of home-based agents:

Many agents are now home based.

- An agency's full-time employee may find that it's much easier to work from a home office than at the agency's physical location. The agent likes working from home because of the independence and flexibility it affords. The agency likes it because it requires less office space and fewer resources. Not that home-based agenting is a good idea for everyone. Peer interaction is lost and plenty of self-discipline is required.

- The owners of a mom-and-pop agency may decide that the overhead costs of a conventional storefront location are financially unfeasible but that working out of a home location is viable and affordable. So they decide to operate the agency entirely from home.

- An agency may have a part-time seller of travel (often called an independent contractor) who prefers to work out of his or her home. Such outside agents may have a full-time job in another field and sell travel to their circle of friends, relatives, and coworkers. The agency with which the seller is affiliated is usually called a **host agency**.

It should be noted that not too long ago home-based agents were thought of as unprofessional dilettantes. That stereotype has changed as many skilled agents have relocated their workspaces to their homes and as home offices in all fields have become far more common in our society.

Appointed Agencies

If a travel agency wishes to sell air tickets (and many agencies still do), it must be officially authorized to do so. That is, it must be "appointed" by the *Airlines Reporting Corporation* (ARC) and *the International Airlines Travel Agent Network* (IATAN). Both organizations require that certain factors be in place before an appointment can occur, including sound financial resources, experienced personnel, and the ability and willingness to promote and sell travel. The criteria for appointment are precisely spelled out and may change from year to year.

Travel agencies don't need to be appointed by ARC and IATAN to sell cruises, hotels, car rentals, and tours. However, certain suppliers in these categories may require the agency to be ARC-, IATAN-, or perhaps CLIA-appointed before commissions can be paid or industry discounts to agents become available. Any travel agency must also satisfy general state, county, and city business requirements, as well as any government requirements specific to sellers of travel.

Although not necessary, travel agencies can choose to belong to certain trade associations. The most popular associations among travel agents include *CLIA*, the *American Society of Travel Agents* (ASTA), the *National Association of Career Travel Agents* (NACTA), the *Outside Sales Support Network* (OSSN), the *National Association of Cruise Oriented Agencies* (NACOA), and the *Association of Retail Travel Agents* (ARTA).

Corporate Travel Management

Many companies—especially smaller ones—rely on conventional travel agencies to handle all of their employees' travel logistics. Increasingly, though, corporations have realized that, like data processing and personnel costs, travel is a very controllable expense.

In some cases, therefore, they ask that the travel agency with which they do business have a branch-like, "in-plant" office on the client company's premises. It may be staffed by the travel agency's personnel, by company staff, or by a mix of both.

Many companies—large ones especially—do not contract with travel agencies but create their own *corporate travel departments* (or *travel management divisions*). The travel agent–like employees of these divisions are usually called **corporate travel managers**. Sometimes they're labeled *corporate agents*, with the title corporate travel manager reserved for the person in charge of the department.

Corporate travel management personnel have many duties. In addition to arranging travel, they do the following:

- Set corporate travel policy (for example, a traveler must book advance purchase fares whenever practical)

- Plan meetings, conferences, and convention programs

- Negotiate with suppliers

- Manage travel budgets

A good travel agent can recommend a cruise to meet a client's expectations.

© Losevsky Pavel/www.Shutterstock.com

- Arrange personnel relocation and housing

- Communicate with management in other departments of the corporation

Because they're considered regular corporate employees and have so many additional responsibilities, corporate travel managers are usually paid better than regular travel agents. Several agency chains specialize in business, government, or military travel. The military is a huge purchaser of travel and travel-related products and services.

Travel Agent: Sales or Service Person?

Look at This & That, "For Work or Pleasure," and you'll see that business agents are primarily service providers, whereas those agents dealing with vacationers are salespeople. Of course, a leisure agent must also provide great service, and corporate agents sometimes practice certain sales strategies.

For Work or Pleasure?

It has often been observed that agents who deal primarily with business travelers have different personalities and approaches from those who work mostly with vacationers. Perhaps this is the result of the unique client psychologies involved, or perhaps it's the agent's psyche that draws him or her to specialize in one form of travel or the other.

Here are some of the differences in the ways a leisure agent and a corporate travel agent work. Many are generalities, yet they do describe the fundamental differences between the two sectors:

Corporate Agents	Leisure Agents
• Respond to requests	• Inform and suggest
• Are somewhat sensitive to travel costs	• Are extremely sensitive to travel costs
• Deal with logistics	• Deal with vacation "dreams"
• Are seen as service people	• Are more likely to exert their sales skills
• Usually work with short lead times	• Are more likely to work with long lead times
• May make plenty of changes as a trip departure approaches	• Are less likely to make changes once a trip is booked
• Often communicate through the traveler's assistant, not the traveler	• Almost always deal directly with the traveler
• Know a lot about the selected destinations their clients usually go to	• Know details about many more destinations
• Usually hear about how a trip went	• Hear about how a trip went if something went wrong
• Just about every caller books travel	• Often deal with "phone shoppers," so a majority of callers *don't* book

Careers

Careers in the Travel Agent Industry

Here are some of the jobs associated with travel agencies:

- Senior executives, directors, managers, owners
- Human resources/training specialists
- Travel agents (leisure and/or corporate)
- Outside sales representatives
- Group specialists

- Cruise, groups, destination, corporate travel specialists
- Clerical support
- Vendor negotiators
- Accountants
- Technological support

The sales skills in all travel sectors are examined in detail in Chapter 10, but let's look briefly at the typical steps that good travel agents take with leisure clients:

1. They provide a warm and cheery *greeting*.

2. They *ask questions* to determine the client's needs. This process is usually called *qualifying*.

3. They do *research*, if necessary, to find the right products and services for the client.

4. They *make recommendations* that meet the client's needs.

5. They *overcome objections* that the client might have to the recommendations.

6. They *enhance the sale* by recommending additional products or services (**cross-selling**) or perhaps better options than the client had in mind (**upselling**).

7. They *close the sale* by getting agreement and payment from the client.

8. They *follow up* to make sure the trip went well.

How Agents Obtain Information

Before the 1990s, travel agents were just about the only people who could swiftly and easily access travel information. For example, if consumers wanted to compare airline schedules and prices, they had to call every airline, compare what they learned from each, then call back to book the best option (assuming it was still available).

THIS & that

Resources

Here are the Web-based resources that are most useful in an agency situation (and for other travel sectors too):

- **Business Travel Planner:** Information on destinations, hotels, airport transfers, and so on.

- **The Hotel & Travel Index:** Brief information and ratings for most of the world's hotels, with maps, destination information, and booking information.

- **The Official Cruise Guide:** Information on just about every cruise ship, major port, and itinerary in the world.

- **The Star Service Online:** Superb, in-depth analyses of worldwide hotels and cruise vessels. No ads.

- **Travel42:** A reference resource that bundles the *Weissmann Reports*, the *Star Service Online*, and several other resources into one interactive package—all for one price.

- **Weissmann Reports:** Excellent resource for destination information.

This has changed. Through the Internet, consumers largely have the same access to information that travel agents do. So agents have reengineered their jobs, stressing their value-added assets—knowledge, experience, accountability, and the other benefits discussed earlier—the kind that most travelers don't possess.

So how do agents access the information that's not already "in their heads"? The primary source is the CRS/GDS, which was described in Chapter 2. Agents also use the Internet, discovering—through repeated trial and error—which sites are the most content-rich. That they're able to do all this electronically is one reason home-based agenting has become so much more practical. And remember, these systems permit not only information resources but also booking capabilities. In some cases, big online agencies pay modest fees to agents for each transaction they carry out online with them.

Agents also use more traditional resources. They generally have access to at least several industry sources on hotels, as well as detailed

Business travel is a major sector of the travel industry.

© AVAVA/www.Shutterstock.com

Careers

The Expert Is in

What must leisure travel agents do to succeed? At the very least, they must:

- Have a detailed understanding of the products and services from those suppliers they sell most frequently
- Know those destinations their clients most often visit
- Have solid research and computer skills
- Be familiar with the logistics of travel and be able to find out about related issues like passports and visa requirements

- Know at least a little about basic bookkeeping and accounting
- Possess sharp sales, service, and communication skills
- Devote at least some time each year to expanding their expertise through training programs, reading trade publications, and doing some personal travel

destination geography reference tools. They can use toll-free numbers to contact suppliers for information and to book travel. And they can consult brochures.

It is interesting to note that certain experiential product suppliers, such as cruise lines and tour operators, report that the typical travel agent contacts them about three times per booking, whereas a customer who buys directly from them via a toll-free line averages seven calls per booking. This suggests that consumers are not as adept at dealing with travel as agents are. It also explains why such suppliers value travel agents. If travel agents were to vanish, cruise lines and tour companies would have to double or triple their reservations staff to handle the volume of calls. This could change. However, for now, most consumers still feel that a travel agent is a more reliable source of information on experiential products than Web sites are.

More This and That

Here are some miscellaneous things you ought to know about the travel agency business:

- Because of the cut in airline commissions, most agencies charge clients fees for making air bookings and reservation changes.

- About one-quarter of travel agents are paid straight salary, one-quarter have salaries based entirely on commissions earned, and half are paid on a combination of both.

- The trade publications that agents most commonly read are *Travel Weekly*, *Travel Agent*, *TravelAge West*, *Agent@Home*, and *Vacation Agent*. Most agents read one magazine in depth each week and skim the others if there's time. These publications have companion Web sites that offer late-breaking news, training modules, and other features in addition to the print magazine content.

- Consumers are most likely to consult travel agents about cruises, tours, and complicated trips.

- Consumers who use travel agents tend to be wealthier, better educated, and spend more on travel (twice as much) than those who don't.

- E-mail and texting have become significant ways for travel agents to communicate with clients. This is especially true for agents with specialties, who often sell to clients who live well beyond the agent's local community.

- Organizing and operating group departures is a major source of revenue for many agencies.

- It's important for a travel agency to have "errors and omissions" insurance, which protects them from damages that may occur because of mistakes made by an employee in planning a client's trip. Specialized insurance companies provide it.

- About 80 percent of all cruises and 85 percent of all tours are sold through travel agencies.

Review Questions

1. List at least five reasons people decide to use travel agents to plan their trips.

2. What kinds of travel agencies are there?

3. How does the way a corporate travel agent works differ from the way a leisure agent works? Give at least seven differences.

4. What resources do travel agents use to access information?

5. What skills does a travel agent typically need?

It's All About You Questions

1. Would you consider working as a travel agent? Give three reasons why or why not.

2. Working from home is not limited to travel agents. In fact, it is estimated that about a quarter of all businesses are home based. What do you think are three advantages and three disadvantages of working from home?

NAME DATE

Activity 1: Searching

Enter "travel agency" in your Internet search engine, and then browse through the first 40 Web addresses you find. What patterns or categories of sites did you discover? Was it sometimes difficult to distinguish agencies from tour operators? What unexpected sites did your search produce? Describe your experience.

Now select something you are interested in when you travel (for example, diving). Try to use your search engine to find travel agencies or agents that specialize in that interest. How did you do it, what was the outcome, and why?

Activity 2: Let Your Fingers Do the Walking

Look up "travel agencies" in the Yellow Pages of your telephone book. Answer the following questions based on the listings and ads you find.

1. What agency would be the first one you would call? Why?

2. Which might be your second choice to call? Why?

3. Do any agencies indicate that they belong to any travel associations such as ASTA or CLIA? About what percentage of agencies indicate such an affiliation?

4. Do any agencies indicate specialties? Which specialties are named?

5. How many (what percentage) give a Web site address?

6. Are any well-known brand names (for example, American Express or AAA) indicated? Which ones?

NAME   DATE

Gale Hospitality, Tourism and Leisure Database Assignment

The following assignment requires access to the Gale Hospitality, Tourism and Leisure Database. Check with your instructor to see if you have access to this database.

Find the article *Help Them Count the Ways* in the Gale Hospitality, Tourism & Leisure Collection.

Read the entire article and then come up with 10 things a travel agent should find out from clients when selling "romance travel."

6

Better by the Bunch: The Tour Industry Today

KEY TERMS

- Adventure tour
- Affinity tour
- All-inclusive tour
- Customized tour
- Day tour
- Deadheading
- Ecotourism
- Escorted tour
- Fly-drive tour
- Ground operator
- Group desk
- Group/tour rate
- Groups manager
- Hard adventure
- Hop-on, hop-off
- Hosted tour
- Inbound operator
- Incentive trip
- Independent tour
- Intermodal tour
- Meet-and-greet service
- Motorcoach tour
- Mystery tour
- Narration
- Optional
- Outbound operator
- Pied piper
- Public tour
- Receptive operator
- Seat rotation
- Site tour
- Soft adventure
- Split itinerary
- Student tour
- Tour
- Tour manager
- Tour operator
- Transfer service
- Trip director

After studying this chapter, you'll be able to:

- Describe the many kinds of tours that exist

- Explain why tour manager jobs are in such demand

- Determine what motivates people to take a tour

- Explain how tours are priced and sold

Photo courtesy of Frank Marini

Frank Marini

CURRENT POSITION/TITLE:

Vice President of Sales, Collette Vacations

SHORT DESCRIPTION OF WHAT YOUR RESPONSIBILITIES ARE:

I oversee the company's Travel Agents Strategy & Focus.

EDUCATION:

BA, University of Rhode Island

FIRST JOB IN TRAVEL/HOSPITALITY INDUSTRY:

Mailroom clerk at Collette Vacations while in high school

FIRST PAID JOB (IF DIFFERENT FROM ABOVE):

Dishwasher at Magic Menu Restaurant

FORMER POSITION:

President of Contiki, a tour company for 18- to 35-year-olds

FAVORITE PART OF WHAT I DO:

Making someone's lifelong travel dreams a reality

THING I WISH I DIDN'T HAVE TO DO:

Going through 150+ new e-mails per day

SOMEONE WHO INSPIRES ME:

My Mom & Dad

STRANGEST OR FUNNIEST CAREER-RELATED THING I'VE EVER EXPERIENCED:

Teaching Australians on a tour to Switzerland how to make snowballs (they had never seen snow) and then having a full-on snowball fight with them. Priceless.

FAVORITE QUOTE:

"Ideas are easy, execution is hard."

SOMETHING ALMOST NO ONE KNOWS ABOUT ME:

I competed in the Junior Olympic Trials for the Hammer Throw. I also play bass guitar in my rock band, THE CLOSERS.

A vacation should be fun, don't you think? But it doesn't always turn out that way. You arrive at the hotel and it's overbooked. You can't figure out where the best place to eat is or what sights you should see. You finally decide on a place to dine but can't find parking—and the traffic! Then you get home, gather your receipts, do some math, and figure out that the trip cost you three times more than you expected.

You're not the first to discover that travel can be stressful. In fact, as you learned in Chapter 1, the word *travel* comes from a French word that means "to work," and that word, *travailler*, is rooted in the Latin word *tripalium*, which was a device for torturing. Although it might not be torture, some people decide that all that trip planning work isn't worth it. Many decide to take a tour instead. Let's find out why.

Kinds of Tours

Before delving into the reasons many people choose to travel by tour, let's clarify what a tour is. In the travel industry, a **tour** is defined as *any preplanned (and prepaid) package to one or more places that includes two or more travel components* (for example, flights, lodging, admission to attractions).

Tours may be highly structured or loosely organized and can vary in duration from short sightseeing trips to continent-crossing adventures that last several weeks. No matter how many types of people there are—and wherever they want to go—there seems to be a tour made just for them.

Escorted Tours

"When I'm on vacation, I don't want to worry about anything." That's a commonly heard statement from people who favor **escorted tours**, *structured journeys on which the tour participants are accompanied by a travel professional who sees to their needs.*

They would rather leave the planning, driving, and hassles to somebody else. Of course, an escorted tour almost always involves a group of people. The group may be preformed (from a school or club, for instance) or consist of people who separately bought the tour package and are meeting for the first time.

On an escorted tour, *the person in charge of ensuring an enjoyable travel experience* is called the **tour manager**. From the moment of

Touring has been around for a long time.

© ChipPix/www.Shutterstock.com

arrival at the first destination until the departure for home from the final destination, the tour manager accompanies the tour group and performs many key responsibilities. Typically, the tour manager will:

- Coordinate all travel logistics, such as hotel check-in, baggage handling, and group transportation

- Guide the travelers through the tour's itinerary, keeping everyone well informed and on schedule

- Offer fun and fascinating commentary while traveling and sightseeing, often in conjunction with local sightseeing guides

- Handle any and all problems, personality conflicts, and emergencies

- Sometimes accompany the group on the first and last days' flights

In the travel industry, a tour manager may also be called a *tour leader, tour director, tour escort, tour conductor, tour guide*, and, in Europe, *tour courier*.

The preferred mode of transportation for escorted tours is the motorcoach. Ah, a bus, you say? Not in the tour business. Buses are those bare-boned vehicles that take passengers to school or work. Motorcoaches, on the other hand, are large, well-powered vehicles (sometimes costing $500,000 and more) that are custom-built for touring. They transport groups (and their luggage) over long distances in relative luxury, with comfortable seats, video screens, and large windows for easy viewing.

Motorcoaches also are often used for local sightseeing, to transport charter groups, and as regular intercity transportation. *An escorted tour in which a motorcoach is the main mode of transportation to and from destinations and attractions* is called a **motorcoach tour**.

Several studies have shown that an aversion to bus transportation is the single most important factor that prevents travelers from taking a group tour, despite the comparative comfort of modern motorcoaches. That's one reason **intermodal tours**, which *combine different types of transportation into one package*, have become increasingly popular. Traveling by motorcoach may be augmented by a train trip, a cruise, or even a bicycle caravan. Not surprisingly, intermodal operators tend to downplay the role of motorcoaches in their packaging.

> ### insider info
> Tour managers may get commissions on anything the group members buy during a "shopping" stop. Often these stores are more expensive than others.

> ### insider info
> Tour managers rarely have to pay for lodging or meals during a tour. They get "comped." (From "complimentary," or free.)

Today's motorcoaches are ideal for touring.

© Gilles Lougassi/www.Shutterstock.com

Popularity Contest

The job of tour manager is one of the most popular, appealing, and competitive in the travel industry. Leading tour operators are deluged with hundreds of inquiries a year for tour escort employment. Why the flood of applications?

- *Lifestyle*: Tour managing has great allure. Like the rich and famous, tour directors travel to exotic locales, stay in high-end hotels, and feast on fabulous food—and get paid for it! Plus, tour managers are often independent contractors, free to choose when and where to work. They become the group members' "celebrity," their focus of attention. If you like being in the limelight, tour managing may be a good job for you.

- *Salary and benefits*: Tour directors are generally well compensated. According to one study, the average starting salary in the United States for a tour director is $70 per day. Someone with significant experience averages $100 per day, and those with multiple language skills far more. More important, they also earn sizable tips, receive some living expenses, and, in some cases, get commissions from **optionals**, *additional tour features not included in the main package* (also called *add-ons*). In fact, top tour leaders, working 30 to 40 weeks a year, can make about as much as an airline pilot or a major travel industry executive.

- *Experience*: A lot can be learned in a classroom, but the real-world experiences gained from escorting tours have helped tour managers climb the ladder in the travel industry. Actually, the experience gained from conducting tours also benefits those going into law, medicine— really any profession where problem-solving and people-dealing skills are valuable. Having to solve problems immediately, appease problematic passengers, negotiate with hardnosed hotel clerks, or entertain stressed tour members when the motorcoach breaks down builds character and tests one's skills. Most tour managers will tell you that tour escorting makes you a better person.

The Downside of Tour Managing

Although tour conducting may seem to be a dream job, it *is* demanding. Here are some of the reasons why:

- *Stress*: On the road, a tour leader must cope with constant pressure. Dozens of people, some of whom may be difficult or demanding, are in his or her care. Tour conducting certainly isn't a 9-to-5 job. If someone calls at 4 in the morning with a problem, the tour director must deal with it. In reality, a tour conductor is on duty 24 hours a day.

- *Life on the road*: Like traveling salespeople, tour conductors live out of a suitcase. (No wonder many tour managers are single.) Those who do have a family must live with long periods away from home. Moreover, what tours are scheduled and which ones are offered to the tour manager are often unpredictable, which makes it even more difficult to maintain a normal life.

- *Unstable work situations*: Tour operators may treat escorts as freelancers yet frown on them working for competing companies. And working as an independent contractor has its pluses, but pension plans, health insurance, and the rest of the benefits associated with full-time work are usually not among them. Companies often limit tour directors to a few destinations. They expect escorts to be fully available during high seasons. And they'll certainly stop offering tours to a tour manager who turns down too many trips.

Hosted Tours

Hosted tours are similar to escorted tours. But the "host" (a tour representative) only meets with the tour travelers when they need to see him or her. Usually the host doesn't travel with the group but is available (at a desk in the hotel lobby, for example) to answer questions, book extra trip components, and solve problems. Hosted tours appeal to people who desire independence in their trip but also want easy access to someone who can help them with their needs.

Independent and Fly-Drive Tours

Not everyone is a candidate for an escorted or a hosted tour. In fact, some people hate the idea of a group tour. When they think of a group tour, they perceive a trip with limited freedom, forced companionship, and uncomfortable bus rides. They would rather be in charge of their own travel experience than have someone else do it for them.

These people are not alone. In fact, the most popular type of packaged tour is the **independent tour**. To qualify as independent, *the tour package must include overnight accommodations, plus one or more other travel components.* For instance, a traveler who wants to go to Austria could buy a two-week package that includes air transportation between the United States and Austria, seven nights in a hotel in Vienna, seven nights in an apartment in Salzburg, an Austrian Railpass or car rental, and other services (such as a visit to the world's largest strudel maker), all for one price.

insider info

Many tour companies will arrange FITs (trips assembled from scratch, rather than a package) for a travel agent to resell to his or her clients.

Interior of a luxury motorcoach.

© Quin/www.Shutterstock.com

Independent tours attract travelers who wish to set their own itinerary yet want the value for their dollar that powerful volume tour companies can offer. In the United States and Canada, independent tours outsell escorted tours four to one.

Just as the name suggests, **fly-drive tours** are similar to independent tours but with only two necessary ingredients: air transportation and car rental. They may also include other travel components such as accommodations and sightseeing. But if you don't fly and drive, you're not on a fly-drive tour.

Hybrid Tours

In recent times, all sorts of variations of traditional tours have appeared. One increasingly popular version of these hybrids resembles an escorted tour, but features large blocks of free time (including entire days) for tour members to explore a destination on their own. Each tour operator has its own term to describe this type of tour: flexible, select, and free & easy are some of the terms commonly used.

City, Site, and Personal Tours

Day tours are *tours that last fewer than 24 hours*. Most *city tours* would fall into this category. On this type of tour, a *city guide* points out the interesting sights (most likely historical or architectural) of the area. City tours are usually conducted via motorcoach, minibus, van, or as part of a walking tour.

One increasingly popular version is called the "**hop-on, hop-off**" tour. A fleet of buses (often refurbished open-top double-deck buses from London) follows a route with predetermined stops. Passengers can get on and off at any stop along the way. Another bus and guide will stop there in 10 or 15 minutes. This way, sightseers can customize their trip, stopping at places they are interested in for as long as they want and bypassing those they don't find interesting.

Sometimes a city guide will serve double-duty and drive the vehicle, becoming a *driver-guide*. Groups constitute most city tours, but individuals can go on their own

The Name Game

A tour itinerary typically has a name that's chosen to define its purpose, identify the destination, and promote the journey. For instance, "Fall Foliage" excursions are popular in New England in September and October, when the countryside explodes with color. A "Civil War" tour might visit sites such as Gettysburg, Antietam, and Appomattox Court House—places that are steeped in American history.

A park ranger gives a tour of Mesa Verde, Colorado.

private tours. Widespread in developing countries—or wherever entrepreneurial taxi drivers are in business—*personal* or *private guides* (often using their own vehicles) take individuals on exclusive tours to see the sights.

Tours conducted at a specific building (such as the U.S. Capitol), *attraction* (such as Mt. Rushmore), *or limited area* (such as San Francisco's Chinatown) are called **site tours**. In the travel industry, all such sites are referred to as attractions. The tour may be given on foot or in some sort of vehicle (for example, the *Maid of the Mist* boats at Niagara Falls).

Other Types of Tours

Some of the most intriguing successes in the tour business today are tours that are highly specialized and that target niche, or specialty, markets. Some are organized bicycle trips of Europe. Others consist of roller-coaster enthusiasts who visit the nation's greatest amusement parks. The first escorted tour ever—organized by Thomas Cook—was made up of people who shared one common trait: they didn't drink alcoholic beverages.

One type of niche tour, an **adventure tour**, *features physically active, exotic, and/ or sometimes demanding experiences.* For example, you can join an expedition to Mt. Everest. The package may include hotel accommodations, a round-trip flight, three meals a day, a climb up the mountain, and more. (Your gear and a helicopter rescue are extra.)

insider info

Some cities, including Washington, D.C., require applicants to pass a test to become a licensed tour guide.

An adventure tour may include whitewater rafting.

"Soft" adventure tours feature activities that most fit travelers can do, such as hiking, zip-lining, and river rafting. **"Hard" adventure** implies that the traveler has special skills, training, and, often, special equipment. Examples include diving, windsurfing, and rock climbing.

People who embrace the "leave no trace" philosophy have made **ecotourism** an appealing segment of not just the tour business but of the entire travel industry. When traveling to natural areas, ecotourists strive to *conserve the environment while also sustaining the well-being of the local people*. Ecotourism is sometimes referred to as *sustainable tourism* and often overlaps with the soft adventure market.

A group tour that has more to do with economy than ecology is an incentive trip. Combining business with pleasure, an **incentive trip** is *a reward for a company's most productive employees*. For example, a real estate company might fly all of its agents who reach a certain sales level to Las Vegas for a week, all expenses paid (except for losses at the blackjack table, of course).

The company can benefit by offering travel as an incentive (as opposed to, say, a washing machine) because group activities can be planned to reinforce company spirit and efficiency. Incentive houses (specialized tour companies or divisions of large travel agencies) and the companies they deal with see this as a win-win situation for everyone. The profits that the incentive program has produced pay for the trip and generate higher revenues for, in this case, the real estate company.

While accumulating wealth is the aim of incentive trips, accumulating knowledge is the purpose of **student tours**. Sometimes called *study tours*, they typically *involve*

insider info

One tour company specializes in a consumer segment that generally *doesn't* take tours: 18- to 35-year-olds. Its name: Contiki. The appeal: tour members share many common interests.

preformed school groups that visit a destination to enhance their learning experience. For example, a Latin club might visit Rome; a band might travel to Pasadena to march in the Tournament of Roses Parade; or a debate team might travel to the national convention in San Antonio.

Tours made up of high school students or younger students are accompanied by teachers, and usually parents, acting as chaperones. A college's students—and alumni—are often attracted to study tours sponsored by their school. A professor who has highly specialized knowledge of the history and culture of the destination often leads these tours. For example, an Egyptologist may escort a cruise down the Nile; an archaeologist may be the guide to Mayan ruins; or a Classics professor might be the star of a cruise to Greece and the Mediterranean.

Meet-and-greet services are related to tour experiences. Often, tour companies (especially independent tour operators) hire *guides or other "greeters" to welcome and escort travelers from the airport to their hotel, assisting them with their luggage as well.* Business travelers use such services too, sometimes as part of a convention package. Individual travelers or small groups may purchase meet-and-greet services. Cruise lines and escorted tour companies use meet-and-greet personnel to direct their passengers from the airport terminal to their motorcoaches to transfer them to the ship or to begin their tour.

Telling Terms

Here are some commonly used tour industry terms that go beyond what is defined in the main body of the text:

- **Deadheading:** (1) Making a trip or a segment of a trip without passengers; (2) driving an empty motorcoach somewhere.

- **Group/tour rate:** A special rate charged by a hotel to tours.

- **Groups manager (on a cruise):** A "one-stop" service person who facilitates all logistic matters for groups on a ship.

- **Mystery tour:** A tour in which the destination and itinerary are kept secret from the clients until they embark on the tour.

- **Narration:** A commentary provided to passengers on a tour, also called "guidespeak."

- **Seat rotation:** The policy of having passengers on a motorcoach change seats several times a day to ensure seating fairness.

- **Split itinerary:** An itinerary in which part of the tour group does one thing while the other part does something else.

- **Trip director:** A tour manager for an incentive company. Larger companies reserve this title for the person who directs all personnel and activities for a particular incentive trip.

Who Owns Tour Companies?

Travelers from the United States and Canada spend more than $11 billion yearly on tours. And according to the U.S. Travel Data Center, one out of every five people who takes a trip of five nights or longer does so through a packaged tour. The businesses that put together these packages are called **tour operators** (also called *tour companies, tour packagers, tour brokers,* or *wholesalers*). *Tour operators contract with suppliers* (for example, hotels, restaurants, airlines, motorcoach operators, and other transportation companies) *and attractions* (such as theme parks, historical buildings, and museums) *to create multiday tour packages.* They then sell the tours, either directly or through travel agents, to the public.

Travel agents especially like to sell tours because they can make a relatively high commission based on most of a client's vacation activities (even meals and airfare) with minimal arrangement hassles. In some cases, travel agencies become, in effect, tour operators, as well, by running their own group departures.

Tour operators generally belong to several associations. *The National Tour Association* (NTA) is composed of tour companies, suppliers, attractions, and destination marketing organizations (you'll learn more about these in Chapter 8). *The United States Tour Operators Association* (USTOA) limits full membership to fewer tour companies (the larger ones) and minimizes the role of suppliers in its organization. Both associations offer a valuable benefit: consumer protection plans that help reimburse tour clients in the event that a tour company with which they have booked a trip goes bankrupt. A third association is the *American Bus Association* (ABA), which represents the interests of motorcoach companies and tour operators.

insider info

It is usually best to choose an escorted tour company that has a "seat rotation" policy. This prevents tour members from staking out their "own" seats for the whole tour.

Why People Take Tours

Almost everyone feels the need to get away once in a while—from work, school, or their everyday routine. We see travel as a reward for our hard work. The fact that tours eliminate much of the drudgery and headaches of traveling makes the reward seem even more attractive. We've touched on some reasons why people take tours. Let's take a closer look.

Time and Money

Travel may be a reward for work, but it can turn into a booby prize if you fritter away your hard-earned money by wasting time and making the wrong choices on your trip. A tour that's thoughtfully arranged and conducted promises travelers that they'll get to their destinations and see the sights in a reasonable amount of time and comfort. Plus, the group purchasing power of tour operators enables them to pass along savings to consumers. Often, tour members can get a bigger bang for their buck with a more upscale travel experience than they could by booking the trip components on their own.

insider info

Off-season departures usually represent much better values than peak-season travel.

Quest for Knowledge

According to one poll, 84 percent of tour travelers rated "learning" as the most important benefit of a tour. And nearly half of those polled couldn't wait to share what they learned with their family and friends once they got home. You'd have to do some serious research to learn what a well-trained guide can comment on. Plus, a really good guide can go beyond any guidebook and truly bring a locale to life.

Camaraderie

It's not surprising that lasting friendships are often forged among people who were strangers at the beginning of a tour. Most likely, because of the tour's destination, activities, and price, its members will have similar interests and be of comparable socioeconomic status.

Tours in which the group members already know each other are called **affinity tours**. These groups are made up of members from specific clubs, schools, religious groups, or corporations. Physically challenged travelers book tours with specialized companies, knowing that the trip has already been thought through to accommodate their needs.

Lack of Options

In some cases, booking a tour to a location may not merely be the best choice—it may be just about the *only* choice. For example, tour operators frequently corner the market on hotels in an area for a special event such as Mardi Gras in New Orleans, the Running of the Bulls in Pamplona, or the Super Bowl. The only way an average consumer can get a room may be through a tour package. Although tourists

THIS & that

Get on the Bus

Tightly allied to the tour business is the motorcoach industry. One segment of the business operates intercity transportation services. The largest and best known is *Greyhound*. A second segment is the charter motorcoach business. These independently owned companies (they may also be part of a franchise) rent or lease motorcoaches to groups, schools, sports teams, cruise lines, and, often, to tour operators. Tour companies rarely own their own buses. A third segment, **transfer services**, specializes in *operating buses or vans between airports and hotels*. A fourth sector consists of companies that use motorcoaches to give city tours. (The best known is *Gray Line*.) And, of course, city transit systems—usually controlled by the city government—facilitate transportation within a city's metropolitan region via buses, streetcars, and subways. Note that some of these segments can overlap. A charter bus company, for example, may also operate airport transfers, and an intercity company may charter coaches to a tour operator.

might not appreciate this business strategy (if they're aware of it), they are often pleasantly surprised by how much they enjoyed the tour and become converts to group travel.

People will often join a group tour when visiting places where they perceive they might have difficulties with the local language and customs, or if safety is a concern. It wouldn't be easy, for example, for people to go to Antarctica by themselves. Most tourists who visit Tanzania, China, and Russia do so as part of organized groups.

Guests at a resort on a Segway tour.

What Determines Price?

How do tour companies price their tours? It depends on the where, when, and how long of the travel components. For instance, a short flight to a heavily visited destination will probably differ in price from a long flight to an out-of-the-way place; a room in Edinburgh will cost more in the summer than in the off-season; and it will cost more to rent a car for two weeks than for a day. A rundown of the travel components of a tour is usually listed on the tour's itinerary and, often, in the company's brochure.

A tour that offers most of its features for one price is called an **all-inclusive tour** (also called an *all-expense tour* or *inclusive tour*). Clients know and pay for most of their vacation costs before they even leave home. The travel components typically or partially covered in an inclusive tour are lodging, transportation, meals, and admissions to attractions.

When buying or selling a tour, you should keep in mind that price isn't always the best measure of *value*. Two tours, which at first appear identical, could be offered at very different prices, and yet the more expensive tour may be the better value. For instance, the hotels on the more expensive tour may be rated higher and have better locations than those on the less expensive tour.

How Tours Are Sold

Tour operators sell their tours to the general public and to preformed groups. *Packages offered to the public* are often called **public tours**, or *per-capita tours*. Tour companies will advertise a series of tours with departures on a regular schedule. For example, a company might promote a baseball tour: seven-day motorcoach

insider info

The tour has only some meals included? Check to see if they're mostly breakfasts. If they are, those "nine meals included" may be less impressive than they seem at first.

insider info

The quality of the hotel brands a tour utilizes usually reflects the tour's overall quality.

Touring for the Rich and Famous

Several tour operators, such as *Travcoa* and *Abercrombie & Kent*, target very upscale travelers. Although their tours are pricey, the features are rather astounding. For example, they may limit groups to 18 passengers so that the tour members' experience can be more personal and attentive. Tour participants not only stay at the best hotels, but in the best *rooms* of those hotels. If they dine at a restaurant other than

the one the group visits, they will be reimbursed by the tour company for their meal. Or let's say that, because traffic is light, it takes only an hour to get to an attraction on their motorcoach. However, because of heavy traffic, the return might take three hours. So—and this really happens—they'll be flown back to their hotel in helicopters.

tours going to Major and Minor League games, departing from Chicago every Sunday from April to September. People find out about the tour from the company's brochures, catalogs, Web site, or ads, and then pick the departure date they want. They book the tour either through a travel agent, who may even have recommended the company and tour in the first place, or with the tour company directly. If the tour doesn't fill up (or at least meet a minimum number), the tour company may cancel the trip and try to move the clients to another departure date.

Tours tailored for a preformed affinity group, at a special price, are usually called **customized tours**, or *charter tours*. Potential tour participants usually find out about them from flyers, meetings, e-mails, word-of-mouth, or an organization's newsletter. Often *a person within the organization will spearhead the trip*; this person (for example, a teacher at a school) is called a **pied piper**.

A company that concentrates on tours in a particular city, area, or country is called an **inbound operator**. For instance, someone in Peru might purchase, through a travel agent in Lima, a tour to visit Utah's national parks. The Peruvian agent will book the tour with an inbound operator—a company in the United States (perhaps a branch of the same international company the agent works for). Once that traveler (and the tour's other passengers) arrives in Utah, the inbound operator, who often works with a local ground operator, caters to the tour member's needs.

An **outbound operator** *takes groups from a particular city or country to another city or country*. The Internet and the travel sections of the Sunday newspaper are filled with companies that take groups of Americans on regularly scheduled trips to, for example, Australia. There is no set rule on how outbound tour operators utilize tour conductors. Escorts may travel with the group from the start of the tour, they may meet the group at the destination, or the outbound operator may contract with an inbound operator and use its tour leaders.

insider info

In some countries, colleges offer a degree in tour guiding. It's a requirement to work as a tour manager or guide.

Careers

Careers in the Tour Industry

Here are some of the careers you might pursue in the tour business:

- Senior executives, directors, and managers
- Clerical support
- Reservationists
- Tour conductors

- Tour guides
- District sales managers
- Human resources/training specialists
- Tour planners
- Drivers
- Technological support

More This and That

Here are a few additional insights into the tour industry:

- *A type of inbound tour operator that specializes in serving other tour companies' arriving groups in a limited geographic area* is called a **ground operator**, also known as a *land operator* or **receptive operator.**

- Surprisingly, many banks—especially in the midwestern and southern parts of the United States—offer escorted tours for their depositor-customers. Many of these banks outsource their group departure planning to regular tour operators; others do it all themselves.

- A **group desk** is *a division of an airline's reservations department that takes care of group reservations.*

- Some tour companies are, in fact, divisions of airlines and cruise lines, with tours operated in conjunction with flights or cruises from the parent company. Travel agencies also may assemble their own tours. Many of today's largest tour operators began as divisions of travel agencies.

- More than 700 tour operators are members of NTA, an organization that brings together those who package travel—group as well as individual trips—with suppliers and destinations that represent the various components of a trip.

Review Questions

1. What are five responsibilities of a tour manager?

2. Explain three disadvantages of a career in tour conducting.

3. Identify the following types of tours: independent, intermodal, and inclusive.

4. What are three factors in determining how a tour is priced?

It's All About You Questions

1. Did your opinion of what a "tour" is like change at all after reading this chapter? In what way?

2. Is there a place you've always wanted to visit and where you'd consider taking a multiday tour in order to see it? Explain your reasons.

NAME   DATE

Activity 1: How Outgoing Are You?

To succeed, a tour manager must be outgoing. Assess how much of a "people person" you are by doing the following exercise.

"If I had to choose between the following two options (A and B), in most cases and most of the time I would rather:"

	A	B
_____	**1.** Attend a sporting event	Watch it on TV
_____	**2.** Go to a party	Read a good book
_____	**3.** Visit with friends	Work on a hobby
_____	**4.** Watch a team sport such as football	Watch an individual sport such as gymnastics
_____	**5.** Go shopping with family or friends	Shop on my own
_____	**6.** Take a cruise vacation	Get away from it all on a near-deserted island
_____	**7.** Play cards with friends	Work on a jigsaw puzzle
_____	**8.** Be a therapist	Be an author
_____	**9.** Take aerobics classes	Take long walks alone
_____	**10.** Be a talk-show host	Be a sculptor
_____	**11.** Talk on the phone	Do some gardening
_____	**12.** Call a person and thank him or her directly for a favor	Send a written thank-you note or e-mail to the person

Total A's _____   Total B's _____

Your instructor will help you assess your "gregariousness quotient" from your answers to the above choices. Adapted from _Conducting Tours_, by Marc Mancini, Delmar Cengage Learning.

Activity 2: Touring the Internet

Visit the Web sites of the following tour companies and decide which you'd pick for an escorted tour of Australia:

Brendan Vacations: http://www.brendanvacations.com

Collette Vacations: http://www.collettevacations.com

Contiki: http://www.contiki.com

Tauck World Discovery: http://www.tauck.com

Travcoa: http://www.travcoa.com

Your #1 choice:

Explain in a short paragraph why:

You want to visit Hawaii for a week or so. Which of the following independent tour companies would you select?

Classic Vacations: http://www.classicvacations.com

Pleasant Holidays: http://www.pleasantholidays.com

United Vacations: http://unitedvacations.com

Your #1 choice:

Why?

Gale Hospitality, Tourism and Leisure Database Assignment

The following assignment requires access to the Gale Hospitality, Tourism and Leisure Database. Check with your instructor to see if you have access to this database.

Find the article *Guiding Star* in the Gale Hospitality, Tourism & Leisure Collection.

- If you were visiting Los Angeles, would you take this tour? Why or why not?

- What do you think of Brian Donnelly's approach to tour guiding?

- Would you *enjoy* doing one of these tours?

Magic at Sea: The Cruise Industry

KEY TERMS

- Air-sea package
- Berth
- Bow
- Cruise consolidator
- Deck
- Gangway
- Gross registered tonnage
- Inside stateroom
- Outside stateroom
- Pax
- Port
- Repositioning cruise
- Seating
- Space ratio
- Stabilizer
- Starboard
- Stateroom
- Stateroom steward
- Stern
- Tender
- Zodiac

After studying this chapter, you'll be able to:

- Determine why people do or don't go on cruises

- Describe different types of cruise lines and ships

- Reveal what a cruise experience is like

- Explain how cruises are priced and sold

Photo courtesy of Kristin Karst

Kristin Karst

CURRENT POSITION/TITLE:

Executive Vice President and Co-Owner, AmaWaterways, a global river cruise company

SHORT DESCRIPTION OF WHAT YOUR RESPONSIBILITIES ARE:

Responsible for global sales and charters, and managing more than 100 team members

EDUCATION:

MBA in Economics of Tourism and Business Management, University of Dresden, Germany; later taught there

FIRST JOB IN TRAVEL/HOSPITALITY INDUSTRY:

Worked at a travel agency during school breaks

FAVORITE PART OF WHAT I DO:

To have helped create a business from scratch and to now influence the spirit and attitude of those who make its success possible

THING I WISH I DIDN'T HAVE TO DO:

To have to be constantly focused; it would be nice, sometimes, to just relax.

SOMEONE WHO INSPIRES ME:

Rudi Schreiner, my husband

STRANGEST OR FUNNIEST CAREER-RELATED THING I'VE EVER EXPERIENCED:

Having to decide whether to eat fried tarantula on a recent trip to Cambodia

FAVORITE QUOTES:

"Everyone has a fair turn to be as great as he pleases." (Jeremy Collier); "Happiness depends on ourselves." (Aristotle)

SOMETHING ALMOST NO ONE KNOWS ABOUT ME:

Sorry, I promised to keep it a secret.

Did you ever see the movie *Titanic*? The film portrays one of the most tragic disasters in maritime history, when, in 1912, the huge, new vessel struck an iceberg and sank. More than 1,500 lives were lost. But here's an equally intriguing story. People exiting the theater after seeing *Titanic* were asked, "Having seen this movie, would you consider taking a cruise?" Despite the horrors they had observed on screen, 9 out of 10 said "Yes," they wanted to cruise. What stayed in their minds wasn't the misfortune. It was the romance, the luxury, and the magic of a sea adventure on a great ship.

Such is the appeal of cruising today. That's why each year more people cruise, more ships are built, and more dollars are spent on advertising. For two decades now, cruising has been one of *the* success stories of travel. Let's examine the phenomenon more closely.

Why People Cruise

Fun, adventure, and romance—these are just a few of the things that entice people to book a cruise. But there are seemingly as many reasons to go on a cruise as there are items at a well-stocked cruise ship buffet. Naturally, the cruise industry has extensively researched the topic. Here are their findings on why people take cruises:

- **Getting away from it all.** Unless you make your living on a fishing boat or pirate ship, chances are that leaving land and unwinding at sea will be a special experience.

A cruise ship visits the Greek Islands.

© JCVStock/www.Shutterstock.com

- **Luxury and service.** At one time, the pampered service provided on cruise ships was reserved for the rich and powerful. No more. Now everyone can have breakfast in bed, lounge on deck, and relax in a hot tub.

- **Interesting destinations.** You can sail to some of the world's most exciting places—on all seven continents—on a cruise ship. Ships can travel a great distance, stopping at the most interesting ports along the way. Cruises are an excellent way to sample a specific geographic area. Factors such as road conditions and distances between destinations make cruising the best option (for most people) when visiting places such as Alaska, the Caribbean, and the fjords of Norway.

- **You can do it all.** Work out or dine whenever you feel like it? Take a seat for blackjack or for afternoon tea? Cruises offer a vast variety of activities, events, ports, and dining options to occupy your time.

- **You can also do nothing.** Some people's idea of a vacation is to pack in as many activities as possible, but others prefer to relax. On a cruise, people are free to do as they wish. Sleep in. Relax by the pool. It's your choice.

- **Something for everybody.** Because of the many dining, entertainment, and activity options, a cruise can satisfy virtually anyone. Can you think of another vacation experience that can make that claim? In fact, a cruise can be so fulfilling that many companies hold their meetings, retreats, or incentive trips on cruise ships (even chartering a whole vessel).

- **A learning experience.** Cruising exposes you to different people and cultures. On many cruises, expert lecturers make the vacation experience that much more enriching. Some passengers choose specialty cruise lines that make the learning experience their primary selling point.

- **A friendly experience.** A cruise ship offers many opportunities to socialize and meet new people. By your choice of ship and destination, you're bound to encounter people with similar interests.

- **A romantic experience.** Before Leonardo DiCaprio and Kate Winslet kissed on the *Titanic*—and even before TV's *Love Boat*—people have known that a cruise ship is a good place to spark a relationship. In fact, a *Cosmopolitan* magazine survey showed that 80 percent of cruise ship passengers feel more amorous at sea. Who can argue with that?

- **A safe experience.** Although crime, terrorism, and accidents can happen anywhere at any time, cruising represents one of the safest travel options available. The ship is tightly managed and secured. Access onto and off the ship is strictly controlled. Safety devices and construction features make the chance of fire—or an iceberg—sinking the ship highly unlikely. Increasingly stringent sanitation procedures make illness onboard less probable.

- **A trendy experience.** Studies show that people tend to book a cruise in reaction to the most powerful form of advertising: word-of-mouth. Plus, positive images of cruising on television and in movies promote the idea that a cruise ship is an "in" place to be.

- **A no-hassle vacation.** For those looking at stress-free escape, cruising is it. A cruise ship minimizes your concerns and maximizes your leisure time. Unpack just once. Transportation, food, and lodging are all part of one seamless experience.

- **A prepackaged vacation.** Generally, a cruise is categorized as an inclusive vacation. In other words, you get many of the core components of your vacation in one price. Although the degree of "inclusiveness" can vary from cruise to cruise, a cruise package generally includes stateroom accommodations; toiletries (such as shampoo); most, if not all, meals; entertainment; onboard activities; fitness facility access; and, of course, transportation by the ship. Sometimes included, sometimes not, are port charges (the fee that ports charge the ship to dock), government fees and taxes, transportation to get to the port (for example, air), and transfers between the airport and dock. Usually not included are gratuities, alcoholic beverages and soft drinks (but beverages are often less expensive than at a hotel), spa services, shore excursions (such as tours), optional activities, and laundry service.

- **A vacation value.** Dollar for dollar, travelers find they get more for their money on a cruise than on a similar land-based vacation. As vacationers price out transportation and accommodation costs, they often forget that charges for things such as food, gasoline, and entertainment can easily add 50 percent to the cost of a "normal" vacation. Studies show that consumers regularly rate cruising as a better value than other vacation choices.

With so many good reasons to go on a cruise, it is no surprise that, on average, 95 percent of cruise passengers rated their cruise experience as very or highly satisfying. But cruise lines and travel agents sometimes have trouble convincing people who haven't taken a cruise to take their first one. Often, these objections in the consumer's mind are based on long-standing (and debatable) conceptions about the cruise experience. What are the roadblocks in people's minds? Take a look at This & That, "Jumping the Barriers," for the most common objections to cruising—and what can be said to counter them.

Kinds of Cruise Lines and Ships

The diversity of cruise vessels and the cruise lines that operate them is quite surprising. Let's divide them into three general categories: *mass-market*, *specialty*, and *miscellaneous*.

Mass-market cruise lines and ships are the ones that probably come to mind when you think of cruising. Cruise companies such as *Carnival*, *Norwegian*, and *Royal Caribbean* offer value-priced itineraries and operate large, sometimes huge vessels that accommodate anywhere from 1,000 to 5,000 passengers. Most of these ships feature multiple dining facilities, a swimming pool or two, a casino, a large showroom (and several smaller entertainment venues), an exercise facility and spa (where you can get a massage), shops, a small medical facility, a reception area (often in an atrium), and, of course, cabins (which are usually referred to as **staterooms**).

insider info
The larger the ship, the more choices and options there usually are.

insider info
Among the unusual features of some ships: a bowling alley, a pool with waves, a miniature golf course, a climbing wall, a "water coaster," and an ice-skating rink.

insider info
The shorter the cruise, the younger the passengers tend to be.

THIS *&* **that**

Jumping the Barriers

Objection	Counter
1. Expense	• Cite cost on a per-day basis • Compare to a similar land-based vacation • Stress inclusiveness and value • Recommend a cruise line that mirrors their budget • Suggest a repositioning cruise
2. Boredom	• Show a daily activity log • Cite their favorite activities • Cite testimonials from other clients • Recommend an active cruise • Mention the people-meeting nature of cruising
3. Elderly passengers	• Recommend a cruise with a younger passenger profile • Point out brochure photos of younger people • Explain this was once true, but no longer • Cite a testimonial from another client of about the same age as your client
4. Formality	• Recommend an informal cruise product • Explain alternate "casual" dining options • Look up dress requirements as stated in the brochure's information section
5. Regimentation	• Recommend a flexible cruise product (for example, upscale cruises, sailing ships, and adventure/education cruises) • Cite the "do-it-all-or-nothing-at-all" nature of cruising • List flexible features (such as multiple dining options) • Suggest independent pre- and postcruise packages
6. Limited port time	• Select itineraries that offer maximum port time • Suggest shore excursions as an efficient way to experience a port • Offer pre- and postcruise packages
7. Confinement	• Recommend a ship with a high space ratio • Recommend an ocean-view stateroom or one with a verandah • Sell up to a larger stateroom or suite • Reinforce that ships are really large, floating resorts
8. Forced socializing	• Underscore the do-it-all-or-nothing-at-all nature of cruising • Recommend a product with many dining choices and/or open seating • Sell up to a product with all open-seating dining • Suggest a stateroom with a verandah

Jumping the Barriers (*continued*)

Objection	Counter
9. Navy experience	• Stress the features inconceivable on a military ship (such as entertainment and pampering)
	• Emphasize that this isn't a seagoing military base but a seagoing *resort*
10. Too much food	• Cite healthy, "spa" dining options
	• Point out exercise opportunities
11. Ship safety	• Explain how safe today's cruise ships are and how the few problems that have occurred have been rapidly contained
	• Underscore the fact that security is emphasized on today's vessels
12. Terrorism	• Explain how cruise lines take aggressive precautions to avoid such problems
	• Point out that the lines avoid trouble-plagued ports and regions
	• Say that a ship is a highly controlled environment, where unusual situations are quickly noticed
13. Too far	• Underscore that it's worth it
	• Choose a closer embarkation port or one that requires fewer plane changes
	• Remind them that, once there, a cruise maximizes their vacation time
14. Motion discomfort/ getting sick	• Explain how ship stabilizers minimize motion
	• Inform them of Sea Bands®
	• Recommend that they discuss the problem with their physician; pills or Transderm Scop patches may be prescribed
	• Recommend a river cruise, where motion is rare
	• Book during a time of the year when winds and waves are minimal
	• Cite the aggressive efforts cruise lines are taking to keep their ships highly sanitized
15. Level of knowledge	• Give more information
	• Help them visualize themselves on the cruise
	• Describe how they'll feel on a cruise
	• Loan them a video about cruising

Source: Adapted from *The CLIA Guide to the Cruise Industry* (p. 158), by Marc Mancini, 2011, Clifton Park, NY: Delmar Cengage Learning. Copyright 2011 by Delmar Cengage Learning. Printed with permission.

Certain "premium" lines (for example, *Holland America*, *Princess*, and *Celebrity*) offer more lavish ships and experiences, selling to more moneyed consumers. But they still may be considered mass-market because they attract almost as many passengers as do the less expensive companies and operate ships almost as large.

Specialty cruise companies focus on narrower segments of consumers:

- *Luxury cruise lines* appeal to wealthy travelers, operate smaller vessels, and offer astonishing levels of service.

- *Education and adventure cruise lines* target people who want their cruise to be built around learning and exploration-type experiences. They generally use small vessels and visit ecologically interesting places.

- *Masted sailing ships* have real sails and reproduce an experience that once dominated seafaring. They can be found at all value levels and attract people who want to relive the romance of yesteryear.

- *Riverboats* fall into two categories: paddlewheelers that sail on the Mississippi and its tributaries, re-creating a Mark Twain-like adventure, and contemporary riverboats that ply such legendary rivers as the Nile, the Danube, and the Rhine.

Some kinds of cruise adventures fall into truly miscellaneous categories. The cruise vessels that sail Norway's fjord-lined west coast also carry cargo and serve as transportation for locals. Huge ferry ships transport people overnight (with entertainment) between Scandinavia and Europe's mainland. There are large "condo"

A river cruise ship sailing the Nile.

© Jose Ignacio Soto/www.Shutterstock.com

Big, Bigger, and Biggest

THIS & that

What criteria does the cruise industry use to size its ships? Several, in fact. A ship can be measured by the number of staterooms, how many passengers it can accommodate, and its **gross registered tonnage** (**GRT**). GRT is *a measurement of the volume of enclosed public spaces on a ship*. Open areas (such as the promenade deck) or sections used only by the crew (such as the kitchen and bridge) aren't factored into the measurement.

This is how the cruise industry generally classifies the size of ships based on GRT and how many *passengers* (**pax** in industry terms) the vessel can accommodate:

- *Very small ship:* Less than 10,000 GRT; under 200 pax

- *Small ship:* 10,000–20,000 GRT; 200–500 pax

- *Medium ship:* 20,000–50,000 GRT; 500–1,200 pax

- *Large ship:* 50,000–70,000 GRT; 1,200–2,000 pax

- *Megaship:* 70,000 GRT or more; over 2,000 pax; the very largest megaships are now over 200,000 GRT and carry more than 5,000 passengers.

Another measurement used in the industry is the **space ratio**, which reflects *the space, or "elbow room," passengers will have onboard*. Usually, the higher the ship's space ratio, the less crowded its guests will be. The space ratio is calculated by dividing the GRT by the vessel's passenger capacity. For example, a megaship with a GRT of 100,000 that can accommodate 2,500 passengers would have a space ratio of 40. Space ratios range from 15 to 70, with most ships falling between 25 and 40.

---

ships, with apartment-type lodging, each unit individually owned, where some people live year round (or can lease their units for part of the year). People can book trips on barges that cruise canals, and others travel via freighter ships. Some choose to rent a houseboat or sailboat for their vacation. One ship is, in fact, a floating university. In Semester at Sea, students receive college credit from the University of Virginia while visiting some of the world's greatest ports.

The Ship Experience

With all of the choices of cruises and destinations, it's hard to come up with a truly typical itinerary. But because almost half of all cruises go to the Caribbean region (the Caribbean and the Bahamas), a seven-day cruise to the western Caribbean is a good example.

Before You Sail

Some cruise lines include transfers from the airport to the port in their package, most others require you to pay extra for this service, or to make your own arrangements. A "meet-and-greet" person will be at the airport to facilitate your transfer to

insider info

Most cruise ships operate on a "cashless" system. Here's how it usually works. You register your credit card when you check in for your cruise, either in advance online or at the port. All onboard transactions are billed to your room. On the last night of the cruise, an itemized statement is left in your stateroom. If all the charges are correct, you don't need to do anything and your credit card is billed. If you question any charge, you'll have to settle it at the ship's guest services desk.

A Western Caribbean Itinerary

THIS *& that*

Day	Destination	Arrive	Depart
Sat.	Ft. Lauderdale, Florida		4:30 p.m.
Sun.	At sea		
Mon.	Ocho Rios, Jamaica	8:00 a.m.	5:00 p.m.
Tues.	George Town, Grand Cayman	7:00 a.m.	3:30 p.m.
Wed.	Cozumel, Mexico	10:00 a.m.	7:00 p.m.
Thurs.	At sea		
Fri.	Key West, Florida	7:00 a.m.	4:00 p.m.
Sat.	Ft. Lauderdale, Florida	7:00 a.m.	

insider info

It is a good idea to fly to the port city a day early. If you fly into the port on the same day your cruise is leaving and your flight is delayed or canceled, you could literally "miss the boat."

the dock. You get on a motorcoach and your luggage is loaded onboard. You won't need to deal with your bags again until you reach your stateroom. The cruise line intends to minimize every hassle on your vacation.

When you arrive at the port terminal, you check in (as you would at a hotel's front desk), pass through a security gate, and make your way up the **gangway**, *the walkway connecting the ship with the dock.*

As you board the ship, you're welcomed by several members of the ship's crew. A photographer may capture the moment, one of many instances during the cruise. You'll be able to purchase the photo later in the ship's "photo gallery." A crewmember may escort you to your stateroom. You'll notice that the room is smaller than a hotel room, but everything is efficiently designed to maximize the space. Now is a good time to review the materials handed to you during check-in and the in-room literature. Soon, your **stateroom steward** (*the person who maintains your stateroom*) arrives with your luggage and introduces him- or herself.

A lifeboat drill must take place on every ship within 24 hours of departure; often it occurs before the ship sails. It'll be noted in the ship's daily activity log, and a public address announcement will inform you when it happens.

Bon Voyage

A festive highlight of any cruise is when the ship leaves the dock and heads for open water. A celebration may be taking place on the pool deck where, with tropical beverage in hand, you wave goodbye to the stress of civilization, to the rhythm of a live Caribbean steel drum band.

Another cocktail reception might follow somewhere else on the ship. But the big event of the day is your first dinner at sea. The main dining rooms on some cruise ships offer two **seatings,** *set mealtimes for dinner and sometimes lunch.* You may have indicated your preference with your travel agent when you booked your trip. The maitre d' will escort you to your table, where you'll meet your dining companions for this voyage.

This traditional form of cruise dining—with set meal times and preassigned seating—is being replaced, in many cases, by a more flexible approach. Pioneered by Norwegian Cruise Line's "Freestyle Cruising," it provides the kind of options and choices that appeal to many of today's consumers. As a result, quite a few vessels now feature flexible restaurant hours, open seating, and as many as 25 dining venues. In fact, one of the reasons cruise ships have become so huge is to make possible the kind of variety that customers want.

After dinner, you might take in a Las Vegas-style revue in the main showroom, relax in a lounge, or try your luck in the casino. As you're swiftly discovering, a cruise offers a wealth of options (Figure 7–1).

At-Sea Days

While most days of this cruise will be spent visiting ports, your first full day will be spent at sea. What will you do? Whatever you wish. It's a cruise. The choice is yours. You can order room service for a private meal, dine in the main dining room, or eat at any other of the seemingly endless possibilities onboard.

Perhaps you're hungry for details about this ship. You could attend the ship's orientation meeting and the "port talk" preparing you for the next day's destination. Or maybe you just want to unwind. You could work out in the gym, relax in the spa (make sure to book your massage appointment early), or lounge by the pool.

Before you know it, it's time for dinner. After the meal and a show, you decide to call it a night. The port talk informed you about Dunn's River Falls, Jamaica's most famous waterfall, and tomorrow you're going to climb it.

In-Port Days

You wake up and gaze out your window to discover that while you slept the ship arrived at Ocho Rios. You take a motorcoach to Dunn's River Falls. After your adventure, you head into town for some shopping, then back to the ship for some relaxation. In the next few days, you'll swim with stingrays, visit Mayan ruins, and tour Ernest Hemingway's house.

The End of the Cruise

The last evening of the cruise, you enjoy the farewell dinner and a show, settle any outstanding charges at the purser's office, then head back to your stateroom. You pack your suitcase and leave it outside your room for a crewmember to pick up. You won't see it again until after you've disembarked, so you keep with you whatever you'll need overnight.

insider info

If a ship has set mealtimes and assigned seating, it's often better for couples to request seating at a large table (6 to 10 persons). At smaller tables, they'll feel forced to make conversation with their tablemates.

insider info

If a cruise has many days at sea on its itinerary, a large cruise ship will feature more things to do.

FIGURE 7-1
A sample daily activity log.

Courtesy of Holland America Line

ACTIVITIES & ENTERTAINMENT

	6:00am - 7:30pm	**Goofy's Pool** is open for family fun and sun. Deck 9, Midship.
A	6:00am - 12:00am	**The Quiet Cove Pool** is open for adults. Deck 9, Forward *(Guests 18 & older)*
	7:00am - 6:30pm	**Mickey's Pool** is open for use. Deck 9, Aft *(This is a non smoking area).*
A	8:00am	**Tone Zone:** Total body shaping - your muscles will thank you! Vista Spa, Deck 9, Forward.
	8:00am - 4:00pm	**Bridge, Cards & Board Games:** Find a spot to play, Fantasia Reading & Game Room, Deck 2, Midship.
	8:00am - 12:00am	**Quarter Masters Arcade** is open for your enjoyment, Deck 9, Midship.
	8:00am - 4:00pm	**Bridge, Cards & Board Games:** Find a spot to play, Fantasia Reading & Game Room, Deck 2, Midship.
A	9:00am	**Walk A Mile:** Instructor led walk in the sunshine and seabreeze. Preludes, Deck 4, Forward.
	9:15am	**Deep Sea Fishing:** Please meet in Sessions Deck 3, Forward.
	9:30am - 3:30pm	**Parasailing:** Please meet at Marge's Barges, Castaway Cay, ten minutes prior to your assigned departure time *(Located just past the Post Office).*
	9:45am - 3:00pm	**Bahamian Hair Braiding:** Cash or Key to the World Card accepted, Castaway Cay. *(subject to availability)*
	10:15am	**Power Walk!** Join your Cruise Staff and exercise in paradise. A great way to see the island! Meet at the Post Office, Castaway Cay. *(Approximately 2 1/2 miles)*
	11:00am - 3:00pm	**Game Room in the Grouper Pavilion:** Join *Castaway Joe* for a game or two in the Grouper Pavillion, Castaway Cay. Ping Pong, Pool & more!
	11:30am - 3:00pm	**Beach Bonanza.** Join *DJ L.A.* for some fun in the sun with your favorite requests. Gazebo, Castaway Cay.
	11:30am	**Island Games:** Join your *Cruise Staff* for some fun in the sun at the Gazebo! Castaway Cay.
	1:00pm	**Informal Scrabble Tournament:** meet in Sessions, Deck 3, Forward.
	1:00pm	**Deep Sea Fishing:** Please meet at Marge's Barges, Castaway Cay *(Located just past the Post Office).*
	1:30pm	**Volleyball Challenge:** Team up for some friendly competition, Family Beach, Castaway Cay.
	1:30pm - 2:30pm	**Family Whale Dig Exploration:** Every beachcomber is sure to dig this exploration, Monstro Point.
	3:00pm - 6:30pm	**Disney Vacation Club:** Stop by our desk to learn about the wonderful world of resort ownership. Deck 4, Midship.
	3:30pm - 5:30pm	**Island Music:** Enjoy the tropical sounds of *Kool Breeze*. Goofy's Pool Gazebo, Deck 9, Midship.
	4:30pm	**DISEMBARKATION PRESENTATION & DISCOVER THE MAGIC** Join *Jim*, your Cruise Director for the information you will need for your journey home, followed by our special farewell featuring the Programmers and the Children. Walt Disney Theatre, Deck 4, Forward.
	4:30pm	**ALL ABOARD!** Disney Magic prepares to sail.
	4:30pm	**Friends of Bill W.** meet in Fantasia Reading & Games Room, Deck 2, Midship.
	4:30pm - 6:30pm	**Mickey's Slide** is open for use. Deck 9, Aft (HEIGHT AND AGE RESTRICTIONS APPLY).
A	4:45pm	**Stretch & Relax:** Finish the cruise off right! Come and unwind... Vista Spa, Deck 9, Forward.
	5:30pm	**Port Departure:** *Disney Magic is* expected to sail for Port Canaveral. 225 Nautical Miles, Total Distance Traveled 2037 Nautical Miles.
	5:30pm	**Jewish Sabbath Service:** Conduct your own service in Off Beat, Deck 3, Forward.
	5:30pm - 6:00pm	**Formal Portraits** taken in the Atrium Lobby, Deck 3, Midship & Deck 4, Midship.

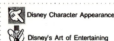 Disney Character Appearance
 Disney's Art of Entertaining
Disney's Navigator Series
 Disney Behind-the-Scenes
Shore Excursion
A Guests 18 & Older

CHARACTER APPEARANCES

Meet some of your favorite Disney Friends:
9:40am - 10:00am
Castaway Cay Post Office *(beside the ship)*
10:00am - 10:20am
Castaway Cay Post Office *(beside the ship)* & Scuttle's Cove
10:20am - 10:40am
Castaway Cay Post Office *(beside the ship)* & Scuttle's Cove
10:40am - 11:10am
Scuttle's Cove, Castaway Cay.
3:45pm - 4:05pm
Gangway, on the pier.
10:15pm
'Til We Meet Again
Atrium Lobby, Deck 3, Midship

Movies
Deck 5, Aft

Bad Company (PG13)
12:00pm - Running Time 1:57
Lord of the Rings (PG13)
2:30pm - Running Time 2:58
Lilo & Stitch (PG)
6:00pm - Running Time 1:35
Lilo & Stitch (PG)
8:30pm - Running Time 1:35
Bad Company (PG13)
10:30pm - Running Time 1:57

Castaway Cay Crate
Straight from the beaches of Castaway Cay to your stateroom, this crate is packed with chips, crispy pralines, 2 Bahama Mamas with Castaway Cay coolies, a compact radio and Calypso Crunch Mix,
$43.00.
Contact Guest Services Desk for more information.

Family Activities

Bahamian Hair Braiding
9:45am - 3:00pm
Power Walk
10:15am
Island Games
11:30am
Beach Bonanza
11:30am - 3:00pm
Family Whale Dig Exploration
1:30pm - 2:30pm
Family Talent Show
7:30pm
Walk the Plank
7:45pm

FIGURE 7-1 (Cont.)
A sample daily activity log.

Courtesy of Holland America Line

FUTURE CRUISE SPECIALS!

The Magic and Wonder doesn't have to end! Stop by the Cruise Sales Managers Desk, Deck 4, Midship (Port Side) from 8:00am - 9:30am; 4:00pm - 6:30pm or 7:30pm - 11:00pm today, & meet with Donna, your Cruise Sales Manager to learn about how you can book your next Disney Cruise Line Vacation while on this voyage and secure an exclusive onboard offer.

DUELING PIANOS FAREWELL PARTY!
Deck 3, Forward

♪ 7:30pm - 8:30pm Rockin' Bar

★ **FAMILY TALENT SHOW** ★
Join your fellow guests, Fidelio & Carl for a fun event!

off beat
♪ 10:15pm
ADULT TALENT SHOW!

11:15pm - 11:45pm
FAREWELL ROWDY REQUESTS
One last chance to hear your favorite songs!

Discover the Magic

Our special show featuring the children of the Disney Magic.
Don't miss this special farewell!
5:00pm
Walt Disney Theatre, Deck 4, Forward.
Immediately following the Disembarkation Talk

ESPN
SKYBOX
Deck 10, Midship
Check out the latest scores of your favorite teams.
3:00pm - 11:00pm

ADULT ACTIVITIES

Walk a Smile Mile
9:00am

Dabarkation Presentation
4:30pm

Elegant Piano Selection
7:45pm - 8:30pm & 9:15pm - 12:00am

Adult Karaoke
9:30pm - 10:30pm

Adult Talent Show
10:15pm

Rock the House
10:45pm

Dueling Pianos Finale
11:15pm

5:45pm - 6:30pm	**Dancing & Listening Music** with *Ben & Dana*. Promenade Lounge, Deck 3, Aft.
6:00pm - 7:00pm	**Family Time:** Explore Disney's Oceaneer Club and Lab, Deck 5, Midship. *(Adult accompaniment, please)*

6:30pm & 8:30pm

Disney Cruise Line proudly presents

FAREWELL VARIETY SHOW

starring

Gary Delena & Eric Brouman

Walt Disney Theatre, Deck 4, Forward

As a courtesy to all Guests we kindly advise that the saving of seats is not permitted in the Walt Disney Theatre.

Please be advised Crew Members are available at the entrance to the Walt Disney Theatre, 30 minutes prior to show time for assistance with wheelchair seating.

7:30pm - 8:30pm	**Your Shopping in Paradise** guide, *Kerrie*, is available at the Shore Excursion Desk, Deck 3, Midship.
7:30pm - 8:30pm	**Pin Trading:** Collect and trade with your fellow Guests in the Atrium Lobby, Deck 3, Midship. *Helmsman Mickey Pin available tonight.*
7:30pm - 8:30pm	**Family Talent Show:** Join your fellow Guests, *Fidelio & Carl*, for this fun event. Rockin' Bar D, Deck 3, Forward.
7:30pm - 9:00pm	**Disney Vacation Club:** Stop by our desk to learn about the wonderful world of resort ownership. Deck 4, Midship.
7:30pm - 9:00pm	**Formal Portraits** taken in the Atrium Lobby, Deck 3, Midship & Deck 4, Midship.
7:45pm	**Walk The Plank Game Show:** Join your *Cruise Staff* and the *Pirate Captain* for this fun game that tests you *Disney Magic®* knowledge in Studio Sea, Deck 4, Midship.
7:45pm - 8:30pm	**Cheese & Grapes** are served to accompany a fine selection of wines, Sessions, Deck 3, Forward *(Guests 18 & older)*
7:45pm - 8:30pm	**Dancing & Listening Music** with *Ben & Dana*, Promenade Lounge, Deck 3, Aft.
7:45pm - 8:30pm	**Sparkling Moments:** Kir Royal - Bellinis - Champagne and strawberries available for purchase in the Atrium Lobby, Deck 3, Midship.
7:45pm - 8:30pm	**Elegant Piano Selections** with *Daryl Lockhart*, Sessions, Deck 3, Forward *(Guests 18 & older)*

SPECIAL NOTE: Out of respect for Adult Guests, Beat Street and all lounges on Deck 3, forward are for Guests 18 years and older after 9:00pm. Sessions is an adult only bar at all times.

9:15pm - 10:00pm	**Elegant Piano Selections** with *Daryl Lockhart*, Sessions, Deck 3, Forward *(Guests 18 & older)*
9:30pm - 10:30pm	**Adult Karaoke** with *DJ L.A.* Rockin' Bar D, Deck 3, Forward *(Guests 18 & older)*
9:45pm - 12:00am	**Dancing & Listening Music** with *Ben & Dana*, Promenade Lounge, Deck 3, Aft.
10:15pm	**'Til We Meet Again...** A final farewell from the Characters and Mainstage performers of the Disney Magic. Atrium Lobby, Deck 3, Midship.
10:15pm - 11:15pm	**Adult Talent Show.** Your final chance to sing along with *Fidelio & Carl* in Off Beat, Deck 3, Forward *(Guests 18 & older)*
10:45pm - 2:00am	**Rock the House:** with *Free Reign & DJ L.A.*, Rockin' Bar D, Deck 3, Forward *(Guests 18 & older).*
11:00pm - 12:00am	**Elegant Piano Selections** with *Daryl Lockhart*, Sessions, Deck 3, Forward *(Guests 18 & older)*
11:15pm - 11:45am	**Dueling Pianos:** *Farewell Favorites Finale*. Join *Fidelio & Carl* in a "So Long" sing-a-long of the most popular requests & skits of the voyage. Off Beat, Deck 3, Forward *(Guests 18 & older)*

Careers

Career Opportunities in the Cruise Industry

What jobs exist in cruising? Before exploring that topic, let's examine who does what on a cruise ship:

- The *captain* is in charge of all the ship's operations.
- The *staff, deputy captain*, or *first officer* is in charge when the captain is busy (with social functions, for instance). He usually also oversees ship safety and security.
- The *chief engineer* is in charge of all mechanical operations.
- The *chief medical officer*, or *doctor*, looks after the health of the passengers and crew. Ships with 100 or more passengers must have a doctor onboard.
- The *chief radio* or *communications officer* oversees all shipboard communication systems, including emergency transmissions, ship-to-shore calls, Internet communications, and in-room programming.

As well as being in charge of sailing operations, the captain oversees the staff of the ship's hotel operations:

- The *hotel manager*, *hotel director*, or *chief purser* operates very much like the manager of a land-based resort or hotel.
- The *purser* has responsibilities similar to those of a hotel's front-desk manager or assistant manager.
- The *shore excursion manager* is in charge of operating and booking port-based packages.

- The *cruise director* oversees the entertainment and informational opportunities onboard.
- The *executive chef* controls the kitchen, supervising the preparation of all food and beverages.
- The *food and beverage manager* watches over the serving of meals and beverages.
- The *head housekeeper* or *chief steward* makes sure that the ship is kept—well—shipshape.

To maintain their impressive level of service and safety, these officers supervise a potentially very large staff. The largest megaships may have more than 2,000 crewmembers aboard. Most of the crew on a ship are foreign-born, but North Americans do staff front-desk, entertainment, spa, fitness facility, excursion desk, and other positions where English-speaking skills are required.

Large cruise lines, most of which operate out of Florida, offer land-side job opportunities at their headquarters, as well as at domestic ports that their ships frequent and cities that represent important markets for their cruises. Another possible career is as a cruise-specialist travel agent. Like airports, cruise ports—often under local government control—employ many administrative, service, and security personnel. The *maritime port management industry* largely deals with freight, but in cities such as Miami, Ft. Lauderdale, and Vancouver, cruise-related activities play an important role in the operations mix.

The next morning, you'll have an early breakfast and disembark the ship. On some ships, passengers may leave whenever they wish; on others, they're divided into groups and wait for their group to be called. You then claim your luggage, go through Customs and Immigration, and head for the airport on the motorcoach, reminiscing about the wonderful cruise experience you've just had.

Who Owns Cruise Lines

The issue of cruise line ownership is a complex one. Several large companies own most of the two dozen major cruise lines. For example, Carnival Corporation owns *Holland America, Princess, Seabourn, Cunard,* and *Costa,* as well as its own Carnival brand. Royal Caribbean owns *Celebrity* and *Azamara.*

Also, a cruise line may be headquartered in the United States but have its ships registered in another country such as Panama, the Bahamas, or Liberia. The reason: it frees the companies from the hiring, work hour, and other regulations that would be enforced if they were registered in the United States. This is called a "flag of convenience" arrangement. The ship flies the flag of the foreign country where it's registered.

What Cruises Cost

As we've touched on before, one of the appeals of cruising is that passengers can price most of their vacation up front. Cruise line Web sites and some brochures provide prices for each sailing, with information on what's included and what's not. The prices

insider info

Making a phone call to or from the ship is expensive. Communication through onboard Internet centers, however, is a somewhat reasonable alternative.

insider info

There's often a $15 to $25 cover charge to dine at some of the alternative restaurants on ships with multiple dining venues.

A standard stateroom.

© CAN BALCIOGLU/www.Shutterstock.com

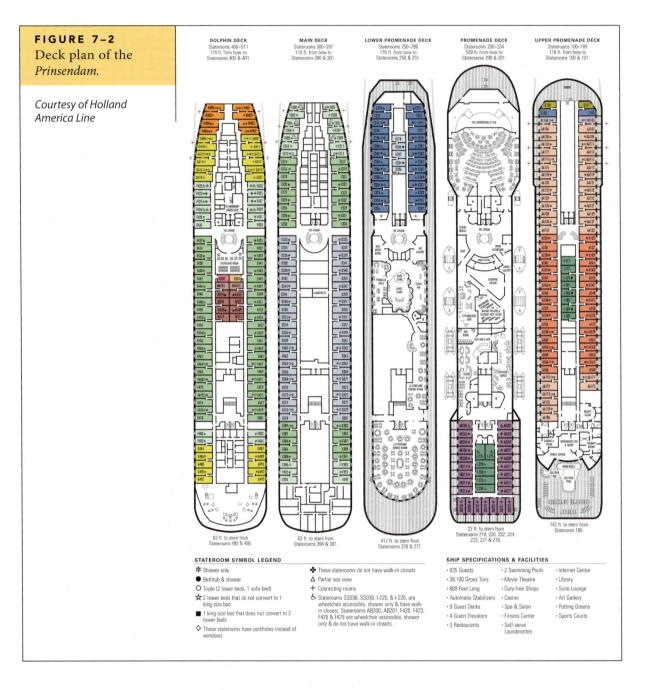

FIGURE 7–2
Deck plan of the *Prinsendam.*

Courtesy of Holland America Line

quoted are per-person, based on double occupancy (two passengers per stateroom). Primarily, prices are based on the type of stateroom requested, and, *in general*:

- The higher the deck the stateroom is located on, the greater the cruise price will be.

- **Outside** (often called "ocean-view") **staterooms** cost more than **inside staterooms** (which are usually windowless). Outside staterooms with obstructed views (for example, by a lifeboat) are less expensive than those with a clear view.

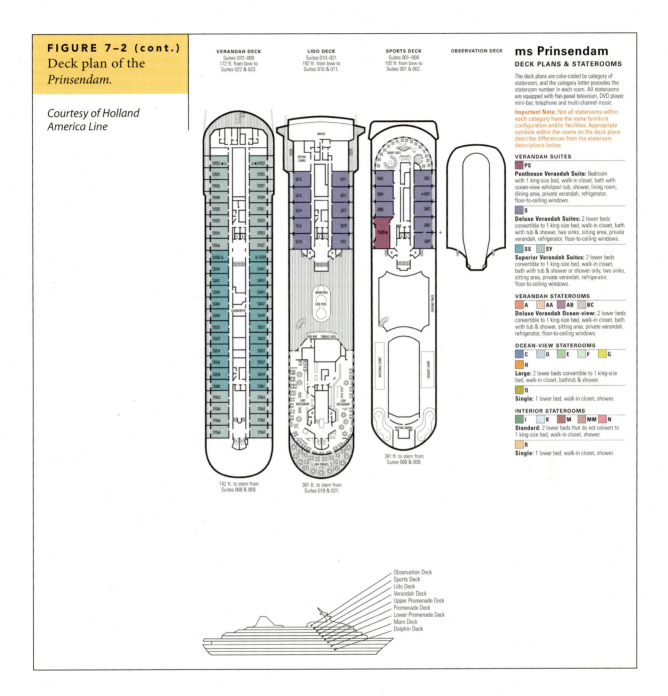

FIGURE 7–2 (cont.)
Deck plan of the *Prinsendam.*

Courtesy of Holland America Line

- An outside stateroom with a verandah (a private balcony) costs more than an ocean-view room. On some newer ships, all of the outside staterooms have balconies.

- Larger staterooms are typically priced higher than smaller ones.

- Suites (rooms with separate sitting areas) cost more than regular staterooms. Extra amenities (such as robes, champagne, and butler service) are usually included. See Figure 7–2 for an idea of where the various types of staterooms are located.

Other factors can affect the price of a cruise:

- Passengers can often lower the price of a cruise by booking six to nine months in advance. Cruise lines offer promotional fares to push early bookings.

- However, if a ship isn't fully booked, the cruise line may offer a last-minute sale.

- Because staterooms are based on double occupancy, the fare of a third or fourth guest in the room is usually discounted. (Conversely, a single passenger in a double-occupancy room will pay a higher fare.)

- Cruise lines price their itineraries on seasonal demand (a concept introduced in Chapter 1). For example, booking a cruise in winter, the low season for Mediterranean cruises, will garner passengers substantial savings. Summer is the high season, when they'll pay the most; somewhat lower prices can be had in spring and fall, the shoulder seasons.

- Traveling on a **repositioning cruise**—*when a ship is moving from one general cruise area to another*—is another way to grab a bargain. For example, after summer in Alaska, the ship travels down North America's west coast, eventually repositioning to cruises in Mexico's waters for the winter.

Pre-, Post-, and Off-Ship Experiences

It is entirely possible to have a great cruise vacation experience and never leave the ship. But for many passengers, what happens on shore is just as—or more—important than what happens at sea. Port experiences can be divided into three categories: *precruise*, *intermediary port stops*, and *postcruise*.

Precruise and Postcruise Packages

You can certainly arrive in the departure port city and immediately embark the ship for your cruise. Most cruise vacationers do it that way. But frequently, passengers decide to extend their vacation either before or after, in or around the city where their cruise begins and/or ends. A consumer can purchase an **air-sea package** that consists of *airfare, airport-to-dock-to-airport transportation, and perhaps lodging*. The package can be obtained directly through the cruise line or built component by component. Of course, a travel agent can put together a more extensive package that includes a car rental, tours, and more.

Intermediary Port Stops and Shore Excursions

Cruise lines do an excellent job of informing their guests about the options available to them at the places they'll be visiting. Facts about the history and culture of

Vancouver is a common starting point for cruises to Alaska.

the destination, shopping and sightseeing tips, and information about the tours and excursions available for purchase are given at port talks aboard the ship, on the cruise line's Web site, via literature provided before sailing, through in-room brochures, and during video presentations.

When a ship arrives in port, passengers have four options:

1. They may elect to stay onboard. This is most probable if they've already seen the port or if they want easier access to certain onboard amenities (such as spa services).

2. They can explore the port on their own.

3. They may buy a tour or activity from a vendor (usually waiting for them at the dock).

4. They may go on a shore excursion that they purchased from the cruise line before the cruise or onboard the ship. Occasionally, some or all shore excursions are included in the price of a cruise (usually on very upscale or river cruises).

Excursions offered by a cruise line can range from sightseeing tours aboard a motorcoach to underwater exploration in a submarine. It really depends on the cruise line and the destination. Typical excursions in the Caribbean include city

insider info

If you buy a shore excursion from the cruise line and something goes wrong, the ship will probably wait for you. If you buy one independently at the dock and a problem arises, the ship probably will sail without you.

Huge ships have become the norm.

tours, golf excursions, shopping expeditions, and scuba diving. In Alaska, passengers might get a close-up view of a glacier from a helicopter or go fly-fishing. On a Mediterranean cruise, they could sample wine and cheese in a bistro one day and explore Pompeii and Sorrento the next.

Telling Terms

Here are some additional cruise-related terms you should know:

- **Berth:** A bed on a ship. Also, the place where a ship docks.

- **Bow:** The front of the ship.

- **Deck:** A floor of a ship.

- **Port:** A place a ship visits. Also, when facing forward on the ship, the left-hand side.

- **Stabilizer:** An underwater device that helps reduce a ship's motion.

- **Starboard:** When facing forward, the right-hand side of the ship.

- **Stern:** The back of a ship.

How Cruises Are Sold

How do people typically purchase a cruise?

- *Travel agents* are responsible for about 80 percent of cruise bookings. Why travel agents? Can't consumers simply buy a ticket for a cruise like they would an airline ticket? As you learned earlier, customers are reluctant to buy complex and costly experiences on their own. And they may know that no two cruise lines—or even ships—are alike. Good travel agents will find the right price and personality match between their client and a cruise. Agencies are often able to offer their clients better deals on their preferred cruise lines. To the cruise lines, travel agents are essential promoters for their vacation experience. Cruises are good for travel agencies, too, because they're comprehensive packages, yielding commissions on virtually everything the consumer does on vacation.

- *Tour companies* offer cruises through their brochures, mailings, and Web sites. To create greater value, a few package a pre- or postcruise tour as part of their offering.

- Somewhat like airline consolidators, **cruise consolidators** *buy blocks of staterooms from a cruise line, sometimes at the last minute, and offer them to the public at a discounted price.*

- *Cruise lines* sell their product directly to consumers, through Web sites or toll-free numbers.

insider info

Among some of the better-known entertainment that has appeared as a regular offering on ships: Blue Man Group, Cirque du Soleil, Second City, and performances of *The Lion King*.

More This and That

Here are some additional insights into the cruise industry:

- The Caribbean is the world's most popular place to cruise, followed by Europe, Alaska, Mexico, the Panama Canal, trans-Atlantic, South America, the South Pacific, the northeast United States/Canada, Hawaii, and Bermuda.

- Small boats, called **tenders**, *transport passengers to and from shore if the ship is too large or the port is too shallow for docking directly at the pie*r. In exotic places like Antarctica, passengers might board *a large inflatable rubber boat* called a **zodiac**.

- On most ships, smoking is limited to certain designated spaces. A few ships allow smoking practically everywhere onboard.

- Many cruises feature themed sailings, such as jazz, history, or baseball. These often appeal to people who would not otherwise take a cruise.

Review Questions

1. What are five reasons people go on a cruise?

2. Explain three reasons people *don't* go on cruises and how a travel agent might overcome the client's hesitance.

3. Give an example of a geographic area you think would be best visited on a cruise and why.

4. What are three factors that determine how a cruise is priced?

It's All About You Questions

You want to visit Greece and Turkey. You are not sure whether to do it on an escorted tour (one targeted to passengers about your age) or a cruise (where there's more age diversity). Decide which one you would select, then give five reasons you chose it and five reasons you "rejected" the other one.

Activity 1: Interviewing a Cruiser

Do you know someone who has taken a cruise? Ask that person the following questions and sum up their answers.

1. What was the number-one motive you had for going on your first cruise?

2. Were there other reasons?

3. Where did you go on your cruise(s)?

4. Did you have any negative preconceived notions about cruising? Were those notions changed by your cruise experience?

5. What are your favorite things about cruising?

Activity 2: Profiling the Lines

Five cruise lines, with their Web site addresses, are listed below. Each line has at least one thing about it—often emphasized through a tagline or slogan—that sets it apart from other cruise lines. For example, Carnival calls its vessels "the Fun Ships" because of their emphasis on fun and entertainment. Write two or three sentences that summarize what kind of cruise line each is, with special emphasis on which factors set it apart from the others.

Norwegian Cruise Line: http://www.ncl.com

American Cruise Lines: http://www.americancruiselines.com

Seabourn Cruise Line: http://www.seabourn.com

AMA Waterways: http://amawaterways.com

Hurtigruten: http://www.hurtigruten.us

Gale Hospitality, Tourism and Leisure Database Assignment

The following assignment requires access to the Gale Hospitality, Tourism and Leisure Database. Check with your instructor to see if you have access to this database.

Find the article *Cruise Pampering: Waves of Pleasure* in the Gale Hospitality, Tourism & Leisure Collection. Spas aren't limited to resort hotels. They're among the most popular services on cruise ships too.

- If you had a free spa treatment on any cruise line mentioned here, which would it be? (Give the specific treatment and the cruise line.)

- Use the Internet to look up the cruise line that offers the service you chose. Would this be a cruise line you would sail? Why or why not?

8

Extra Specials: Other Segments of the Travel Industry

KEY TERMS

- Convention and visitors bureau
- Convention center
- Couchette
- Destination marketing organization
- Familiarization trip
- Fleet
- Inventory
- Lot
- Meeting planner
- Options
- Tourist office

After studying this chapter, you'll be able to:

- Explain the motives behind renting cars and choosing rail travel

- Describe the car rental and rail travel industries and experiences

- Interpret how car rentals and train travel are priced

- Identify the many types of destination marketing organizations and what they typically do

- Describe how other suppliers fit into the travel industry "landscape"

Photo courtesy of Jason Coleman

Jason Coleman

CURRENT POSITION/TITLE:

Chief Visionary, Jason Coleman, Inc.

SHORT DESCRIPTION OF WHAT YOUR RESPONSIBILITIES ARE:

I own a cruise-oriented agency and do it all. I'm Chief Officer of Everything.

EDUCATION:

BS in Marketing Management, California State University, Dominguez Hills; Master of Tourism Administration, The George Washington University

FIRST JOB IN TRAVEL/HOSPITALITY INDUSTRY:

Conference & Meeting Planner for an educational association

FIRST PAID JOB (IF DIFFERENT FROM ABOVE):

Butcher in a meat market

FAVORITE PART OF WHAT I DO:

Being creative in everything, from planning client itineraries to marketing and much more

THING I WISH I DIDN'T HAVE TO DO:

Talk on the phone. If I didn't have to do so much work by phone, I'd set up my office on a cruise ship and live at sea.

SOMEONE WHO INSPIRES ME:

Walt Disney for his creativity and ability to understand the customer so thoroughly

BEST CAREER MEMORY I HAVE:

Receiving ASTA's Young Professional of the Year award

STRANGEST OR FUNNIEST CAREER-RELATED THING I'VE EVER EXPERIENCED:

I got up in front of about 800 college students at an event I planned to thank them for a great, successful conference. What came out was "thanks for a great sex conference."

FAVORITE QUOTE:

"My only hope is that we never lose sight of one thing, that it was all started by a mouse." (Walt Disney)

Air, lodging, travel agencies, food services, tours, and cruises: these sectors almost surely first come to mind when you think of the travel industry. But there are other supplier groups—some huge—that have a significant impact on the travel business. Let's take a look at some of the most important ones.

Car Rentals

Have you ever rented a car? If so, you probably had contradictory feelings. On one hand, to drive a make and model of car that you haven't experienced before is an exciting, even exhilarating change of pace. For example, you may never have considered buying a convertible. But on vacation in a warm and sunny place, why not rent one?

On the other hand, there's the stress of the unfamiliar. How do you adjust the mirrors? Where is the trunk release? Did you think you were switching on the headlights and instead started the windshield wipers? For many people, though, the benefits of renting a car far outweigh the drawbacks. Let's look at what motivates a person to rent a car.

Car Rental Motivations

Most people rent a car for some or many of these reasons:

- **To get around easily.** The flexible transportation a car provides is perhaps its greatest strength. You can drive directly to your hotel or motel, take unplanned side trips, and stop wherever or whenever you like, all while carrying your luggage with you in the trunk. Trains, taxis, and buses rarely permit that kind of freedom.

- **To best navigate and experience a place.** Some destinations with extensive highway systems, such as California and Florida, are ideal for auto travel. That's what most locals favor to get from place to place. New England's back roads are best experienced from a car. And what better way to sense the soft, sweet beauty of Hawaii than in a convertible?

- **To save money.** If three or four people travel in a car, it usually costs less, when you figure the cost of the rental on a per-person basis, than if they were traveling by train or plane.

- **To do business.** Business travelers represent an important and highly profitable segment of car renters, and their reasons aren't always purely practical. Some, for instance, rent luxury cars to impress their clients.

- **To replace your own car.** Did an accident put your car out of action? Was it stolen? Then your insurance company may authorize a car rental while your own auto is repaired, located, or replaced. Car dealerships and repair shops likewise have agreements with car rental companies that permit you—at a special rate or even free of charge—to have a rental vehicle while your own vehicle is serviced. These *replacement market* car rental locations are usually situated near clusters of car dealerships and repair shops, rather than at airports.

- **To try out a car you're thinking of buying.** A surprising number of auto renters have this secondary motive in mind when they rent a vehicle for other purposes. Rental companies don't guarantee a specific make, year, or model, however. They just promise that a car in the category requested will be available. You also may want to try out a car you might not ordinarily drive or can't afford in the "real" world. In other words: have a fantasy experience.

- **Because you prefer driving vacations.** Many people, especially those who genuinely like to drive, feel more comfortable with a car rental experience than any other transportation mode once they arrive at their vacation destination.

Rental cars aren't always the best option, though. There is a downside. Driving, especially over long distances, can be tiring. Unfamiliar roads, scarcity of parking, the cost of tolls and gasoline, heavy traffic, foreign-language signs in other countries, safety issues, and similar factors can sometimes tip the scales in favor of alternative transportation.

The Business of Car Rentals

As with a hotel or a travel agency, a car rental location may either be corporate-owned or a franchise. Some car manufacturers have major stock in car rental

A car rental provides flexibility at many destinations.

companies. Competition in the field is fierce, profit margins are often razor-thin, and many factors have an impact on the business. If fuel prices rise, for example, large cars and SUVs can suddenly go out of favor. If airfares drop, a sudden surge in car demand may result because so many more people will be flying and many of them will need to rent cars at their destinations.

The car rental industry relies heavily on its relationships with other suppliers. Some aggressively court travel agencies, and others target corporate travel managers. Car rental desks are sometimes located at large hotels.

The relationships between car rental firms and air carriers are especially strong. Frequent flyers can receive air mileage points on their car rentals. Airline service people often ask callers if they need to book a car. When passengers book their air tickets online, they're automatically asked if they need a car rental. And tour operators with fly-drive programs have close relationships with car rental companies.

As with any large business, the car rental business has many job titles particular to its industry. *Rental sales agents* work the car rental desks at airports or at the car lots. *Service agents* prepare and clean the cars. *Shuttle drivers* transfer customers between the airport and the rental lot, and *mechanics* see to it that the cars are kept in tip-top shape. *Reservationists* work at the car rental call center. *Managers* work at all levels and departments. Even more than the hospitality industry, the car rental business offers rapid promotions.

What Car Rentals Cost

The number-one factor that determines a car rental's cost is the *category* or *class* of car the renter selects. Each category is designated by a letter code; the coding pattern varies from rental company to rental company. Here are the usual categories, in

THIS & that

Join the Club

Most major car rental firms feature car rental "clubs," which allow members certain special privileges such as expedited check-in, lower-mileage cars, and, as in the case of National, the ability to select your own vehicle. Major clubs are:

Hertz:	#1 Club	Dollar:	Express
Budget:	Fastbreak	Alamo:	Insider
Avis:	Preferred	Payless:	Perks Club
Thrifty:	Blue Chip	Enterprise:	Plus
National:	Emerald Club		

order of price from least to most expensive. (There are sometimes exceptions, of course.)

- **Subcompact or economy:** Very small cars that have few amenities, comforts, or options. They appeal to very cost-conscious customers or those who won't be doing much driving during their rental. They're ill suited for three or four people or for those with lots of luggage.

- **Compact:** Small cars that are a little larger than subcompacts, are a bit more comfortable, and come with more options.

- **Mid-size** or **intermediate:** Fairly small, these autos feature a good selection of options and can accommodate three or four people with some comfort.

- **Full-size** or **standard:** Often called "family cars," these can seat three, four, or more people comfortably, have plenty of trunk space, and many amenities.

- **Premium:** These cars rank higher than full-size but aren't quite as luxurious as our next category.

- **Luxury** or **deluxe:** These are among the largest and most upscale cars you can rent. Examples are Lincolns and Cadillacs. They provide great comfort and spaciousness. They appeal to those who want to experience or convey a prestigious image. They're also ideal for long trips and for four or more passengers.

- **Specialty:** This is a catch-all class, which most car rental companies further subdivide into separate categories. Among the possibilities are SUVs, convertibles, vans, minivans, jeeps, trucks, sports cars, and exotic or super-luxury brands such as Mercedes or Jaguar. Some rental companies specialize in renting motorhomes.

Many words used in the car rental industry are the same as those used by auto dealers: the *place where cars are kept* is called the **lot**; the *number of cars available* is referred to as **inventory**; and the *makes and models of cars offered by the entire company* is its **fleet**. Another dealership term: *additional, extra-cost features* are called **options,** or *amenities.*

Telling Terms

Note also that many of these categories are broken down into two- or four-door models, with two-doors sometimes a little less expensive to rent.

Other factors determine what you pay for a car rental:

- **What the rental basis is.** Most car rental companies offer an *unlimited-miles* plan. No matter how many miles you drive, the daily rate will be the same. Most rental companies define a "day" as 24 hours from the time you pick up the car. Return the car 25 hours later—most companies allow a 59-minute "grace period"—and you'll be charged an extra hour at a hefty rate or even for an extra day.

  An alternate approach is the *time plus mileage* plan. There's a charge for each day, usually lower than the unlimited-miles rate, *and* a per-mile charge. A variation: you have a *time with mileage cap*. You're allowed a certain number of miles (for example, 200 miles per day times the number of rental days) at no additional charge. Drive more miles and a per-mile cost kicks in.

- **How many days are involved.** Most rental contracts charge either on a daily or a weekly basis (which, at many car rental firms, starts at *five* days). Weekly rates usually represent a sizable discount, per day, compared to the daily rental rate. The reason: leisure travelers are most likely to use them. However, if you take a weekly rate but return the car early, you'll still be charged the full weekly rate— or maybe even more. For example, if the rental rate is $50 per day or $190 per week and you return the car after only four days, you'll have to pay $200—$10 more than if you kept it for seven days!

- **What insurance you take, if any.** In many cases, driving a rental car is covered by your personal auto insurance, your homeowner's insurance, or the insurance provided by the credit card you use to book the car rental. Some renters, however, decide to purchase the rental company's coverage. Why? To avoid a possible increase in premiums for their personal car insurance in the event of a car rental mishap claim or to avoid the hassles of dealing with their insurance company at all. See the Telling Terms, "Cover Me!" for an explanation of the types of car rental coverage options that most rental companies offer.

- **Whether you take the fuel option.** Most car rental companies offer "fuel options." For example, the service representative tells you that you must return your car with a full tank of gas or be charged a hefty gasoline price for them to refuel it. But if you take the fuel option, you'll be buying a full tank of gas from the rental company at a price below what you'd pay at a gas station. Sounds like a great idea, except for one thing: the only way you can profit from the deal is if you return your car with a virtually empty gas tank—a rather nerve-wracking thing to do. Otherwise, the rental company gets all that fuel you didn't use, but have paid for, for free. Though it can be a hassle, usually it's better to gas up on the way to returning your car.

insider info
Some car rental companies give a monetary incentive to service people who successfully sell up to a higher category level or sell additional options.

insider info
A great idea: rent a car with a GPS or use your own (or your smartphone with a GPS app). It's worth it unless you're very familiar with the destination.

insider info
Renting and driving a car in a developing country is not a great idea.

- **On which days you drive.** Drive on weekdays and you pay a higher daily rate. Drive on weekends and it's lower. Each company has its own definition of when a weekend period starts and ends. Like the airline "stay over Saturday night" policy, this results in business travelers paying more and leisure travelers paying less.

- **Where you rent.** As with hotels, certain markets, especially those that attract plenty of business travelers, tend to have higher average rates. Others, especially those like Florida that have more vacationers, feature lower rental prices.

- **During which season you rent.** As with every sector of the travel industry, low travel periods often feature better rental rates, and peak seasons are marked by pricey ones.

- **How many cars are available.** Usually, the rental rates among companies at a certain airport will be roughly the same, no matter which one you book through. However, if the number of cars available at one company's lot is much larger than at its competitors', then that company will drop its prices to help move its inventory.

- **If there's an additional driver.** Some car rental companies charge an extra fee for an additional driver, others don't, and with still others, it depends on who the driver is. For example, a spouse or business partner might not trigger an extra charge, but a friend would.

- **How the car is booked.** A travel agency that has a preferred relationship with a car rental company may have access to better prices. Low, Web-only fares are also common in the car rental industry.

- **What taxes are levied.** Taxes of all sorts often add considerably to the cost of a rental.

- **Which coupons are used.** Car rental companies frequently issue coupons that represent a percentage or set dollar discount, free day, or upgrade.

- **If the renter requests special amenities.** Ski- or bike-racks, child safety seats, navigation systems—all of these amenities and more may cost the renter extra.

- **Which company you work for or organization you belong to.** Many companies and organizations (for example, auto clubs) negotiate special contracted rental rates for their employees or members. Similarly, car rental firms may offer special conference-only rates to attendees.

- **If there's a drop-off charge.** In many cases, if you pick up a car at one location and return it to another, either a higher rate structure or a "drop-off charge" will kick in.

- **When the car is booked.** As with air and lodging, you usually pay more for a car rental if you wait until the last minute. As you've learned, though, the reverse can be true: oversupply of cars at a certain location can lead to lower prices.

Cover Me!

Here are the most common forms of coverage, or protection plans, that rental companies offer, either bundled in packages or each priced separately:

- CDW (Collision Damage Waiver): If the car is involved in an accident, there will be no charge to the renter for repairs or for "loss of use" (revenue that the rental company isn't getting while the car is being repaired).

- LDW (Loss Damage Waiver): If theft or vandalism involving the car occurs, this coverage relieves the renter of financial liability. Sometimes LDW is incorporated into CDW.

- PAI (Personal Accident Insurance): This covers bodily injury to the driver and, in many cases, to passengers.

What about other forms of liability? A car rental agreement usually automatically includes, at no extra cost, liability coverage for damage to other cars, other persons, and property. But this is only up to a certain amount, usually dictated by local law. Renters who want coverage beyond these limits (and those of their personal auto policy) can buy ALI (Additional Liability Insurance) or ELI (Extended Liability Insurance). ALI and ELI add additional insurance coverage past what the renter's regular car insurance or rental company insurance provides.

How Car Rentals Are Sold

Car rental companies sell their product much like other travel suppliers: through travel agencies, via toll-free numbers, online, and even at their service counters. It's often the case, too, that personnel at the service counter will make special offers to the renter when he or she picks up the car (for example, an upgrade to a better category for much less than if the higher-category vehicle had been booked in the first place).

More This and That

Here are some miscellaneous bits of information you should know:

- Most car rental companies generally require the driver to be *at least 25 years of age* (renters under 25 may have to pay a surcharge), possess a valid driver's license, and have an accepted credit card or pay a large cash deposit.

- The largest car rental facilities are usually at or very near airports, but smaller ones can be found in other locations (such as adjoining hotels or near car dealerships).

- Reselling their older cars is a significant business for car rental firms. In some cases, the car rental company operates its own used car lots. In other cases, major car manufacturers forge a buy-back agreement with car rental firms; the manufacturers and their dealers then resell the cars.

- Procedures and practices for renting cars in foreign countries vary. In some nations, automatic transmissions are uncommon; in others, air conditioning is an extra available only in more expensive cars. Car rental firms in certain countries won't allow you to take their cars to other nations. For example, because of high rates of theft and accidents, some northern European locations do not allow drivers to journey to places such as Italy or southern France. One key fact: your personal auto insurance or credit card coverage may not cover you in other countries. Always check.

- Some companies specialize in renting recreational vehicles (RVs). In turn, a huge network of RV parks and campgrounds in North America and (to some extent) Europe cater to the needs of RV vacationers.

- European car delivery programs are an interesting hybrid of car rental and purchase. You buy the car in your own city but arrange to pick it up at its factory in Europe. The price is usually thousands of dollars lower than if you bought it at home. You use your new car to drive around Europe, then drop it off at a preassigned port. The car is shipped to your home dealership, and you take delivery a month or two after you return. The money you saved through overseas delivery helps defray the cost of your trip too.

Let's remember that there's a whole segment of car travel that has nothing to do with car rentals: traveling for business or pleasure *in your own car*. Some experts claim that as much as 85 percent of multiday vacation trips are done via the family automobile.

Careers

Careers at Car Rental Companies

Here are some of the jobs that car rental companies provide:

- Senior executives, directors, and managers
- Reservationists
- Rental sales agents
- District sales managers
- Clerical support
- Human resources/training specialists
- Maintenance personnel/mechanics
- Service agents (cleaning)
- Fleet supervisors
- Shuttle drivers

Rail Travel

Are passenger trains a thing of the past, the present, or the future? It depends on your perspective, outlook, and experience. If you've never been on a train, you probably think of it as something from old movies. If you commute by rail, it's very much a thing of your present. And if you've ever been on a high-speed train, you may well view it as a thing of the future.

Rail travel can be efficient, romantic, and inexpensive. It also can be a frustratingly inefficient and sometimes costly way to get around. Your perception probably depends on what kinds of trains you've been on because there are many variations of rail travel.

Kinds of Passenger Rail Travel

Here are the four major categories of rail travel:

1. **Transportation rail:** From commuter trains that take people to and from work or school, to long-distance trains that cross continents, and everything in between, rail travel can be a nation's key form of transporting both business-people and leisure travelers (for example, in Japan and Britain) or a means of transportation that's secondary to automobiles and planes (for example, in the United States).

2. **High-speed trains:** These "bullet trains" represent a subdivision of the transportation category but provide such a different kind of service that they merit their own section. Bullet trains travel well over 100 miles per hour and often represent the fastest way to get from place to place. Amtrak's *Acela* (in the U.S. northeast), Japan's *Shinkansen*, and France's *TGV* are the best-known trains of this type.

3. **Specialty trains:** Usually privately owned rather than publicly run, these trains are attractions unto themselves. In some cases, they offer super-deluxe experiences; perhaps the most famous of these are Europe's legendary *Orient Express* and Africa's *Blue Train*. In other cases, they provide the best way to experience a place like the Grand Canyon, Mexico's Copper Canyon, Alaska's interior, or the Canadian Rockies. Some, usually called scenic railways, go only a few dozen miles, with restored old train cars. Others, such as India's luxurious *Palace on Wheels*, travel for more than a week.

4. **Local rail:** Subways, streetcars, monorails, and more—these forms of public transportation provide a vital service to the world's great cities. San Francisco's cable cars may be the most famous of all.

Of course, freight trains are a major industry as well. In some countries, they take precedence over passenger trains. In the United States, for instance, a passenger train may have to wait on a sidetrack to permit a freight train to pass.

insider info

Train stations, especially those built in the early twentieth century, can be attractions unto themselves. It's often worth getting to such a station early just to experience it.

insider info

When in Moscow, ride the subway. It has some of the most astonishing subway stations in the world, with marble walls and crystal chandeliers.

Amtrak and Via Rail Canada

THIS & that

Amtrak is the private, federally subsidized corporation that operates most long-distance passenger service in the United States. Canada's counterpart is called *VIA Rail Canada*.

Why People Travel by Rail

Having already hinted at some of the factors that motivate people to travel by rail, here are the specifics:

- **To save time.** In an age of lengthy security procedures at airports and clogged roads and highways, rail travel often represents the fastest way to get from place to place, especially when high-speed trains are involved. This is most true for trips of 200 to 500 miles or so. In cities, subways often cover distances far more swiftly than cars or taxis can. Rail travel, of course, is not always the quickest form of travel. In many countries, inefficient rail systems result in maddeningly slow trips. For long trips, air is almost always faster.

- **To experience the environment.** Specialty trains and local transportation rail lines enable passengers to have an up-close, often leisurely, and personal experience of the ever-changing landscape. Even long-distance train travel

A high-speed train.

© Oleksiy Mark/www.Shutterstock.com

helps passengers form intimate portraits of a place, with the "back porches" of cities, towns, and countryside passing by the train's panoramic windows. This is one reason many rail services operate "glass-domed" cars that permit an unobstructed and dramatic view of the scenery.

- **To travel in comfort.** Intercity and cross-country trains often have wider seats and a much better pitch between seats than do aircraft. The ride is quiet and smooth. Moreover, passengers can get up and walk around—something that's hard to do on a plane and impossible to do in a car or a bus.

- **To meet people.** Rail travel easily lends itself to socializing, usually in a train's dining or lounge car.

- **To save money.** In some cases, it's quite economical to travel by train, streetcar, or subway. First-class seats on trains are almost always less expensive than those on planes. Also, trains usually depart from midcity railway stations. There's no need to take an expensive cab ride to and from the airport. Special rail passes provide especially good value.

- **To "travel back in time."** Many specialty trains enable you to experience what was the dominant form of travel in the nineteenth and early twentieth century. Their restored train cars are marvels of Victorian engineering or Art Deco design. For that matter, train travel itself, in any form, provides an evocative slice of nostalgia.

- **To "conquer" bad weather.** A snowstorm can halt air, car, and motorcoach travel. Unless it's a huge storm, rail travel is largely unaffected. (Thunderstorms can delay air travel too.)

- **For a feeling of safety.** Although train accidents do occur, many people perceive rail travel as a more secure and comforting form of transportation than air travel. After all, it is *on the ground*. For frequent travelers who are fearful of air travel, rail is usually the transportation of choice.

Rail Passes

Many rail systems, both local and long-distance, offer special passes for purchase. For a set number of days and for a single price, the pass permits unlimited use of train service. The pass can cover travel in a region, state, nation, or—as in the case of the well-known *Eurail pass*—a large group of participating countries. In some cases, the pass can be bought at the destination you're visiting. More commonly, though, it must be purchased in advance, before you arrive at the place you intend to visit. This makes it possible to offer such deeply discounted passes exclusively to visitors from elsewhere, who will almost surely use them for sightseeing. There may be passes available at the destination, too, but not quite as value-priced.

insider info

Many countries offer *youth passes*, which are priced lower than any other rail passes.

Of course, rail travel does have its drawbacks. In some countries, trains can be slow, stop too often, break down too easily, be poorly maintained, or are overcrowded. If you take a multiday trip, you may wish to have sleeping accommodations onboard, but in many countries, they're expensive. You lose some flexibility, too, because unlike in a car, you can't just stop to see something special. And not all places are accessible by rail; you can go only where the tracks go.

The Onboard Experience

What's it like to take a long-distance train excursion? That depends where you are. In the United States or Canada, typically you'll board your train at a city-center *railroad station* or *terminal*. You may purchase your tickets in advance (for example, from a travel agency, on the Web, or via a toll-free phone number) or wait until you arrive at the station.

About 20 to 30 minutes before departure, an announcement will be made, on a large schedule board and/or a public address system, that your train is ready for boarding at a specified track. After perhaps a security screening, you'll board the train, your luggage in tow or facilitated by a porter. You'll seek out your train car, based on the class of service you've chosen.

As with air travel, your seating may be in coach, business, or first class. Usually, though, only two classes of service are offered. Meals, seating comfort, and other amenities will vary—as it does with air travel—according to which class of service you chose to pay for. You'll have a specific assigned seat if you're in business or first class, and perhaps an assigned one if you're in coach. Often, though, coach is open seating, with a first-come, first-served policy. You'll place your luggage either in an overhead bin or in a luggage compartment at the entrance/exit areas at each end of the car.

Once aboard, you have that wonderful freedom that train travel promises: you can read, nap, walk around, get some food in the dining car, or socialize in the lounge car. Not all trains, however, feature dining or lounge cars. Some just have a snack bar. Others serve meals at seats, from a rolling cart—you buy what you wish—or by flight attendant-like staff in first class. The meal service approach depends on the route. Early on in your journey, a *conductor* will ask to see your ticket to make sure that you're in the right seat and the right class.

insider info

When you're ready to board the train, walk along the platform toward the cars farthest from the entrance. They're probably less crowded.

Suppose your journey is an overnight one. You may choose to sleep in your seat. Or you may have booked one of the train's *sleeping compartments* or *bedrooms* in a *sleeping car*. Small and cozy, each bedroom may have a private, enclosed shower, sink, and toilet. If not, then the restroom and shower for the car and all its guests is nearby. One final thing about U.S. train travel: curtained, bunk bed–style sleeping accommodations no longer exist. They remain, as memories, only in old movies.

Foreign Rail Experiences

In many countries, rail travel isn't just an alternative to air or car travel; it's the dominant form of travel. As a result, service is much more frequent than it is in Canada or the United States, with far more places accessible by rail. In many developing nations, train travel may be well below the standards you expect and is quite an adventure. Specialty trains in such countries, though, can be impressive.

In industrialized nations, however, rail travel often represents the best way to get around. The journey would be much like the one described for the United States and Canada, with certain exceptions:

- Some foreign trains have small compartments within each rail car, with doors opening onto a corridor that runs along one side of the car. Movies set in Europe feature them prominently. Each compartment has two rows of two or three seats on each side, with passengers facing one another.

- As with U.S. and Canadian rail transportation, passengers can sleep onboard, either in their seats or in small, bedroom-like compartments. However, many foreign trains, especially European ones, feature **couchettes**, *a bunk in a passenger compartment*. Configured like regular passenger compartments during the day, couchette compartments are converted by the porter into sleeping quarters at night. The two lower seats each turns into a couchette, and one or two couchettes above each of these fold out from the wall.

  Couchettes are certainly an intimate sleeping arrangement, considering that usually the people overnighting in these cramped quarters may not know one another. More startling is that they're preassigned with no regard to the sex of the occupants.

- Foreign trains tend to have only two classes of service, with less difference between the two than in the United States or Canada.

insider info

In a few developing countries, people sometimes ride a train sitting on the railcar's roof. Not a good idea.

Careers

Careers in Rail Travel

Rail transportation offers many potential careers. Here are some of them:

- Senior executives, directors, and managers
- Clerical and sales support
- Accountants
- District sales representatives
- Human resources/training specialists
- Dispatchers
- Ticketing agents
- Onboard attendants/conductors
- Maintenance personnel
- Engineers

- It's critical that when you board a foreign train, you know precisely which car to board. Some cars may go to one destination, but others will be "decoupled" from the engine and connected to another train and go somewhere else. So you might be going to one place—but your rail car won't. Signs posted on the car's exterior usually indicate that car's destinations and, fortunately, the conductor will usually rectify a mistake before it's too late when he or she sees your ticket.

More This and That

- The most traveled rail route in the United States is the Northeast Corridor, from Boston through New York City, Philadelphia, and Washington, D.C.

- Amtrak tickets are handled very much like airline tickets (including as e-tickets). In fact, Amtrak works through the Airlines Reporting Corporation (ARC).

- On some specialty train journeys, such as the one that goes through Mexico's Copper Canyon or Alaska's Denali National Park, passengers don't sleep on the trains but overnight at hotels along the way.

- Some rail journeys are packaged with pre-, post-, or even midtrip land accommodations, just like cruises. Other packages offer rail transportation in one direction and air transportation for the return. Rail-ski packages are also quite common.

Destination Marketing Organizations

Strictly speaking, they're not suppliers, but **destination marketing organizations (DMOs)** represent a major force in tourism. What's a DMO? It's *an organization whose mission is to promote a place.*

DMOs can represent virtually every size and type of place. A notable neighborhood, a town, a city, a region, a state, a province, an island group, a nation, a group of nations, a continent—all of these can operate a DMO service. As you learned in Chapter 1, they can also go by many names. *Tourist bureaus* or **tourist offices** usually represent a country. Headquartered in their home country, they often maintain offices in key cities across the globe, where the employees work closely with their local embassy or consulate. **Convention and visitors bureaus** (**CVBs**) usually operate out of a city, region, state, or province. The biggest ones have satellite offices or sales representatives in other places.

What do DMOs do? First, they use every medium at their disposal to reach the traveling public. If you've read a brochure or seen an ad in a travel magazine, online, or on TV that promotes a place—with no direct mention of a specific supplier—that promotional piece probably was paid for by a DMO. DMOs also work indirectly, issuing press releases that may be picked up by the news media and transformed into stories. They may provide all manner of logistic and informational support to, say, a magazine writer who is doing an article about their destination. And they may

operate offices, Web sites, and/ or toll-free lines that consumers can access to obtain information, advice, brochures, and promotional materials.

DMOs also aggressively court travel suppliers such as tour operators and cruise lines. In fact, in order to get tour companies to visit their destinations, representatives of DMOs make up as much as 70 percent of the attendees at such events as the National Tour Association's annual conference. The biggest DMOs often sponsor meals or entertainment for the thousands of NTA members who attend the conference.

The Chateau Frontenac hotel projects Quebec City's charm.

DMOs target travel agents too because they know that agents have a major influence on where their clients go. They run ads in publications to entice the agency community, host receptions (for example, breakfasts) that agents attend, and sponsor training programs (consisting of live classroom instruction, print workbooks, videos, and/or Web-based text). After agents finish the study program, they take a test. Pass it and they're awarded a "specialist designation" that provides them with special benefits like low-cost, agent-only **familiarization trips** (**fams**), special communications, and, most important, instant credibility with consumers seeking guidance on that destination.

DMOs, Big and Small

Here are two examples of how DMOs can represent almost any size of place. The city of Oslo, Norway, has its own modest DMO, VisitOSLO. So, too, does the region that includes and surrounds Oslo. Norway has a *tourist board*, which cooperates with Sweden, Denmark, Finland, and Iceland in an alliance called the Scandinavian Tourist Boards.

A similar layered approach can be found in Hawaii: Waikiki Beach has its own promotional organization, as does the city it's in (Honolulu), the island it's on (Oahu), the state it's in (Hawaii), and, of course, the nation it's part of (the United States).

How DMOs Are Funded

Three financial models are typical among DMOs:

- *A DMO may be funded entirely by the government of the destination that it represents.* In a time of government budgetary constraints, this approach has become increasingly rare. DMOs also find it difficult to operate under this model because the political forces and expectations that come to bear on them can be frustrating.

- *A DMO may be funded entirely by its member-suppliers.* In this model, hotels, restaurants, attractions, stores, sightseeing companies, and others contribute a yearly membership fee to their DMO. In turn, the DMO integrates the

Insuring Travel

It would be wonderful if all went well on a trip. This doesn't always happen, however. Travel is a complex experience. Things can easily go wrong. Suppose your flight is canceled and you miss your cruise departure. Or your luggage gets lost. Perhaps the tour company you're booked with goes out of business before you leave—or worse, while you're on your trip. And what if you have an accident or become ill before your vacation begins? Won't you lose those nonrefundable deposits you've already paid? Travel insurance potentially covers all of these scenarios and more. It's a great way to protect your travel investment and to obtain ready-made solutions to most unforeseen events.

The details of coverage are usually complex and change frequently and are beyond the scope of this book. Many coverage details have to do with *preexisting medical conditions*—Does the traveler already and knowingly have a medical condition that could interfere with his or her trip?—and those factors that insurance may not cover (for example, problems caused by war or a terrorist act). It *is* important, however, to understand that three models for travel insurance predominate:

- The insurance may be supplier-generated. That is, a cruise line or tour operator provides the coverage. This isn't really insurance in the strictest sense. It simply means that if something goes wrong, the supplier will take care of the costs involved. The advantage is that supplier-generated insurance is usually inexpensive. But there are disadvantages. For instance, what if the supplier goes out of business (that is, "defaults")? Who will cover the loss? Another drawback is that supplier-generated insurance usually covers a limited number of situations.

- The insurance may come from an insurance company. Although more expensive than supplier-generated insurance, "regular" travel insurance covers many more situations, applies when suppliers default, and usually offers a 24/7 assistance center accessed by a toll-free number, which helps provide solutions to unexpected occurrences. Such insurance can be obtained directly from the insurance provider or, more commonly, through a travel agency.

- The insurance may come from an insurance company but through the supplier. Many suppliers acknowledge the limitations of self-generated coverage. They therefore contract with an insurance company to provide their coverage. If the supplier defaults, the customers will still be covered.

member-suppliers' products into its promotional efforts. The challenge for this model is to keep all members pleased with a balanced promotional campaign.

- *A DMO may be funded by a mix of government and member-supplier support.* This is the most common operational model today.

Closely allied to the DMO sector are *sports marketing commissions*, which work at bringing major sporting events to a place. Festivals, world's fairs, and similar events are also magnets for tourism.

Miscellaneous Travel Suppliers

Here are three other significant travel supplier segments you should know about: meetings and conventions, shopping venues, and attractions.

Meetings and Conventions

Meetings and conventions represent a huge portion of travel-related business. Many major cities have vast **convention centers** that *provide space for the conference and display booth needs of major associations and corporations*, sometimes with thousands of delegates in attendance. These convention centers also accommodate local events such as boat, car, and home shows, and health/wellness expositions. Events at convention centers bring substantial business to other local suppliers such as hotels, motorcoach companies, tour operators, and food service providers.

The meetings and conventions business operates on a smaller scale too. In fact, most meetings and conventions are modest in size and scope. In such cases, hotels

© Perfect Illusion/www.Shutterstock.com

A convention center benefits not just attendees but also the local economy.

host the attendees, providing meeting space and food services in conference rooms and ballrooms located on the hotels' property.

Critical to the success of such event functions are **meeting planners**, *specialists who help plan, negotiate, coordinate, operate, and conduct follow-up evaluations of a convention or relatively large meeting.* They may work for the company or association that's staging the event, for a company that specializes in meeting planning, or as independent contractors.

Shopping Venues

It's amazing how some people love shopping, and they often carry that love over to their travel experiences. In turn, a huge business has grown to facilitate this passion for shopping:

- Virtually every attraction has at least one souvenir outlet. In fact, it's essential to their profitability.

- Streets at cruise ports are lined with jewelry stores, clothing boutiques, craft shops, and who knows what else to appeal to cruise passengers.

- Virtually every international airport has duty-free shops, where goods are sold minus their import tax. In reality, the price is only a little bit better than what you would pay at home.

- Some malls, such as the gigantic Mall of America near Minneapolis, the West Edmonton Mall, and the huge outlet malls just outside Las Vegas, derive much of their income from tourists.

Milan's Galleria Vittorio Emanuele II, built between 1865 and 1877, inspired many of today's shopping malls.

© Rob van Esch/www.Shutterstock.com

Attractions, Activities, and Events

Many motives compel travelers to visit a destination. One of these reasons is to see or experience something special (an attraction). A famous building, structure or monument, a natural wonder, an unusual neighborhood, a theme park, a re-created historic village (an "outdoor living history museum")—these all can be classified as attractions. Attractions usually work closely with DMOs, tour operators, and others to enhance an attraction's ability to entice and please visitors.

Attractions have been a travel motivator for a very long time. As you learned in Chapter 1, the Seven Wonders of the World were "must see" attractions for voyagers thousands of years ago. The Pyramids are the only wonders that remain, though "pieces" of the other six can be found at their original sites and in museums, especially London's British Museum.

Just about every city that attracts tourism boasts a concentration of significant attractions: New York City has the Statue of

North America's First Attraction

When the first European explorers arrived in what is now New York and New England, one of the first things Native Americans told them about were the gigantic waterfalls that were well inland, to the northwest. Even to the indigenous people, Niagara was something to behold (and a sacred place, as well).

During the eighteenth and nineteenth centuries, Niagara Falls became a magnet for tourism. New rail lines and roads provided easy access. Hotels, restaurants, and museums lined the best vantage points. Colored lights illuminated the falls at night. A powerful boat, the *Maid of the Mist*, carried passengers right up to Niagara's cascades. Tunnels dug into the rock behind the falls allowed visitors to experience the falls *from behind*. Daredevils crossed tightropes laid across the Niagara River, and others plunged over the falls in barrels. And Niagara became *the* place to honeymoon.

But Niagara had a limitation: it was a seasonal attraction. From mid-October to May, cold, sometimes blustery weather undermined its appeal. Tourism basically shut down for the winter.

To overcome this, local officials and merchants introduced an event for the holiday season, a "Festival of Lights." It was immediately successful. They then received permission to open two huge casinos. The result: Niagara Falls has now become a popular destination year-round.

Liberty, the Empire State Building, Rockefeller Center, Ground Zero, Times Square, and several world-class museums; Orlando has about a dozen major theme parks. But try to name an attraction in North Dakota. Not easy, is it? That may be why it has the least tourism of any U.S. state. Actually, North Dakota does have interesting things to see, but they're not well known.

Sometimes a single famous attraction is all that you need. Machu Picchu—the "lost city of the Incas" high in the Andes Mountains—is on the wish list of many travelers.

Of course, an *activity* can be an attraction. People go to Mt. Tremblant north of Montreal, Canada, to snowboard and ski, to Tanzania to see the amazing wildlife, and to Chuuk Island in Micronesia to dive among the shipwrecks that remain there from World War II.

As previously noted, special events can generate strong visitor interest. For example, some tour companies operate only one departure yearly: a tour to Pasadena for the Rose Bowl and Rose Parade. That's all they need to make their business profitable.

insider info

When a major theme park's gates open, it's best for visitors to proceed to the far end and work their way back. They'll encounter shorter wait lines.

Review Questions

1. Give at least five reasons a person might rent a car.

2. Cite at least six factors that can affect the cost of a car rental.

3. Give at least five reasons someone would choose to take a long-distance rail journey.

4. In what significant ways might a foreign rail experience differ from a U.S. or Canadian one?

It's All About You Questions

1. If you had to make a list of seven attractions that you've never seen but would love to see, what would they be?

2. What one thing in your city or town would you show first to a friend visiting from out of town?

Activity 1: Bon Voyage and Buon Viaggio

Let's say you're planning to visit France and Italy and will be able to spend two weeks there. You've decided to do so independently because you don't want to take a tour or a cruise. How would you personally choose to do it: by car rental, rail, or air? Explain your choice.

NAME   **DATE**

Activity 2: Motoring Around Los Angeles

Pretend you'll be renting a car to drive around Los Angeles in July, visiting key tourist sites. How important will each of the following factors be? Be prepared to explain your reason behind each choice.

Factor	How important?		
1. A well-known car rental company (for example, Hertz)	Very	Somewhat	Not very
2. A large car (for example, full-size)	Very	Somewhat	Not very
3. The color of the car (assuming you have a choice)	Very	Somewhat	Not very
4. The proximity of the car rental facility to the airport	Very	Somewhat	Not very
5. Availability of car rental insurance from the car rental company	Very	Somewhat	Not very
6. Price	Very	Somewhat	Not very
7. Unlimited mileage option	Very	Somewhat	Not very
8. A nonsmoking car	Very	Somewhat	Not very
9. You get frequent-flyer miles from an airline for renting the car	Very	Somewhat	Not very
10. The car has GPS for no extra charge	Very	Somewhat	Not very

Gale Hospitality, Tourism and Leisure Database Assignment

The following assignment requires access to the Gale Hospitality, Tourism and Leisure Database. Check with your instructor to see if you have access to this database.

Find the three articles under the title *Fast Train Phobia* in the Gale Hospitality, Tourism & Leisure Collection.

After reading all three, determine what you believe to be the single most important reason the United States doesn't have more high-speed rail service.

9

Here, There, Almost Anywhere: The Geography of Travel

KEY TERMS

- 24-hour clock system
- Cape
- Cay
- Continent
- Ecotourism
- Elevation
- Equator
- Geyser
- Great circle route
- Gulf
- Hurricane
- Island
- Jet stream
- Lake
- Lines of latitude
- Lines of longitude
- Locator map
- Mountain
- Northern Hemisphere
- Ocean
- Peninsula
- Reef
- River
- Sea
- Southern Hemisphere
- Temperate zone
- Tradewinds
- Tropical zone

After studying this chapter, you'll be able to:

- Relate geographic principles to travel concerns

- Define major geographic and destination-related terms

- Locate the world's significant tourist destinations

- Identify where some of the world's great attractions are

Images © C Miller Design; hut image © Keith Levit/www.Shutterstock.com

Photo courtesy of Hugh Riley

Hugh Riley

CURRENT POSITION/TITLE:

Secretary General/ CEO, Caribbean Tourism Organization

SHORT DESCRIPTION OF WHAT YOUR RESPONSIBILITIES ARE:

I lead an organization that represents more than 30 Caribbean governments and the businesses that serve their visitors' needs.

EDUCATION:

City University of New York; Thomas Edison State College; University of Surrey, England

FIRST JOB IN TRAVEL/HOSPITALITY INDUSTRY:

Sales Representative for the Barbados Tourism Authority

FIRST PAID JOB (IF DIFFERENT FROM ABOVE):

Radio Broadcaster in Barbados, the country of my birth, thanks to prior BBC training

FAVORITE PART OF WHAT I DO:

Getting to enjoy the unique beauty of each country I have the honor to represent

THING I WISH I DIDN'T HAVE TO DO:

Squeeze a gallon-sized task into a pint-sized budget

SOMEONE WHO INSPIRES ME:

The ancient poet Virgil who, through my Latin teacher, Earl Glasgow, taught me, "You can, because you think you can." (from *The Aeneid*)

BEST CAREER MEMORY I HAVE:

Setting up supersonic Concorde flights to Barbados. You could leave JFK airport in the morning, have lunch in Barbados, and be back to NYC in time for dinner—all in the same day.

FAVORITE QUOTE:

"When you really want something, the Universe conspires to help you get it." (Paulo Coelho from *The Alchemist*)

SOMETHING ALMOST NO ONE KNOWS ABOUT ME:

At one point, I wanted to be a lawyer or a priest.

The world is a big place. And let's face it, it's too big to describe thoroughly in one chapter. The situation is made even more challenging because most of us have studied very little geography in school. A *National Geographic* survey discovered that nearly half of Americans between the ages of 18 and 24 couldn't find New York on a map, and 27 percent could not locate the Pacific Ocean, the world's largest body of water. Eleven percent couldn't even find the United States on a map. Yet destinations are critical to the travel industry: They're *the* reason people travel. Places are what bring travel alive.

So let's cover at least the highlights of world geography. Let's be practical too. Where most of the world's zinc comes from, or what an alluvial plain is, doesn't matter much to the travel business. Where Orlando, Las Vegas, and Venice are, does. So get ready for your crash course on destination geography.

A Little Information About Maps

What blueprints are to builders, what anatomy charts are to surgeons, maps are to travel professionals. But there's one problem: the only truly accurate map is a globe. Flat maps are terribly distorted, because you can't flatten a ball (what the earth is) into a rectangle (what most maps are). Yet we are best acquainted with flat maps, and we use them the most.

So get out a world map or a globe, consult it as we go along, and keep the following in mind:

- Areas near the **equator** (*the imaginary line that encircles the earth's "middle" and is equidistant from the north and south poles*) are depicted accurately. As you go north (up) or south (down) on a flat map, the regions shown become increasingly distorted, or stretched, making them appear much larger than they really are. For proof, find Greenland (it is between the North American and European continents). It seems huge, doesn't it, perhaps even larger than the United States? The reality is that the United States is four times bigger than Greenland.

- The shortest distance between two points is a straight line, right? Wrong, at least on your flat map. This "shortest distance is a straight line" concept works north to south, but *not* east to west. The shortest distances east to west (or vice versa) are represented on a flat map by lines that *curve toward the poles*. Don't worry about the reason. (It's a matter of the geometry of spheres, if that helps.)

- With the straight-line concept, if you flew from San Francisco to London, you'd expect to look down on the northern United States in midflight. Instead, when you look down, you'll see icebergs. That's because jets take the shortest route to London, curving over northern Canada. (This sort of flight is following a **great circle route**.) Here's another mind-bender: the shortest route from

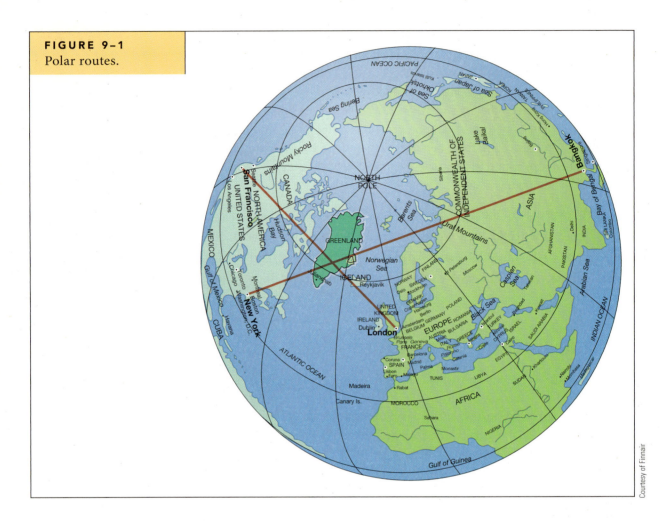

FIGURE 9–1
Polar routes.

Courtesy of Finnair

New York City to Bangkok, Thailand, would be via Helsinki, Finland. It doesn't make sense on a flat map, but use a string to trace it on a globe. You'll see that it really is the shortest route (Figure 9–1).

• Seasons in the **Southern Hemisphere** (*the half of the world south of the equator*) are the reverse of those in the **Northern Hemisphere**. We all know this, but it just seems weird to Americans that in Australia, Argentina, and South Africa, for example, Christmas takes place in summer and Easter occurs in autumn.

• As you look at your map, you'll also notice a grid of lines. (Note that the "boxes" they create get stretched near the poles. It's that same distortion problem we talked about earlier.) The *lines that go north-south* are called **lines of longitude**, and the *lines that go east-west* are **lines of latitude**. Now look at the map's margins. Each line is marked by a degree (for example, the equator is 0 degrees). By matching up these numbers, you can designate any spot on earth by its latitude and longitude: Phoenix, Arizona, is 33 degrees North latitude, 112 degrees West longitude.

• Your map may also illustrate the world's 24 time zones. These time zones tend to parallel longitude lines. As you cross one going east, you pass into the next hour. This is why if you fly from Los Angeles to Washington, D.C., leaving at 8 a.m., the flight might be only five hours long, but you'd arrive in Washington, D.C., at 4 p.m. Conversely, as you cross a time zone (or zones) east to west, you pass into earlier hours. So on your return flight, you'd leave Washington, D.C., at, say, 2 p.m., fly for 5.5 hours, and arrive in L.A. at 4:30 p.m.

- Things get weirder at what's called the *International Date Line* (Figure 9–2). You can perhaps spot it on your map, going north-south—with slight zigzags—down the middle of the Pacific Ocean. If you cross it going west, it becomes the next day (for example, if it's Monday, it instantly becomes Tuesday). If you cross it east to west, it becomes the previous day. (Yes, that's right. If it's Thursday, it becomes Wednesday.) And if you cross it many times during the day, like the astronauts do, you come back a week before you left. (Just kidding.)

If you can't imagine how or why the day changes at the International Date Line, don't worry. Thousands of travel professionals (especially those who deal with trans-Pacific air and sea travel) have applied this principle, using computers, with only the dimmest idea of why it happens.

insider info

As wide as China is, it has only one time zone. The reason: the Chinese failed to attend the 1883 meeting that established the world's time zones.

FIGURE 9–2
International Date Line.

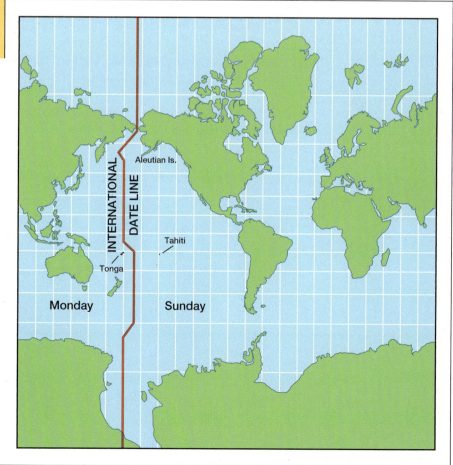

The Winds of Travel

Most people don't realize that although the weather is unpredictable, certain wind patterns are quite predictable and most certainly affect travel:

- In **temperate zones,** *areas between the Arctic or Antarctic circles and the Tropics* (where you probably are as you read this), winds tend to blow west to east. Think about it: this is the direction in which clouds and storms generally move. It's also why things tend to be drier on the east side of temperate-zone mountains (for example, Las Vegas is just east of the Spring Mountains). The biggest effect on travel is that flights going east to west tend to take longer than those going west to east. The aircraft is generally flying *into* the wind. Now you know why that flight we described earlier from Washington, D.C. to Los Angeles took a half-hour longer than when it went from L.A. to Washington, D.C.

- In **tropical zones,** *the regions between approximately 23 degrees north of the equator and 23 degrees south of the equator*, things reverse. Winds here flow from east to west. That's why most resorts are located on the west side of mountainous tropical islands: they get less rain there. Also, these winds (called the **tradewinds**) are closer to the ground, providing pleasant, cooling breezes in otherwise hot climates.

- **Hurricanes**, *storms with winds of 74 mph and above*, can severely alter one's travel plans. Most are born near the equator over tropical waters, then move northward or southward. In the Northern Hemisphere, 80 percent of them occur from August through October.

They're most likely to affect travel in Florida, the Caribbean, the Gulf of Mexico, and Southeast Asia (Figure 9–3).

insider info

Europe almost never has hurricanes.

insider info

Typhoons, cyclones, and hurricanes are different names for the same thing. It just depends on the region of the world where they occur.

FIGURE 9–3
Hurricane areas.

© Cengage Learning 2012

Bodies of Water

More than 60 percent of the earth is covered by water. We are, indeed, a "blue planet." Here are the definitions of the most important bodies of water:

- **Oceans** dominate the earth's surface. There are four oceans: the *Atlantic*, the *Pacific*, the *Indian*, and the *Arctic*. Some geographers claim that there are five, with the *Southern Ocean* as the fifth. Actually, the oceans form one big body of water because they are all interconnected.

- **Seas** are the next largest. They're usually salty and open to (or are even part of) an ocean. A few large lakes are called seas (for example, the *Black Sea*, the *Caspian Sea*, and the *Dead Sea*).

- **Gulfs** are large areas of water that penetrate into land (such as the *Gulf of Mexico*). They usually open onto a sea or an ocean.

- **Lakes** are smaller than gulfs and seas, usually have fresh water, and are mostly or entirely encircled by land. Some, however, are very large (like the *Great Lakes*) and some are salty (for example, the *Great Salt Lake* near Salt Lake City).

- **Rivers** are large streams of water that empty into other bodies of water such as an ocean). The most important to tourism are the *Mississippi* (North America), the *Rhine* and the *Danube* (Europe), the *Nile* (Africa), and the *Amazon* (South America).

Landforms

Many tourist destinations border water. In fact, it's hard to think of any that don't. But all, of course, are on land. Here are the most important landforms:

- **Continents** are the biggest. There are seven: *North America*, *South America*, *Europe*, *Africa*, *Asia*, *Australia*, and *Antarctica*. Some geographers argue that Europe and Asia are one continent because they're on a continuous landmass, which they call *Eurasia*.

- **Mountains** are the world's great, high outcroppings of rock and soil. Among the most famous are the *Rockies* (North America), the *Alps* (Europe), the *Andes* (South America), and the *Himalaya* (Asia).

Kicking back on a tropical isle.

© BlueOrange Studio/www.Shutterstock.com

Volcanic mountains are among the most impressive, including Hawaii's *Kilauea*, which has been erupting continuously for more than two decades.

- **Peninsulas** and **capes** are projections of land into the water. Three examples of famous peninsulas are *Florida*, *Baja*, and *Iberia* (where Spain and Portugal are located). Capes tend to be smaller (for example, *Cape Cod* in Massachusetts).

- **Islands** are landforms completely surrounded by water and are frequent tourist destinations, especially in the tropics.

The Nations We Visit

Have you ever watched the opening or closing ceremonies of the Olympics? It is astonishing how many countries there are (well over 100). What's also amazing is how challenging it can be to figure out even which *continent* some of them are on!

Here's the good news: the majority of these countries have minimal tourism. But that leaves many dozens that do, that you should know at least something about. So here's a list of the most important tourist nations, categorized by continents, with a brief description of each. Follow along on your world map or atlas to make it easier for you to visualize each place we discuss.

Telling Terms

Here are other geographic vocabulary items you should know:

- **Ecotourism:** Tourism that is based on and respects nature.

- **Locator maps:** Special gridded maps, found in travel industry resource books and on Web sites, that represent a small area and help you locate hotels, attractions, and so on.

- **24-hour-clock system:** In many countries, and among travel professionals, time is often expressed as a four-digit number: 7 a.m. is 0700, for example. Afternoon times continue up to the digit 24: 6:30 p.m., for instance, is expressed as 1830.

- **Cays:** Sandy coral islands that are small and low. Also sometimes called *keys* (for example, the Florida Keys).

- **Reefs:** Low ridges, usually made of coral, that rise to or near the water's surface. They're typically just offshore and offer prime diving and snorkeling opportunities.

- **Elevation:** The height, in feet (or meters), of land. The higher the elevation, the cooler it becomes, even in tropical places (for example, it snows atop Hawaii's 13,796-foot Mauna Kea).

- **Geysers:** Jets of steaming water that shoot high into the air. The ones in Yellowstone National Park are famous, especially Old Faithful.

- **Jet stream:** The high-altitude, high-velocity core of those winds that blow from west to east in temperate zones.

North America

See Figure 9–4 for a map of North America.

- The **United States** offers a hugely diversified array of touristic possibilities, from great metropolitan cities (*New York City, Chicago, Los Angeles, San Francisco*, and so on) to those that rely heavily on tourism (*Las Vegas,*

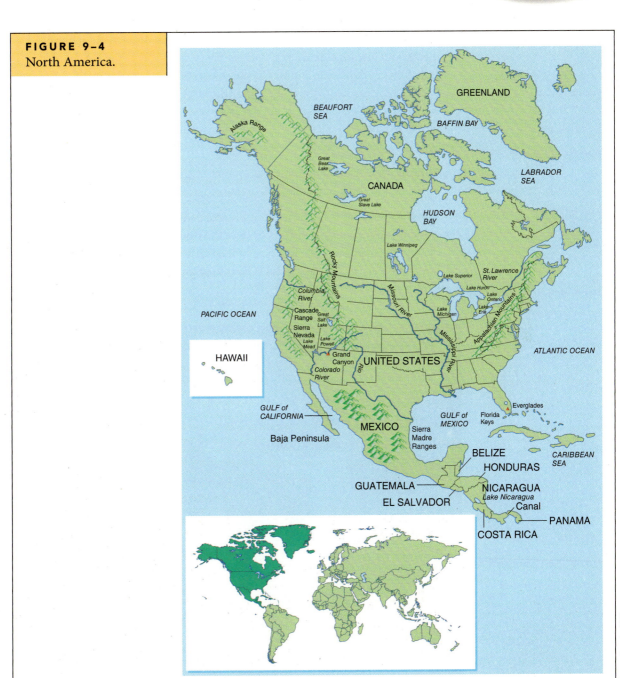

FIGURE 9–4
North America.

Honolulu, and *Orlando*). World-class ski resorts dot its mountains, and prime ocean resorts line its coasts (for example, *Florida* and *Hawaii*).

- **Canada**, because of its northern climate, has an abbreviated summer tourist season. Winter offers plenty of snow-based opportunities too. *Montreal*, *Vancouver*, and *Toronto* are great, cosmopolitan cities, and *Quebec City* and *Victoria* are like little pieces of Europe in North America. *Niagara Falls*, on the U.S.–Canada border, is a world-famous wonder.

- **Mexico** is a land of diverse landscapes, beachside resorts, artistic achievements, and historical treasures. Its *Baja Peninsula* starts at the U.S. border and stretches hundreds of miles to the resorts of *Los Cabos*, at its tip. Mexico's Pacific shore is lined with resort cities (the largest is *Acapulco*). On its Caribbean coast is *Cancun*, a huge seaside resort with nearby Mayan archaeological wonders. Mexico's central region has many towns that still reflect its Spanish colonial past.

- **Central America** and its seven nations are fast-growing destinations, known especially for their ecological and archaeological wonders.

- **The Caribbean** may be the most important collection of islands in the world for tourism. Most visitors explore the islands via cruise ships or stay at the region's major resorts. Not part of the Caribbean but just to its north is the **Bahamas**. Farther north still is **Bermuda**, an island-nation with strong British roots.

Sights like this attract visitors to Alaska.

© Caleb Foster/www.Shutterstock.com

South America

This vibrant, highly diversified continent encompasses 13 countries (Figure 9–5). Here are the most important ones for tourism:

- **Brazil** features some of the most important ecological assets in the world. The mighty *Amazon* carves into Brazil's lush, jungle interior, and *Iguazu Falls*, a series of water cascades over two miles long, lies at the border with Argentina

FIGURE 9–5
South America.

© Cengage Learning 2012

One of the world's best-known events: Carnival in Rio.

and Paraguay. *Rio de Janeiro* is one of the most exciting cities in the world, with fantastic beaches, great cuisine, and one of the world's most dramatic settings for a city. Brazil's *Salvador* region still manifests a strong African heritage.

- **Argentina** feels more European than any other country in South America. At least one-third of its citizens have Italian family names. *Buenos Aires* is reminiscent of Paris, with broad boulevards (including the world's widest), elegant buildings, and many colorful ethnic neighborhoods.

- **Peru** has several absolutely unique attractions. *Cuzco* was the former center of the Incan Empire and still has intriguing ruins. The *Nazca Plain* features huge, mysterious designs drawn onto the ground. They're best seen by air. And *Machu Picchu* is an astonishing city in ruins, perched impossibly high in the Andes.

   Two fascinating island groups belong to South American countries. *Easter Island*, with its huge, mysterious stone statues, lies 2,000 miles west of **Chile** (which governs it); and the *Galápagos Islands*, whose unusual wildlife Charles Darwin made famous, belong to **Ecuador**. The continent of *Antarctica* is often visited by cruise ships that leave from the southern tip of South America.

Europe

No continent attracts more travelers than does Europe (Figure 9–6). In fact, when the World Tourism Organization compiles its tourism statistics each year, a majority of the top 10 most-visited countries in the world usually turn out to be European. History, scenery, skiing, beaches, the arts—all these and more ensure that Europe

insider info
Before going to Peru, you should have your physician prescribe medication to prevent altitude sickness.

insider info
Parking can be very expensive in many of Europe's major cities.

FIGURE 9–6
Europe.

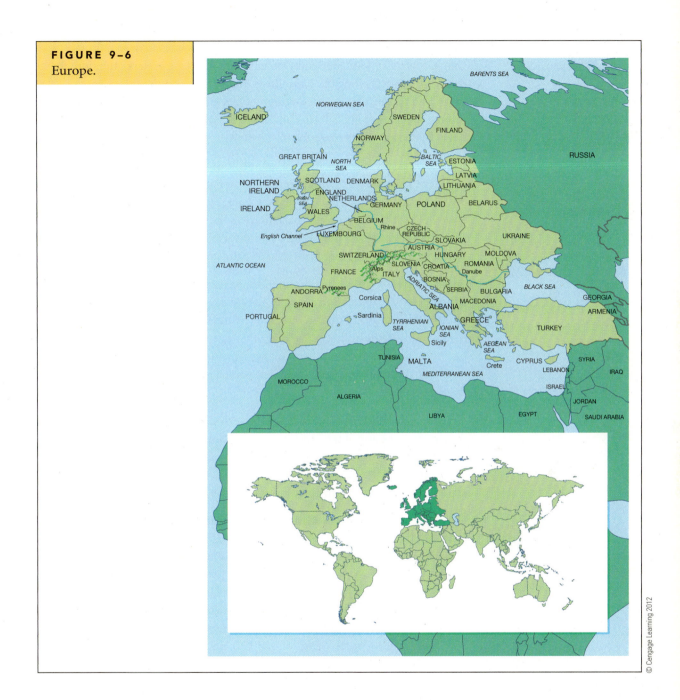

© Cengage Learning 2012

remains one of the most appealing places to vacation and do business. Here are its key clusters of nations:

- The **United Kingdom** (**England**, **Wales**, **Scotland**, **Northern Ireland**) and **Ireland** are immensely popular for travelers, especially those from North America. Their language and culture are familiar and their historical attractions are legendary. *London* can occupy a tourist for weeks, and dozens of fascinating places are easy day trips. *Dublin* is important to Ireland's culture and history.

insider info

In Europe, the *1st floor* is what we in the United States and Canada call the *2nd floor*. Our *1st floor* is their *ground floor*.

- **France** is the largest country completely within Europe. *Paris*—a cultural gem—is its focal point, but many other places merit a traveler's attention: the *chateaux* (castles) along the *Loire River Valley*; *Normandy*, with its seaside towns and historical sites; the southerly *French Riviera*, a place of chic seaside resorts; the mighty *French Alps*; and France's *Eastern Wine Country*, where many legendary wines come from.

- **Italy** is a treasure house of history, architecture, and wonderful cuisine. Northern Italy boasts a striking mix of mountains and lakes. Just to the south are the nation's great, unique cities of *Venice*, *Florence*, and *Milan*. The *Italian Riviera*, like its French counterpart, borders the Mediterranean Sea. Historic *Rome*, farther south, is the country's political and cultural center. Less visited southern Italy has one large city (*Naples*) and countryside charm.

- **Spain** is a highly diversified destination. At its center is *Madrid*, its culturally impressive capital. *Barcelona*, in the country's northeast corner, has some of the world's most unique architecture. Wonderful beach towns line Spain's eastern and southern shores. Several other famous cities and towns are well known to tourists. Among them are *Segovia*, *Toledo*, *Seville*, and *Granada*. The nation of **Portugal**, to Spain's west, has gained great popularity as a tourist destination too.

- **Greece** has been called the Cradle of Western Civilization. Its capital, historic *Athens*, features one of the most famous buildings of all times, the *Parthenon*. Within easy day-trip distances are many historical sites, including *Olympia*, where the first Olympic Games took place in 776 BC. Off mainland Greece's shores are numerous highly picturesque islands.

- **Germany** is a culturally rich land of fairytale castles and towns. *Bavaria*, in the south, boasts the scenery of the Alps and is anchored by the city of *Munich*. Bavaria is what most tourists think of when they imagine Germany. Stretching northward is the picturesque *Romantic Road*, which eventually reaches one of Europe's best preserved medieval towns, *Rothenburg*. Cruises on the *Rhine River* are very popular, and *Berlin*, Germany's capital, is rich with world-class museums.

- **Switzerland** features gingerbread hamlets, deep blue lakes, and dazzling alpine vistas. Its two most important cities are *Zurich* and *Geneva*. Near its border with Italy is that legendary mountain, the *Matterhorn*.

A typically quaint Paris neighborhood.

© F.C.G./www.Shutterstock.com

Careers

Careers and Geography

How can professionals in different sectors of the travel business put geography to use? Here are some examples:

- A cruise activities director may recommend and sell shore excursion tours.
- Airline reservationists can upsell a caller to the comfort of business class on a long overseas flight.
- A car rental representative can suggest a convertible for the client's tropical vacation.
- A hotel clerk or concierge can make shopping, restaurant, and nightlife arrangements for the hotel guest.
- Flight attendants often answer questions about that flight's destination or explain the many places where their airline flies (a key consideration for members of frequent-flyer mileage programs).
- A tour conductor relates all sorts of facts about the destinations that the tour group will visit.
- An incentive trip planner can show corporate clients how certain add-on destinations will enhance their employees' experience.
- A representative from a convention and tourist bureau can show an audience how the destination fulfills their expectations.
- A hotel's sales and marketing director must promote the geographic benefits of staying at his or her property: ocean-view rooms, proximity to attractions or businesses, easy access to public transportation, closeness to trails at a ski resort, and so on.
- Even professionals in the food services industry must think about geography. Location is one of the key elements of whether a theme restaurant (like Planet Hollywood) will succeed or fail.

Adapted from Selling Destinations: Geography for the Travel Professional 5e, *by Marc Mancini,* 2010, Clifton Park, NY: Delmar Cengage Learning. Copyright 2010 by Delmar Cengage Learning. Adapted with permission.

- **Austria** is a first-rate destination. *Vienna*, its capital, lies on the *Danube* and boasts a dazzling array of palaces and other noteworthy structures. *Salzburg*, near the German border, was the birthplace of composer Wolfgang Amadeus Mozart. Austria's southern alpine areas feature some of the world's best skiing.

- The **Benelux Countries** (**Bel**gium, the **N**etherlands, and **Lux**embourg) feature huge cities (for example, *Amsterdam*, in the Netherlands) as well as compact towns (*Bruges*, Belgium) that conjure the region's past.

- **Scandinavia** (composed of **Norway**, **Sweden**, **Finland**, **Denmark**, and **Iceland**) share a common Viking heritage. Its cities are absolutely charming and its scenery is often dramatic (especially along Norway's fjord-lined west coast).

insider info

The world's busiest McDonald's is in Munich, Germany; the world's busiest KFC is in Beijing; there are about 6,000 Taco Bells in Canada and the United States, but none in Mexico.

- **Eastern Europe** has become very popular among visitors. Several of its cities are must-sees, including *Budapest* (**Hungary**), *Prague* (the **Czech Republic**), *Cracow* (**Poland**), *St. Petersburg*, and *Moscow* (**Russia**).

Africa

Have you ever dreamed of visiting the palaces and pyramids of ancient pharaohs? To witness the spectacle of vast, migrating herds? Or even to pay a quiet visit to a family of mountain gorillas? You could do these things in only one place: Africa (Figure 9–7).

Africa is home to dozens of nations, but only a few are typically on a tourist's agenda. Here they are:

- **Egypt** has some of the world's most famous attractions. *Cairo*—Africa's most populated city—has a remarkable collection of ancient artifacts at its *Egyptian Antiquities Museum*. Here rest the treasures of the young pharaoh

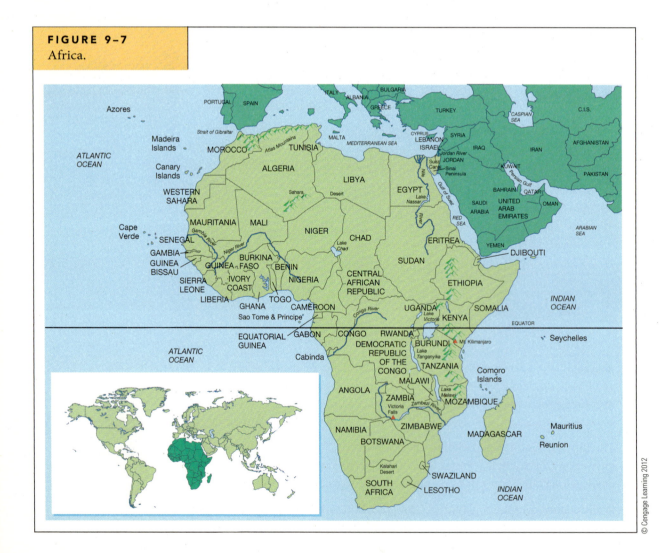

FIGURE 9–7
Africa.

© Cengage Learning 2012

Tutankhamen and the mummies of most of Egypt's well-known ancient rulers. Next to Cairo are the fabled *Pyramids*. Another major center for tourism is located between Aswan and Luxor, along the shores of the Nile River. The area is lined with major temples and tombs.

- **Morocco** is one of Africa's most exotic places, yet it's just across the Strait of Gibraltar from Spain. The city of *Marrakech* is Morocco's most popular destination, but *Fez* (the country's oldest city) and *Casablanca* are also noteworthy.

- **Kenya** and **Tanzania** have made a mission of preserving Africa's ecology and wildlife. For that reason they have long been major safari destinations. Among Kenya's most famous wildlife reserves are *Masai Mara*, *Amboseli*, and *Aberdare*. Tanzania has several important ones as well, including *Serengeti* and *Ngorongoro Crater*.

- On their border, **Zambia** and **Zimbabwe** share one of the world's greatest series of waterfalls, *Victoria Falls*. Zambia also has significant wildlife preserves.

- **South Africa** has gained popularity as a tourist destination. *Johannesburg* and lovely *Cape Town* both serve as departure points for safaris to several major wildlife refuges, including *Kruger*, *Kalahari Gemsbok*, and *Sabi Sand*. **Botswana**, a nation to South Africa's north, also harbors several fine wildlife reserves.

Several tropical and semitropical islands off Africa's coast are prime destinations, too: the **Azores** and **Madeira Islands** (northwest of Africa) and the **Seychelles**, **Mauritius**, and **Madagascar** (to Africa's southeast).

The Middle East

Political turmoil has kept visitors away, but the Middle East—not a continent but a region that links Africa with Asia (Figure 9–8)—is rich with history, much of it associated with some of the world's most important religions:

- **Israel** and **Palestine** have deep significance for Jews, Christians, and Muslims. And, surprisingly, much of it looks like what you might imagine: hillsides covered with olive trees, craggy deserts, and historical biblical structures everywhere. Northern Israel boasts *Nazareth* and the *Sea of Galilee*. Central Israel is anchored by *Jerusalem*, with *Bethlehem* and *Jericho* nearby in Palestine's *West Bank*.

- **Jordan** lies just east of Israel and has many biblical sites. Its most astonishing attraction, though, is *Petra*, a second-century AD city carved out of rocky cliffs and accessed through a dramatically narrow stone gorge.

- **Saudi Arabia**, an important business destination, is most famous for *Mecca*, Mohammed's birthplace and the holiest city in Islam. Muslims must visit it at least once in their lives. Their voyage is called the *hajj*.

FIGURE 9–8
The Middle East.

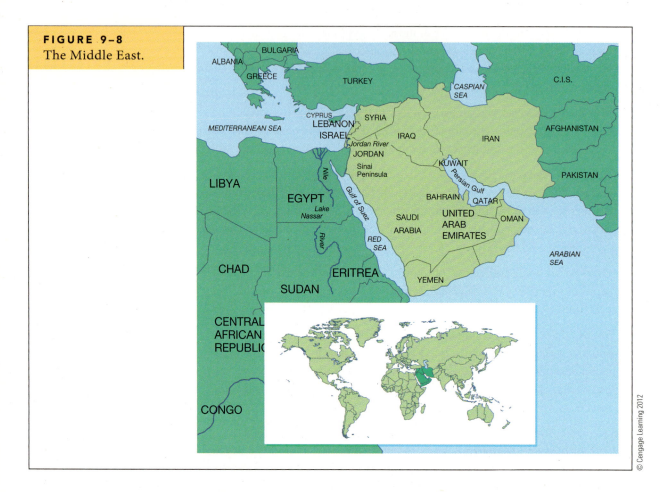

The towering pillars of the temple at Karnak.

- **Turkey** has wonderful sites to explore. *Istanbul* is a vibrant city, with huge mosques, palaces, and marketplaces. Inland *Cappadocia* has hundreds of churches and homes in caves.

Asia

This, the world's largest continent, contains dozens of countries (Figure 9–9). Here are the most visited:

- **China** is noteworthy for its size (the world's third largest country), culture, history, population (over a billion), and legacy left from thousands of years of achievement. It has three major cities that tourists regularly visit: *Beijing*, *Shanghai*, and *Hong Kong*. It also has several famous attractions. Among them are the *Great Wall of China* (best seen on a day trip from Beijing); Beijing's sprawling *Imperial Palace*; and *Xian*, China's ancient capital. Near Xian is an "army" of life-sized terra-cotta warrior statues found buried underground.

insider info

Food in Thailand can be very spicy.

FIGURE 9–9
Asia.

© Cengage Learning 2012

- **Japan** is primarily a business destination, but this country affords visitors a wealth of tourist opportunities. *Tokyo*, its capital, has a unique, fascinating ambiance, with day trips possible to the beautifully situated *Nikko* and *Lake Hakone*, which provides a great view of *Mt. Fuji* (if it's a clear day). *Kyoto*, far to the southwest of Tokyo, was Japan's capital for 1,000 years. It claims to have more than 2,000 temples, shrines, and gardens.

- **Thailand** has long been a favorite country to visit on Asian itineraries. Its capital, *Bangkok*, has many magnificent temples (or *wats*, as the Thais call them). Thailand features several well-known seaside resort cities, including *Pattaya*, *Phuket*, and *Ko Samui*. In Thailand's northwest corner is a lush, teakwood-forested, much less developed area that centers on the city of *Chiang Mai*.

Other nations in Asia attract many visitors, including the following:

- **South Korea** is a country of energy and enterprise; it is well known for shopping and sightseeing possibilities.

- **Taiwan** has dramatic scenery, most especially at *Taroko Gorge*.

- **Indonesia** is best known for its idyllic island of *Bali* and dramatic temple complex at *Borobudur*.

- **Vietnam** is one of Asia's fastest growing tourist destinations, and nearby **Cambodia** has world-famous ruins at *Angkor Wat*.

A temple within Beijing's Imperial Palace.

- **India** offers a huge selection of cities to visit and attractions to see, the most celebrated of which is the *Taj Mahal*.

- **Singapore**—a city-nation—is one of Asia's most prosperous places. Despite its small size, it features many interesting gardens, temples, and ethnic districts.

Australia, New Zealand, and the South Pacific

Australia and its large neighbor island-nation, New Zealand, are wonderfully friendly places to visit. The many smaller South Pacific islands are often cited with any discussion of Australia or New Zealand. (See Figure 9–10.)

- **Australia** is just a little smaller in area than the 48 contiguous United States. *Sydney* is its largest city, with a world-famous bridge and an architectural marvel, the *Sydney Opera House*. Another major tourist area is associated with the *Great Barrier Reef* (the world's longest) and long stretches of beach resorts.

FIGURE 9–10
Australia, New Zealand, and the South Pacific.

© Cengage Learning 2012

Pacific Islanders are proud of their culture.

insider info

When in Australia, visit a zoo. You'll see all sorts of animals found nowhere else.

insider info

Tipping at meals is not customary in Australia, New Zealand, and on most South Pacific islands.

Australia's center, the *Outback*, is arid and nearly empty. In the midst of it all, however, is *Uluru* (*Ayers Rock*), a massive red stone outcropping that's sacred to Australia's indigenous people, the aborigines.

- The people of **New Zealand** are a bit more traditional than their Australian cousins. New Zealand divides into a *North Island*, with Polynesian culture, rolling green hills, mild temperatures, and New Zealand's largest city, *Auckland*; and the more rugged *South Island*, with chillier temperatures and alpine scenery. (This is where *The Lord of the Rings* was filmed.)

- Many Pacific tropical paradises lie between Australia/New Zealand and the Americas. The two most visited are the **Tahitian Islands** and **Fiji**.

Cultural Geography

Geography isn't just about places and things, it is also about people. A big part of travel is discovering the different ways people across the globe think and behave, how their values may differ from ours, and even finding that they may have more in common with us than we might think.

Some of these differences are immediately obvious. If you want to buy something in a Japanese store, salespeople will be almost instantly at your disposal. In Istanbul you will have to bargain. In other places, salespeople seem annoyed that you are even there.

Within the United States you'll find cultural differences too: different accents, different attitudes, and perhaps a different pace of life. Food preferences can vary as well: people from Cincinnati put chili on their spaghetti and Southern New Englanders eat "clam cakes," dine on "lobster rolls," and have their very own type of chow mein, which they place between two slices of white bread, calling it a "chow mein sandwich." To many travelers, cultural variety is often great fun—and it's a great way to expand your thinking too.

Conclusion

So there it is: the world of tourism in a nutshell. But this is just the surface. How can you deepen your knowledge? Take a course in travel geography. Read a good textbook on the subject. Watch travel-related TV shows. Subscribe to a travel magazine. Above all, plan to visit as many of these places as you can. And if you get into the travel business, you will!

insider info

Most visitors to the United States from other nations list shopping as the number-one thing they expect to do.

NAME   **DATE**

Review Questions

1. How can winds affect travel?

2. Describe the major kinds of bodies of water. Give one well-known example of each that is *not* mentioned in this chapter (for example, Lake Superior).

3. Define each important kind of landform. Give one well-known example of each that is *not* mentioned in this chapter (for example, the Yucatan Peninsula).

4. What are the six *continents* besides Antarctica? Name three countries that are found on each (except Antarctica, which has no countries).

It's All About You Questions

1. What place have you been to that is farthest from your home?

2. If you could visit anywhere in the world, where would you go? Why?

3. Is there one place you cannot imagine wanting to go to? Why?

Activity 1: Researching the World

Use the Internet, an encyclopedia, an atlas, or any other resource at your disposal to complete this exercise. Provide a description for each item. Be specific, as the three examples illustrate. Note that none of the items listed has yet been mentioned in this chapter.

Item	Description
Calgary	City in Alberta, Canada
Eiffel Tower	Attraction in Paris, France
Honduras	Country in Central America

1. Tasmania

2. Santorini

3. Dubai

4. Pompeii

5. Bora Bora

6. Haleakala

7. Petronas Towers

8. Montego Bay

9. Monaco

10. Badaling

11. St. Lawrence

12. Monument Valley

13. Stonehenge

(Continues)

Activity 1: Researching the World (continued)

Item	Description
14. Chichen Itza	
15. Djemaa el Fna	
16. Alice Springs	
17. Chateau Frontenac	
18. Branson	
19. Lisbon	
20. Waitomo Caves	
21. Stockholm	
22. The Western (Wailing) Wall	
23. Lombard Street	
24. Charlotte Amalie	
25. Samburu	
26. Sugar Loaf	
27. O'Hare	
28. Ephesus	
29. Graceland	
30. Abu Simbel	

Activity 2: A Wonderful Trip

Review the list of the New Seven Wonders of the World in Chapter 1. Which one of the seven would you most like to visit? Why?

Using the Internet or whatever resources are available to you, determine how you would get there from your hometown. What flight routes would you take? How would you get from the airport to the attraction?

What time of year would you choose to visit it? Consider climate, tourist patterns (high season, low season), and so on.

What other attraction in the same country would you visit on this trip? Why?

NAME   DATE

Gale Hospitality, Tourism and Leisure Database Assignment

The following assignment requires access to the Gale Hospitality, Tourism and Leisure Database. Check with your instructor to see if you have access to this database.

Find the article *Worldwide Convention Centers* in the Gale Hospitality, Tourism & Leisure Collection. This article, though not up to date, rates the top 10 cities for large conventions.

- What three factors seem to be the most important criteria when deciding which cities are best for large meetings and events?

- Which three of these cities would you be most interested in visiting? Why?

THIS CONCIERGE DESK
IS CLOSED
THANK YOU
FOR
VISITING ATLANTA

GEORGIA
WORLD
CONGRESS
CENTER

CONCIERGE
TOURIST INFORMATION

10

Making Connections: How to Market, Sell to, and Serve the Traveling Public

KEY TERMS

- Advertising
- Benefit
- Brand
- Brand-based marketing
- Closed-ended question
- Cross-selling
- Database
- Database marketing
- Demand
- Demographics
- Discretionary money
- Distribution
- Feature
- Intangible product
- Lateral service
- Lead
- Marketing
- Mass marketing
- Niche marketing
- Open-ended question
- Perishable product
- Phone shopper
- Positioning
- Prospecting
- Psychographics
- Publicity
- Qualifying
- Recovery
- Relationship marketing
- Selling
- Stall
- Telemarketing
- Upselling
- Yield management

After studying this chapter, you'll be able to:

- Explain the different types of marketing and the six steps that the marketing cycle usually requires

- Distinguish between transactional and consultative selling, and apply the steps that each entails

- Describe how service is separate from, and overlaps, sales

- Practice the seven steps necessary to achieve service excellence

Images © C Miller Design; hut image © Keith Levit/www.Shutterstock.com

227

Photo courtesy of Jeffrey Anderson

Jeffrey Anderson

CURRENT POSITION/TITLE:

Vice President of Marketing, Avoya Travel

SHORT DESCRIPTION OF WHAT YOUR RESPONSIBILITIES ARE:

Oversee supplier partnerships, develop company strategies, and generate customer interest for the vacations we sell

EDUCATION:

BA in Communication Studies, Azusa Pacific University

FIRST JOB IN TRAVEL/HOSPITALITY INDUSTRY:

Stamping brochures for a penny each when I was 6 years old (then I spent the pennies on comic books)

FIRST PAID JOB (IF DIFFERENT FROM ABOVE):

An "aquatic specialist" at Petco

THING I WISH I DIDN'T HAVE TO DO:

Try to convince my children that when I travel on business, gifts aren't the only reason to be excited when I get home

SOMEONE WHO INSPIRES ME:

My wife or Bono from U2 . . . I'm not sure how to win this one.

BEST CAREER MEMORY I HAVE:

Winning Travel Agency of the Year awards from several cruise lines

STRANGEST OR FUNNIEST CAREER-RELATED THING I'VE EVER EXPERIENCED:

When Norwegian Cruise Line pranked me by having a Marilyn Monroe impersonator sing "Happy Birthday Mr. President" to me at a conference in front of more than a thousand people

FAVORITE QUOTE:

"Trust in the Lord with all your heart . . . and He will make your paths straight." (Proverbs 3:5–6)

SOMETHING ALMOST NO ONE KNOWS ABOUT ME:

I was captain of my college debate team, which won many tournaments nationally and internationally.

L et's say you've bought a cruise ship. (Okay, so that's wildly improbable, but play along.) You rent a berth at the port of Miami, "park" your ship there, decide that your first cruise will set sail on February 1, and that it will visit the Caribbean (you're not sure where) for seven days. You decide that the cruise price will be $299 per person for the entire week. At that price, the cruise will sell itself! You hire a crew and service staff, whom you tell to show up on January 31. February 1 comes along and you're excited! You're there at embarkation, which begins at 1 p.m. No one shows up.

But how can this be? Cruising from Miami to the Caribbean is booming! At a price like that, people should be begging to get onboard. Other cruise lines are making a fortune! Why aren't you?

What's wrong with this picture? You didn't have a marketing plan. You had no sales strategy. And even if, somehow, customers had found your cruise line and ship, it would have been a disaster. Your staff would have been clueless about how to serve the guests onboard.

An extreme, absurd scenario? Of course. However, it does shed light on an everyday truth: to succeed in travel—or in any business—you must have your marketing figured out, you must sell effectively, and you must serve your clientele in the best, most satisfying way. That's what this chapter is all about.

Marketing the Travel Product

To many people, **marketing** is a convoluted, arcane, and nearly impenetrable concept. Really, though, it's quite simple: it's the *process of transferring a product or service from its producer to the consumer*. When you read about the travel distribution system in Chapter 1, you were, in fact, well on your way to understanding what marketing is. And later in this section, when you learn about the marketing cycle, you'll achieve a more thorough understanding of the overall process.

More Definitions

Before continuing, let's take a look at five particular kinds of marketing:

- **Mass marketing** *tries to attract the greatest number of potential buyers*. It tries to be all things to all consumers. In the travel industry, the airlines represent the most obvious example of mass marketing. They try to sell to everybody: business travelers, vacationers, families, couples, price-sensitive consumers, luxury travelers, and just about anyone else with the time, desire, and money to travel.

- **Niche marketing** *targets the needs of a narrow segment of consumers*. It is the opposite of mass marketing. Rather than being all things to all people, it tries

Trekking tours appeal to a clear-cut niche.

insider info

There are still many under-
served niches in the travel
business. One travel agent
set up a cruise targeted to
African American twins. More
than 300 people signed up.

to be something special to a certain group of people with similar interests. For example, a tour company might operate hiking journeys for people between the ages of 18 and 25; a small cruise line might offer "voyages of discovery" to Antarctica to people interested in ecology, enrichment, and learning; a hotel in Jamaica might tailor its product to honeymooners and other romantic couples.

- **Brand-based marketing** *attempts to establish a highly recognizable name (or* **brand***) in the marketplace,* one that becomes known for quality, consistency, and predictable offerings. Some of the best-known brands in the world are travel related: American Airlines, American Express, AAA, Hertz, Carnival, and Hilton are prime examples.

- **Relationship marketing** *emphasizes the connection between a business and its customers.* It tries to understand the particular needs of each potential buyer and make that buyer a sort of "family member." It values loyalty and a long-term business relationship with its customers. Relationship marketers fiercely believe that the focus should not be on the sale but on the person. And they frequently use a customer relationship management (CRM) program to achieve it.

- **Database marketing** *uses information about customers to create an efficient relationship.* This kind of marketing is closely allied to relationship marketing. It relies on **databases**—*organized, usually computerized collections of customer information*—to build a picture of its customers. When suppliers obtain data about a person, they usually enter that information in their databases. As you learned in Chapter 1, they may collect **demographics** (*easily measurable factors*

Acting Your Age

A customer's age is always a factor in what you market and sell. It used to be that buyers bought things according to what *life stage* they were in. In other words, young people would rent a sports car or convertible, a middle-aged person a more sedate car, and an older person a huge car—it was more cushy and safe. Purchases were "age-appropriate."

However, marketing experts have come to realize that another phenomenon has become more predictive: the *cohort theory*. The way you think and buy when you're 18 to 25 becomes the way you think and buy throughout your entire life. Your generation (called a *cohort*) and when and where you grew up influence your behavior at all of life's stages.

For example, young people who grew up during World War II and who served in the military became comfortable with regimentation. In their later years, they preferred fully escorted tours, where every moment was planned. Later, baby boomers rejected regimentation—they wanted to "do their own thing." Thus, independent tours and cruises became popular. And almost surely, today's youth will want easy total connectivity wherever they travel.

such as age, gender, and income) or **psychographics** (*harder-to-measure factors such as attitudes, preferences, and dislikes*). Using the database, the company can then communicate regularly with customers through the postal system (direct mail), e-mail, telemarketing, or social media.

The Major Steps of Marketing

No matter what form marketing takes, it usually follows a predictable series of six steps:

1. *Research:* Before you can market anything, you must figure out if there's a demand for what you want to sell. **Demand** occurs when *people have the desire for something and the money to pay for it.* Large travel companies such as airlines and lodging chains spend millions of dollars researching what consumers want from them. Smaller businesses such as tour operators and travel agencies are likely to rely on more modest research, such as trial and error or picking up on trends early and quickly.

2. *Development:* Once you've determined what the market is asking for, you then design a new product or adjust an existing one to address these needs. For example, if you own an escorted tour company and your research shows that people want more flexibility while traveling, you may decide to factor more free time into the itinerary. Part of the development stage requires research—not market research this time but *product* research. A cruise line executive, for instance, whose market research indicates that passengers want more unusual destinations will have to research which ports would be suitable and what the other cruise companies might be doing along these lines. That's product research.

3. *Costing:* At what price will your new travel product be sold to the consumer? First, you must negotiate with your suppliers, then determine what your costs will be. Once you know your costs, you then decide what percentage profit you wish to make, add the appropriate amount to your costs, and you will have arrived at your selling price.

4. *Promotion:* It's now time to spread the word to the public about your wonderful new travel product. That's called promotion. Two types of promotion exist: publicity and advertising. **Publicity** is *information sent out at little or no cost to you.* Examples are articles in newspapers, tweets, blogs, speeches to groups, newsletter announcements, and client word-of-mouth. **Advertising** is *promotional information for which you must pay,* such as newspaper ads, TV commercials, and brochures.

5. *Distribution:* **Distribution** is *the process of making your product available to consumers.* With an intangible product such as travel, this is a simple process (as opposed to, say, distributing bottles of soda, furniture, or cars). It requires a well-managed sales tracking system, as well as companies (such as travel agencies) that are well informed and motivated to sell your product.

6. *Follow-up:* The wisest experts realize that follow-up is an integral step in the marketing process. Usually it takes the form of follow-up gestures (a thank-you letter) or surveys and studies that gauge customer satisfaction (such as that little guest feedback form in hotel rooms), leading to your ability to fine-tune your product. In a way, it brings marketing back full circle to its first steps.

Now that would be a billboard.

© Vibrant Image Studio/www.Shutterstock.com

Telling Terms

Here are some commonly used sales terms that go beyond those defined in the main body of the text:

- **Discretionary money:** Money used to buy something that a person doesn't necessarily need but certainly may want. Travel is usually a discretionary purchase.

- **Perishable products:** Products that lose their value if not consumed or used by a certain date. Most travel products are perishable. If a seat on a flight is not sold before departure, for example, it will have no value to the airline. It will have "perished."

- **Lead:** A person who might be interested in buying your travel product.

- **Intangible products:** Products that can't be perceived by the senses. Travel is an intangible, as opposed to *tangibles* such as apples, cell phones, and stereos.

- **Stall:** When a person delays or hesitates to purchase something.

- **Phone shoppers:** People who phone many different vendors or agencies to get the best price and, perhaps, better service, professionalism, and so on.

- **Positioning:** The act of making your products or services different and distinct from another supplier's products or services in the marketplace.

- **Yield management:** As explained in Chapter 2, this procedure enables suppliers to maximize profits by adjusting prices to supply and demand, often at a moment's notice. Airlines and hotels rely on yield management the most, adjusting prices upward or downward according to whether sales are meeting what was forecast.

Selling Travel

Selling is *the process of helping someone to buy something.* This definition is sufficiently broad that it encompasses all sorts of selling: a travel agent who sells a cruise to a client, an airline reservationist who sells a flight to a caller, even a Web site that facilitates the booking of a car rental. In other words, selling doesn't necessarily involve a salesperson.

Selling comes in two varieties: transactional selling and consultative selling. Let's look at each.

Transactional Selling

Transactional selling is the simplest form of sales. It requires the least amount of training, fewest skills, and a minimal number of sales steps. It merely facilitates the purchase. Most of the things you buy (from hamburgers to socks to DVDs) are the result of transactional selling. In the travel industry, it is most common for purchasing commodities such as flights, car rentals, and, to some extent, hotel stays.

insider info

Somehow a smile can be "heard" on the telephone.

Here are the six steps that are typical to transactional selling:

1. *The salesperson greets the customer,* ideally in a warm and friendly manner.

2. *The salesperson takes the order.* He may ask a series of closed-ended questions to elicit the customer's logistic needs. (See Telling Terms, "What Kind of Question Is That?" for more on types of questions.) Or the customer may simply tell the salesperson what she wants to buy (for example, "I need a compact car in Orlando from August 15 to 18."). The "order-taker" (as transactional salespeople are often called) may have to ask questions if the customer hasn't fully thought out her purchase or in some way lacks all the information she needs before buying. The order-taker will make recommendations only if the customer has incomplete information and needs help.

3. *The salesperson may try to "upsell the customer."* **Upselling** is *offering customers a level of product or service higher than the one they originally had in mind.* For example, in the car rental scenario, the salesperson may tell the customer she could upgrade her purchase to a full-size car for only $5.95 more per day. This will result in more profit for the company and, presumably, a more comfortable experience for the customer.

4. *The salesperson processes the transaction,* usually through a CRS or GDS. He will:

    *   Do a little research as to the availability of what the customer has ordered (an upsell may occur here, or earlier, as described).

    *   Confirm availability and review various conditions (for example, "if you have to cancel, you must do so at least 24 hours before the car pickup date").

    *   Find out what form of payment the customer wishes to use (for example, ask for a credit card number).

    *   Confirm that the booking has been made.

    *   Provide the customer with a confirmation number for future reference.

    At some point during this stage of the transaction, the seller may also recap what the customer has expressed about her needs, just to make sure there have been no misunderstandings and that nothing has been left out.

    Sometimes, however, customers are not prepared to buy. They still may be unsure, need to do more research, must discuss things with someone else, or are shopping for the best deal. That's why transactional salespeople are taught to always ask for the business and perhaps apply certain "closing" strategies to give the customer an incentive to make a purchase, then and there. (More about these closing techniques soon.)

5. *The salesperson may try to cross-sell the customer.* **Cross-selling** is *offering additional products or services.* The car rental salesperson may ask the

Counter staff at the McDonald's at Madrid Airport are transactional salespeople.

customer if she wishes to purchase auto rental insurance or wants a global positioning system in her car—each, of course, at an extra charge.

6. *Finally, the salesperson thanks the customer,* signaling that the transaction has come to an end.

Transactional salespeople may be *reservationists* (typically a person you call on the phone and who works at a facility called a call center) or *point-of-delivery* employees such as those who work a car rental desk at the airport or a hotel front desk. In many cases, reservationists may do some of the steps described, and then other employees will do the remaining steps. For instance, a phone reservationist at a car rental company might not upsell or cross-sell. Those steps may be left to the point-of-delivery staff.

Because transactions are easy to process, transactional selling is increasingly handled by automated systems such as those on Web sites or telephone voice recognition programs.

Consultative Selling

Consultative selling is a more subtle and skilled form of sales. It requires plenty of knowledge, training and experience, solid research skills, and deeper insight into people's needs. When you buy life insurance or need financial planning advice, you usually deal with consultative salespeople.

In the travel industry, travel agents and, to some extent, hotel concierges are most likely to practice consultative selling. Reservationists and point-of-delivery staff also may have to do some consultative selling with customers who need a lot of advice before purchasing a travel commodity. Consultative selling is most common with

insider info
The most powerful word to use in selling and promotion is *you*.

travel experiences such as cruises, tours, resort packages, and trips assembled by an agent from scratch rather than a package), which are complex and costly. These are situations in which clients feel they need advice, counseling, and guidance.

Many of the steps to a consultative sale will be familiar to you: They're the same ones used in transactional selling. You'll see some additional steps too, as well as expanded versions of those you've already learned:

1. *You greet the client.* As you learned in Chapter 1, in the travel industry, transactional buyers are usually called *customers*, whereas consultative buyers are referred to as *clients*.

2. *You qualify the client.* **Qualifying** is *the process of asking questions to determine a client's needs.* These questions are generally a mix of closed- and open-ended questions.

3. *You research the client's needs.* This may be as simple as checking for availability while the client is present in the office or on the phone. If the trip is complicated, though, the salesperson may be obliged to take some time for more investigation and contact the client later.

4. *You make recommendations.* Based on what you discovered during the qualifying process, you recommend the right travel products and services that will "solve" the client's needs. Ideally, you should do this using *benefits* language, rather than *features*.

   Features are *the facts about a product or service,* and **benefits** are *the "payoff" for that feature.* For example, you learned in Chapter 6 that upscale tour operators often limit the number of passengers on a tour to 18 despite the fact that they may use 40-passenger motorcoaches. This is a feature of upscale tours. But what is the *benefit* of that feature? One that most people never think of—any person on the tour who wants a window seat can have it. That's one of the payoffs that come from using 40-passenger coaches for 18-passenger tours. Because the benefits of any given feature aren't always clear to the buyer, skilled salespeople cite the benefits of what they're recommending as well as the features.

   When recommending, you should recap the client's needs and show how your suggestions address each. You should then give only one or two recommendations, otherwise you'll just confuse the buyer. After all, the client came to you for the one, right idea, not a half-dozen.

5. *You overcome objections.* Sometimes, clients are not entirely convinced that your recommendation is the right one. They may "erect barriers" to the sale. For example, you may recommend a cruise as the perfect solution to their vacation needs, but they are worried that they may get seasick. This is an objection. (For more examples of cruise objections, refer to Chapter 7.)

   Objections can be real. Some people may, in fact, be so prone to motion discomfort that you will have to come up with an alternate recommendation. But their objection may be based on misinformation. Perhaps they don't realize that today's huge ships are highly stable or that their doctor can prescribe a medication that will most likely solve the problem. By informing them, you may be able to counter their objection and continue with the sale.

6. *You must upsell and cross-sell.* Yes, these are the same steps we visited earlier. The important point is that selected carefully and appropriate to the client, these features will almost certainly enhance the vacation experience.

7. *You must close the sale.* The sale is closed when the buyer agrees that the recommendations the seller has made are the right ones and is prepared to pay. If this doesn't occur, the seller's time basically has been wasted. He or she has provided information, nothing more. So it's the duty of every consultative salesperson (and transactional ones too) to ask for the business and use whatever closing techniques seem ethical, honest, and right.

Many closing techniques exist (author Zig Ziglar has identified hundreds). The three most common ones in travel sales, with examples, are as follows:

- **The urgency close:** "It looks like airfares may be going up on Monday. If we book now, we'll be able to lock in this price."

- **The reservation close:** "Let's at least make a reservation now, with no obligation. You'll then have 48 hours to make up your mind." A more powerful commitment will occur if you ask for a deposit.

- **The scarcity close:** "There are only a few cabins left on the sailing date you are interested in."

What Kind of Question Is That?

Two types of questions are typical when qualifying a traveler. A **closed-ended question** *elicits a brief, usually factual answer.* In travel sales, the classic closed-ended questions are *who, what, when, where, how long, how much.* A typical response would be, "My daughter and I are thinking of taking a cruise in early May to the Caribbean for a week. We'd like to keep the price under $1,500 per person, total." Transactional salespeople usually ask only closed-ended questions.

Consultative salespeople, on the other hand, use both closed-ended and open-ended questions. An **open-ended question** *usually elicits a longer and more complex response.*

Open-ended questions are most a[...] with people who have only vag[...] their travel plans. However, pe[...] cise notions of what they wa[...] such questions too, becau[...] needs they've never thou[...]

Here are some ope[...] travel agent might as[...]

- "What do you g[...] vacation?"

- "What's the[...] why?"

- "What a[...]

One important point: if you follow all of these steps of sales and do them well, closing might be quite easy. Studies show that 40 percent of the time, the *client* closes the sale, with no special effort on the part of the salesperson. And, of course, you should cap it all off by thanking the client for the business.

8. *You must follow up.* Yes, it's back. Follow-up—so critical to marketing—is an integral part of sales and service too. Finding out how the trip went may take time, but it builds a stronger bond between buyer and seller, leads to first-hand insights about travel products and destinations, enables the traveler to vent about things that may have gone wrong, and perhaps lays the groundwork for the client's next trip.

Here's How It's Done

Wondering how a consultative sale might unfold? Here's how a travel agent might properly handle a client call. Watch for all the strategies we've discussed:

Agent: Good morning, Acme Travel L.A. This is Karen, how may I help you?

Client: Yes, I'm thinking of taking my children on a trip to Hawaii.

Agent: I'd be glad to help you with that. Okay, let me ask you a few questions. How many children do you have?

Client: Two: a 10-year-old girl and a 12-year-old boy. So it'll be the three of us.

Agent: And when are you thinking of going?

Client: During the first or second week of January. My kids don't resume school until later in January.

Agent: That's good. There are some great values available around that time. How long do you [have] for the trip?

Client: A maximum of nine days, hopefully [inclu]ding one or two weekend days.

[Agent:] Okay. Give me a rough idea of your [price] range.

[Client:] [U]h, about $3,000 to $4,000.

[Agent: Are] you including everything, including [airfare?]

Client: No, I guess only for airfare and hotel and maybe a car rental. I'd like that. I think you need one to get around Hawaii, right?

Agent: Well, that depends. I'm guessing you've never been?

Client: Yes, that's right. I did do some Internet research, so I know about the different islands and such. But I still feel I do need some advice.

Agent: That's what I'm here for. First, let me ask you a few questions. Have you traveled with your kids before?

Client: Yes, but mostly short trips. Now they're at an age, though, when they can better appreciate a vacation like this.

Agent: What do you picture yourself doing on this vacation?

Client: Both of my children love water sports and the beach, so that's really important. I'd like to have lots of reasonable, family-style restaurants nearby or fast food we can bring back to our room. My son would love to see some serious surfing too.

Agent: You're in luck. January waves in Hawaii are usually impressive.

Client: That's great. And my daughter did a project on the history of Hawaii, so she's interested in cultural stuff. I am too.

(continues)

Here's How It's Done (continued)

Agent: That's easily addressed. I want a few more clues to your needs, though, so tell me, what's the *worst* trip you ever took with your children?

Client: Hmm. Interesting question. Probably when I took them to a resort in Mexico. I had almost forgotten about that. I booked a budget hotel. It was clean and nice but the room was really small. We were constantly stumbling over one another. Plus, we had to take a shuttle to the beach. And my daughter Tiffany hates foreign food of any sort, even Mexican.

Agent: Then you made a good choice with Hawaii. Okay. What about you? What do *you* want out of this trip?

Client: For my kids to have a great time. But, yes, I would like to be able to do at least a little shopping.

Agent: All right. I think I have a good sense of what your needs are. Just to make sure, let me go over what you're requesting. There will be three of you—you and your two children. You prefer going in early January for a maximum of nine days, keeping your basic travel costs to under $4,000. Your kids like water sports, your daughter is into the history of Hawaii, and you'd like to do a little shopping. You'd like to keep food costs down, you want roomy lodging. Did I get everything right?

Client: Yes, absolutely.

Agent: Okay, my suggestion would be a package with a company we have a lot of confidence in, Pleasant Holidays. Because of their buying power, they have great values, so we can keep the budget, I think, well within the range you gave me. The package would include hotel, air, one-day car rental, transfers to and from Honolulu airport, even a lei greeting when you arrive, plus all sorts of other little benefits.

Client: Sounds good. But wouldn't our choices be limited in a package?

Agent: Not at all. Pleasant represents hundreds of hotels in Hawaii. Which leads me to something else. I think we should request a condo for you. It would be very spacious, have two separate bedrooms, one for you and one for your children—they'd have their own room, you'd have your privacy. You'd even have a kitchenette, so you could save money on food by shopping for groceries and cooking, if you wish, or you could eat out. It would be all up to you.

Client: I never thought of a condo, but it's a really good solution, if it doesn't cost too much. I'm guessing you're recommending Waikiki.

Agent: Yes. And there are some nice, value-priced condos within a few blocks of the beach. You'll be able to walk there easily. Plenty of reasonable dining choices are nearby, plus shopping opportunities you'd like. You could use your one-day car rental to drive out to Oahu's North Shore to see the surfing and even visit the Polynesian Cultural Center, which is near there. Both your son and your daughter would be happy with that, right?

Client: Absolutely! And you think you could get that for under $4,000?

Agent: I'm fairly sure. Let me just check my computer. May I put you on hold for a minute or two? [Several minutes pass.] Great news. I can get you an eight-day, seven-night Pleasant package, staying at a two-bedroom unit at the Acme Shores, which is only two blocks to the beach, for $1,159 per person, that's $3,477 total.

Client: That includes the transfers and the one-day car rental?

Agent: Yes, it does.

Client: That sounds great.

Agent: By the way, I'd really recommend the Polynesian Cultural Center. It's a mu first-time visitor. Do you want me to in advance for you?

Here's How It's Done (continued)

Client: Okay.

Agent: The admission package I'm thinking of would include a luau. You wouldn't have to worry about it—it would be all set up in advance. Let me check.... The cost would be $92 for you and $68 each for your children.

Client: Go ahead. It sounds like a great idea. It'll save me the trouble.

Agent: One final thought. Did you ever consider visiting *two* islands while you're there?

Client: I did, but what with the additional flight between the islands, I thought it would be too expensive. Plus lodging seems to cost more on the other islands.

Agent: In your research, did any island beyond Oahu stand out, though?

Client: Yes. The Big Island. My kids would love to see an active volcano. So would I.

Agent: And there's plenty of history there too. Let me check something. May I put you on hold again?

Client: Of course. [Several minutes pass.]

Agent: We're in luck. I could book you a package with four nights in Waikiki, three nights on the

Big Island at a similar condo, with all the same features as the original package, plus the inter-island flight and a car for all three days on the Big Island, for $1,489 per person—that's just a little over $150 more per person than the original budget you quoted me.

Client: And we'd get to see two islands instead of one.

Agent: Yes.

Client: Sounds interesting. Let me think about it a bit, then call you back.

Agent: That's fine. But I can't promise this package will still be available. If you feel that this package fits your needs, I say go for it.

Client: You know, I think you're right. [Client gives her credit card information. The agent confirms the reservation online.]

Agent: As soon as your documents arrive, I'll give you a call. I think you and your family will have a wonderful vacation. Thanks so much for bringing your business to us.

Client: Thank you! Bye!

Agent: And an aloha to you!

Other Kinds of Travel Sales

Transactional and consultative selling can take on other forms beyond the ones just described. For example, **prospecting** occurs when *the salesperson proactively contacts potential buyers*—usually new customers—with travel offers. If it's done on the phone, it's called **telemarketing**. Laws limit telemarketing calls to those who request them. But many people are happy to get calls about travel deals they're interested in from travel providers they know and give permission for such calls. Of course, today prospecting is not limited just to telemarketing. E-mail and social ... provide whole new ways to communicate with potential customers.

... companies also regularly buy and sell with one another. A tour company, ... nce, must book hotel space, charter motorcoaches, arrange meals, purchase ... ction tickets, and the like. Considerable selling skills are required to convince ... ur companies that your hotel better serves their needs than a rival's does.

Travel agents must have consultative sales skills.

Serving the Traveling Public

What is service? How does it differ from sales? In truth, the two dynamically overlap. Many of the elements that constitute good service are also integral to selling. For instance, a warm, welcoming greeting is critical to both service and sales excellence. So, too, is efficiency and friendly follow-up.

Perhaps we can separate the two, at least a little, by examining what lies at the core of each. With sales, your goal is to help someone purchase something. The focus is on buying and selling. With service, you're focusing less on the sale itself than on how you treat someone during the sale or, once they've bought it, during the trip itself.

If a tour company's phone reservationist is pleasant, energetic, accurate, and understanding, then she is certainly practicing good service (and probably applying sales techniques too). Same thing for a hotel bellman, a theme park security officer, or a cruise ship stateroom steward who renders service in a cheerful and caring manner. Yet none of the last three are really salespeople, except for the fact that they're "selling" themselves and the companies they represent. They're treating the customer well *after the purchase* has been completed.

Why even bother? You've got their money, haven't you? But part of successful selling is to ensure that your customers will come back. A loyal client is fiercely important to a company's success. A famous U.S. government study revealed that it costs five to six times more to find a new customer than to retain an existing one. Moreover, service excellence leads to fewer complaints, better employee satisfaction,

Careers

Careers in Marketing, Sales, and Service

Here are some of the jobs available in the marketing, sales, and service fields:

- Senior executives, directors, and managers
- Reservationists
- Customer service representatives
- Clerical support
- Human resources/training specialists

- Graphic designers
- Sales representatives
- Accountants/auditors
- Telemarketers
- Advertising executives
- Technological support

strong word-of-mouth praise, and even sometimes justifies charging higher prices than competitors with mediocre service can charge.

Yet service often misses the mark, and badly. Our interactions with service providers prove it on a daily basis. What an opportunity, though! Companies that can provide superior service today are able to position themselves as *the* businesses to buy from.

Service is especially critical to the travel industry, where service experiences are *precisely* what are being promised and sold. Transactional sales must be efficient and gracious. Consultative ones must be caring and creatively sensitive to the client's needs. And, as the travel experience itself takes place, the customer deserves service that's eager and impeccable. Perhaps other industries can survive with indifferent salespeople (finding a helpful salesperson in some stores is almost impossible), but not the travel business. A cruise line that didn't pamper its guests would go broke, and fast.

Delivering Great Service

There's no great secret to delivering superior service in the travel industry. Here are the seven ingredients that usually ensure travel customer happiness:

Acknowledge and greet the customer. The first moment in a client–service son interaction is perhaps the most critical of all. Within seconds, the ner decides whether the upcoming experience will be a good one or not, on the behavior of *one person.* The greeting must be:

rompt: No one likes waiting. And if waiting is inevitable, the service person should acknowledge the customers and tell them she will be right with them.

- *Energetic and friendly:* After all, the customers are excited about the upcoming trip. That enthusiasm shouldn't be dampened in any way.

- *Sincere:* The greeting shouldn't sound automatic, as if it has been done over and over (even if it *has*).

- *Personal:* The service person should use the customer's name, if feasible. He or she should also realize that this is a *person*, not a "thing" to be processed.

2. *Use positive language.* Have you ever had someone say any of the following to you? "It's not my job," "I don't know," "There's nothing I can do." Didn't like it, did you?

   An unfriendly tone or phrase can easily undermine the service experience. A negative connotation may come across in other phrases too, like "You need to," "We're really busy," or "It's company policy." Travel can be wonderful, but it has the potential to cascade into a series of futile moments. Service people must avoid aggravating, in any way, the delicate balance of travel.

3. *Look and act professional.* We've all heard the phrase, "Don't judge a book by its cover." Yet routinely, fair or not, we judge others by outward appearances. This seems especially true in the travel industry, where uniforms are quite common for airline, hotel, cruise, tour, and theme park front-line personnel, among others. Even when uniforms aren't required, a service person should try to look and dress professionally. Keeping your workspace neat is important too.

4. *Pay attention.* Good service people listen carefully, watch attentively, and never let their thoughts drift. They notice when a customer needs help and proactively do something about it. They apply **lateral service**, *taking the initiative to go beyond their job description, when appropriate,* whenever it is required. For example, so long as they're not busy with something else, aircraft mechanics with certain airlines are encouraged to pitch in and help a gate agent when long lines of passengers are trying to check in for a flight.

5. *Do what you're supposed to do—and more.* Nothing impresses a customer more than when you go well beyond what you're required to do. For instance, at Ritz-Carlton hotels, if you ask staff where the hotel dining room is, they won't simply point out the direction—they will escort you there.

6. *Recover from mistakes.* In service terminology, **recovery** means *making right what a customer sees as wrong.* No one wants a dissatisfied client. No one wants a complaint to be left unfixed. But most people don't realize that there's a proven series of steps to correct a problem:

   - **Fix the customer's emotions first.** You must first address the feelings the problem caused. Express your regret. Say that you understand how they would feel the way they do. Take a conciliatory attitude. Give them

The best waiters deliver memorable service.

time, if necessary, to vent their emotions and articulate their explanation. Remember, you can agree with their feelings without agreeing with the logic behind their complaint. Above all, don't argue with them or go into a long explanation of why it occurred. This isn't about logic—at least, not yet.

- **Find out the details.** Once this venting phase is over, obtain any additional information about the problem that you feel you'll need. Take careful notes—that will keep you focused, show that you're attentive, and may be needed later. *Perhaps* you should give an explanation, if you feel that the customer wants to hear it. Then, as a "reality check," recap the situation as you understand it.

- **Agree on a solution.** If you're empowered to do so, propose a solution to the problem right away. If that's premature, promise that you'll look into it and, if possible, give them (and yourself) a deadline for the solution.

- **Follow through.** If you don't make sure the problem is addressed, almost surely the clients will remain dissatisfied—or worse.

Virtual Service

As technology has become more sophisticated, the ability to deliver service and sales transactions through purely automated systems has become increasingly feasible. In some cases, such systems can be superior to human service operations. For example, it was once a time-consuming chore to call an airline to find out if a flight was on time. Long hold times were common. Now telephone voice recognition systems and Web sites can provide the same information in less than a minute, sometimes in seconds. At hotels, operators would sometimes fail to place a wake-up call to a guest, which could lead to a serious inconvenience. Now guests can touch-tone their wake-up call request on their in-room telephone. The system won't forget. On many cruise ships, passengers can select their shore excursions interactively on their stateroom TV—no long lines at the shore excursion desk anymore.

However, all isn't perfect in an automated, self-service world. Too many "press one, press two" choices can drive customers crazy. Automation's greatest flaw is that there's often no one to talk to, or it takes forever to find out how to get to a "live" service person. When a sales or service situation moves beyond a simple transaction, human beings become increasingly vital to client satisfaction. If access to such service providers is hard or impossible to obtain, dissatisfaction will surely result.

7. *Express gratitude.* The way you close your service moment is as crucial as the way you begin it. Upon checkout, a hotel front-desk clerk can thank the guest for staying. Toward the end of a flight, a pilot or flight attendant may acknowledge to the passengers that they had other choices and thank them for choosing to fly their airline. A security agent, after inspecting a person's carry-on luggage, can thank the person for his or her patience.

More This and That

Here are a few additional insights into marketing, sales, and service:

- The *four-part phone greeting* has become a standard in business. It usually goes like this: "Hello, [company's name], this is [person's name], how may I help you?"

- Acknowledging a *person by name* has become a key tactic in travel (as well as in many other businesses). For example, technology permits hotel staff to know the name of a guest who is calling and facilitates their using it during the conversation.

- *Marketing plans* have become a necessity in the business world, including the travel industry. A marketing plan is a detailed, written description of how a company does business and analyzes how it might adjust its approach to current and future conditions in the marketplace.

- Thanks to database marketing, travel companies have been increasingly able to *adjust their promotions to individual customer profiles.* For example, Disney offered a free video on its Orlando-based attractions and lodging. When you called or went online to order it, you were asked a few demographic questions. Afterward, you received one of several videos that was specifically targeted to your demographic group. For example, if you intended to take children to Walt Disney World, you would receive a video edited to highlight families at play. An older couple, however, would get a video showing how Walt Disney World was perfect for them too.

insider info

To an upscale traveler, quality and excellence are more important than anything else, including price.

insider info

A great way to understand your business is to do a SWOT analysis: analyze your **S**trengths, **W**eaknesses, **O**pportunities, and **T**hreats.

NAME   DATE

Review Questions

1. Define marketing, selling, and service.

2. What are the six steps of transactional selling? What are the eight steps of consultative selling? Be prepared to describe each one.

3. How do sales and service differ? How do they overlap?

4. What are the seven steps to delivering great service?

5. What are the steps to dealing with complaints about mistakes made?

6. Define the following: mass marketing, niche marketing, brands, relationship marketing, and database marketing.

7. Name and explain the six major steps of marketing.

It's All About You Questions

Give one service behavior you especially appreciate when you are at the following venues. Here is an example to get you started.

1. At a restaurant: *The server refills your coffee without you asking.*

2. At a hotel:

3. At an airport:

4. At a fast-food place:

5. At a theme park:

NAME   DATE

Activity 1: Analyzing Our Travel Agent

Reread the travel agent scenario in This & That, "Here's How It's Done," on page **238**, and then answer the following questions.

1. What purely transactional steps does the agent take?

2. Which consultative strategies, in general, does she also use?

3. Which *open-ended* questions does she ask?

4. List the benefits statements she uses when describing the trip she's recommending.

5. Are there examples of cross-sells and upsells? What are they?

6. Does the client have any objection to the recommendation? What is it? How is it handled?

7. Does the client go into a stall? How does the agent handle it?

Activity 2: Not Just the Travel Business

Many of the sales, service, and marketing tactics used in the travel industry are employed in other businesses as well. Cite one specific, nontravel example for each of the following:

Strategy   **Nontravel example**

niche marketing   *Stores that sell only refrigerator magnets*

1. Upselling

2. Cross-selling

3. Brand-based marketing

4. Publicity

5. Follow-up gesture

6. Closed-ended question

7. Open-ended question

8. Consultative selling

9. Overcoming objections

10. Scarcity close

11. Urgency close

12. Lateral service

Gale Hospitality, Tourism and Leisure Database Assignment

The following assignment requires access to the Gale Hospitality, Tourism and Leisure Database. Check with your instructor to see if you have access to this database.

Find the article *Work Shows Industry Is Built on Relationships* on the Gale Hospitality, Tourism & Leisure Collection.

List three conclusions the writer of the article came to after participating in the "In Your Shoes" program.

11

Techno-Travel: How Technology Has Changed Everything

KEY TERMS

- Booking engines
- Browser
- CRM programs
- FAQs
- Homepage
- Hyperlink
- Informational site
- Internet
- Microblog
- Opinion site
- Search engine
- Social networking site
- Uniform Resource Locator
- World Wide Web

After studying this chapter, you'll be able to:

- Identify what CRS and GDS systems do and how these tools support the travel industry

- Explain how the Internet has changed the way people buy travel

- Describe how social media have affected the relationship between customer and supplier

- Clarify the many applications CRM programs have in the travel business

Photo courtesy of Lee Rosen

Lee Rosen

CURRENT POSITION/TITLE:

President, Leisure Pops (a point-of-sale software application that helps agents sell and serve their clients better)

EDUCATION:

BS, UC Davis; MBA from University of Southern California

FIRST JOB IN TRAVEL/HOSPITALITY INDUSTRY:

Founder/owner of TRAMS, Inc. (back-office and CRM system for travel agencies)

FIRST PAID JOB (IF DIFFERENT FROM ABOVE):

Working at a car wash

FAVORITE PART OF WHAT I DO:

Putting together all the right pieces: automation, merchandising, leisure travel, and travel agents

THING I WISH I DIDN'T HAVE TO DO:

Open so many e-mails!

SOMEONE WHO INSPIRES ME:

Napoleon Hill: I read his daily motivation. Great motivation for business and life.

BEST CAREER MEMORY I HAVE:

The first time an agent told me how much Leisure Pops was helping them. Getting that check from Sabre when I sold TRAMS to them was also fun...

FAVORITE QUOTE:

Just do it

SOMETHING ALMOST NO ONE KNOWS ABOUT ME:

I played rugby in Durban, South Africa, and also in the U.S. for city, state and national teams

Have you ever seen an episode from the original 1960s TV series, *Star Trek*? Set in a futuristic, high-tech world, Captain Kirk and his crew of the *Enterprise* materialized their meals with "synthesizers," flew their ship faster than the speed of light, and routinely beamed themselves from place to place. None of these exist—at least not yet.

However, *Star Trek* also predicted such "futuristic" devices as large, rectangular video screens, systems that responded to voice commands, and "communicators" that resembled the cell or iPhones of today—except that they were much more clunky-looking.

We tend to forget how drastically, swiftly, and unpredictably our wired (or, better, wireless) world has progressed. Oh, and Captain Kirk? He—or at least the actor who first played him, William Shatner—became the promotional pitch person for one of the world's biggest sellers of travel: Priceline.com.

And what about space travel itself? Several people have already paid to go into space on Russian rockets, and several private companies—including a sister company of Virgin Atlantic and Virgin America—are hard at work making space tourism a reality.

So, yes, technology has had—and will continue to have—a significant impact on travel, tourism, and hospitality. Let's take a look at selected technologies that have become essential tools of the industry. Some will be very familiar to you, others brand new.

CRS and GDS Systems

Today it's hard to imagine, but arranging travel and lodging was once largely done by phone, fax, or regular mail. Beginning in the late 1960s, the airlines saw the potential for then-emerging technologies to generate fast, effective, accurate bookings. They called this technology the CRS (Computer Reservation System). In the 1970s, they extended the CRS's booking capabilities to travel agents.

Within a short period of time, hotels, car rental companies, and other suppliers joined these programs to weave a vast, global linkage of travel and hospitality providers. To reflect this expansion, CRSs began to be called GDSs (Global Distribution Systems).

Quite quickly the entire technological landscape changed again. The Internet was becoming a valuable tool for both individuals and businesses. The airlines were among the first to see the Web as an easy and inexpensive way to sell their product directly to the public. They created user-friendly, Web-based versions of their GDSs. (To use a GDS, airline employees, travel agents, and others had to take special training.) Now anyone could research, compare, and book travel on airline Web sites.

This triggered another fundamental change. For decades travel agents had received commissions of about 10 percent for every airline ticket sold. It was their primary source of income. On their side, the airlines had figured out that it cost less to sell tickets through travel agents than through their own telephone sales staff. Both sides benefited from this longstanding relationship.

The Internet changed everything. It was much less expensive to sell travel through computers than through people. The airlines reduced their own phone reservations staff and, for the most part, stopped paying agents 10 percent to sell their product.

But there were a few surprises. Online agencies like Travelocity appeared suddenly, grew quickly, and captured a significant portion of all travel sales. This provided them with considerable leverage with suppliers, including the airlines. At the same time, conventional travel agents shifted their focus from selling air, to higher-profit, more complicated items, like cruises and tours.

This newfound competition and tough economic conditions forced the airlines to look anywhere for quick cash, so they spun off their GDS systems into separate companies or sold them to other investors. Surprisingly, GDSs have found ways to continue to be valuable tools to travel agents.

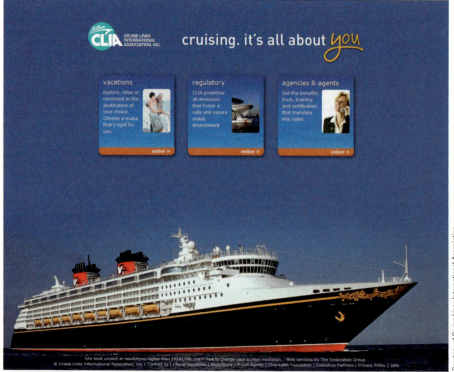

CLIA's homepage.

Almost surely there will be more unexpected twists and turns in this saga. For now, the Web and the GDS continue to be the principal distribution channels for just about every sector and supplier in the travel business. Existing technologies will evolve, others will communicate seamlessly (like the Web and GDS now do), and still others we can't even imagine now will undoubtedly appear.

Travel and the Internet

In just over a decade, the Internet has swept through our lives, dramatically changing the way we research, learn, purchase, and sell. Access to the Internet has become something we take for granted, like TV and radio. And it has had an especially profound effect on the travel industry. As you discovered in Chapter 1, by certain criteria, travel is the number-one product sold on the Net. So let's take a look at how travel and the Internet interrelate, as well as what we might expect from it in the future.

Web Sites

If you were to access the Internet right now and enter the word *travel* into your search engine, the results would be hundreds of millions of sites. If you began sifting through them, a pattern would slowly emerge, with certain site categories predominating. Some of these sites are great for consumers, others are more valuable for travel professionals, and many are useful to both. Here's an overview of the principal types of travel and hospitality sites you'll find:

- **Informational sites:** These sites provide details on places, products, and data (for example, weather forecasts and maps), almost always with links to other relevant sites. The most obvious are those sponsored by DMOs, governments, and travel industry professional organizations. You'll encounter all sorts of unexpected, highly useful Web-based sources of travel-related information, for example, the U.S. CIA (Central Intelligence Agency) site, and even sites that individuals have created as a hobby. Remember, the accuracy of amateur sites is wildly unpredictable. Unlike print-based resources, anybody can publish anything on the Web, accurate or not.

- **Opinion sites:** Information can easily slide into subjectivity on the Web, with experts—or self-proclaimed experts—giving their views on everything about destinations and products. Should you take a cruise on Carnival or Royal Caribbean? What's the finest hotel in Chicago? Which is the best buffet in Las Vegas? There's somebody, somewhere on the Web ready to give you his or her views on each of these subjects, and more.

Opinion sites, which are sometimes subsections of informational and other kinds of sites, can certainly be helpful when planning a trip. But their reviews should be taken with a grain of salt. After all, do the reviewer's tastes and values match yours? A variation of the opinion site is the *chat room*, where you can find the opinions of others and also ask for or exchange opinions with them.

insider info

The major CRS/GDS systems—some of which still exist in some form—were *Sabre* (originally American Airlines's GDS), *Apollo/Galileo* (created by United Airlines), *Worldspan* (from Continental Airlines), and *Amadeus* (several European carriers).

insider info

When visiting an opinion site, keep in mind that people who have a complaint are much more likely to write of their experience than people who were happy with their experience. Also, it is not unknown for a supplier to "rig" the opinion site by asking friends or even employees to write glowing reviews. If you notice a cluster of positive comments submitted over a short period of time, be careful. It may reflect this tactic. If you do consult an opinion site, choose an established one such as *TripAdvisor*, where there are hundreds of comments for each entry. A rating based on two or three opinions cannot possibly be reliable.

- **Supplier bookings sites:** As you've just learned, certain types of suppliers—especially airlines, car rental agencies, and lodging groups—aggressively try to sell travel directly to consumers. Such suppliers recognize that the Net provides a cost-efficient, easily updated way to distribute their products. In turn, consumers view these products as commodities that can easily be bought through the Web. Most cruise and tour operators also have online booking engines, but they find that the buying public usually visits their sites to research, not to buy. As you've discovered, such products are more experiential and complex, so travelers usually want guidance along with the research they've done before making a purchase decision. That counseling usually comes from a travel agent.

- **Travel agency sites:** As you've seen, traditional travel agents swiftly realized that, to survive, they, too, had to embrace Web-based technology. Many of these agencies, even small or home-based ones, now have their own Web sites, often with booking engines to permit online purchases. Expedia, Travelocity, and Orbitz are, of course, travel agencies, too, but they exist almost purely online. However, for consumers who visit their sites for a cruise, tour, or similar product, these online agencies provide ways for their customers to contact a "live" person for guidance and advice. In other words, traditional and online agencies—once very different from one another—are now more alike than most people think.

- **Auction sites:** These companies permit consumers to bid on travel. You enter a price you are willing to pay for a certain generic travel product (for example, a car rental), and the site then tells you if your bid has been accepted and with which supplier. Do bidders know if they're getting the travel product at a good price? Only those who are extremely well informed about current pricing. The most famous travel auction site is http://www.priceline.com. Several auction sites provide more conventional pricing and buying options too.

Strengths of Web-based Technology

Why has buying travel on the Internet become so popular? Here are eight reasons:

1. *It gives access to vast storehouses of knowledge.* You can find out almost anything on the Net, with plenty about travel-related issues. In fact, there's so much information that it can be overwhelming.

2. *It's convenient.* You can research and buy from your home or office, 24/7. Plus, you'll rarely be kept waiting, on hold or at an office.

3. *There's no sales pressure.* You rarely feel that someone is manipulating you into buying. And the site is infinitely patient.

4. *It's interactive.* The give and take between the consumer and the site is quick, flexible, and accurate.

5. *It's visual.* Our society has become increasingly visual. Web sites can provide virtual tours of hotels, live broadcasts from cruise ships, and all sorts of other visuals—the kind that motivate consumers to buy.

Telling Terms

You probably already know the standard terminology of computer and Web-based technology, but just in case, here are some common terms:

- **Booking engine:** A function that enables you to make Web-based reservations in real time.
- **Browser:** Software that permits you to access and retrieve documents on the Web.
- **FAQs:** A list of **F**requently **A**sked **Q**uestions that consumers are likely to want answers to. For example, if you wished to book a tour online, you could access answers to those questions people who are thinking about taking a tour—or have booked one—typically want to know.
- **Homepage:** The first page you see on a Web site. It usually gives basic information and has topics you can click on for deeper information and for booking.
- **Hyperlink (or link):** A graphic or series of words that, if you click on it, takes you to another site.

- **Internet:** A global system of computer networks that enables you to access and communicate with any other computer connected to it.
- **Search engine:** An online program that looks for sites containing words, word combinations, subjects, and other information that match what you have indicated you want to know more about.
- **Uniform Resource Locator (URL):** The "address" of a Web site. For example, the URL of Apple Computers is http://www.apple.com.
- **World Wide Web:** A system within the Internet that organizes information, both text and visuals, into pages that can easily be retrieved and displayed. The public tends to use the terms *Internet* and *World Wide Web* interchangeably (although the World Wide Web is only a part of the Internet, one that goes well beyond the text-only content that the Internet is limited to).

6. *It can be entertaining.* Web sites lend themselves to creative, flashy, and fun buying environments. This is especially useful when selling leisure travel.

7. *It communicates regularly.* If you agree to be put on a supplier's e-mail list, you'll receive special announcements, perhaps a newsletter, and alerts on special offers.

8. *It can customize.* If you volunteer information about yourself to a company's database, it can create a profile that will permit notifications to you of product offers tailored to your tastes.

Weaknesses of Web-based Technology

As great as it is, the Internet isn't a perfect travel sales and booking tool. Here are six of its shortcomings:

1. *It can't "solve" complex trips very well.* Complicated FITs defy technological solutions. Unless the consumer is really adept at manipulating Web-based resources or the site is extremely user-friendly, it's hard to assemble a multi-component trip on the Internet.

2. *It's potentially time consuming.* Although the Internet appears to save time, in fact it can overload you with so many choices and so much data that you don't know where to begin. Buying travel via an inefficiently designed booking engine may take longer than a phone call to a supplier reservationist or a travel agent.

3. *Privacy and security are still an issue.* Many people continue to feel uncomfortable with giving personal information or a credit card number to a "faceless," impersonal system.

4. *Information is often dated.* From a supplier point of view, one of the Internet's strengths is that information can be easily updated. This makes it superior to printed brochures. That's the theory, anyway. The reality is that many suppliers fail to keep their sites current. Even worse, it is often hard to tell *when* the information you're reading was posted. Web sites are still out there in cyberspace for companies that went out of business years ago.

5. *It deals poorly with after-purchase problems.* If something goes wrong, there's often no one to call—or at least it's difficult to find information on how to get a live person for help.

6. *It transacts superbly, but counsels poorly.* Computers are good at asking closed-ended questions such as who, what, when, where, how much, and how long. They're awkward, though, when asking and processing open-ended questions, the kind that good travel agents handle quite well.

Computer programmers are hard at work trying to create a "virtual" travel agent. To some extent, they almost surely will succeed. But equally certain is that, for the foreseeable future, a skilled travel counselor will be able to outperform automated qualifying programs.

Who's Buying?

Computers have almost become everyday household appliances, and Internet access may eventually become as common as telephone service. Still, not everyone favors or even uses the Internet to buy travel. Here are some insights into those who do:

- They tend to be younger and more technologically attuned.
- They tend to have higher incomes, are more educated, and travel more than others.
- They use the Internet, rather than magazines or guidebooks, for research.

THIS & that

- When it comes to buying commodities, they're very price driven.
- Most prefer to book commodities through online agencies rather than through suppliers.
- An overwhelming number of wired consumers say that they'd rather talk to a travel agent when buying complex, costly, and experiential products. Before contacting the agent, though, they do a great deal of Internet research and electronic "window shopping."

Social Media

If there's any need for proof that technology can change our lives swiftly and unexpectedly, it can be found in the proliferation of social media.

One of the most popular Facebook topics is travel.

The story is now well known. In 2004, a Harvard student created a network called Facebook that facilitated communication among students. Within a few years, it—and similar sites—became a multibillion-dollar business embraced by almost all sectors of society.

It also took about a nanosecond for businesses to realize the vast implications of social media as promotional tools. At the same time, it quickly became clear that those who use these media don't like overt sales and marketing promotions.

© 1000 Words/www.Shutterstock.com

That may change. For now, social media is about communicating, not selling. Yes, marketing on social media happens all the time, but it has to be subtle.

It makes sense, too, that travel is especially suited to the Web. Just think of how many of your friends on Facebook write about their travels. In fact, there are Facebook groups that talk about *nothing but travel*.

promotion too!

Kevin Bacon and You

A precursor to the social media phenomenon was, of all things, an online game based on the actor Kevin Bacon. It maintained that any actor was no more than six people away from any other. So actor X worked on a movie with actor Y who worked with an actress on a TV series who later appeared in a movie . . . with Bacon!

THIS & that

By extension, this principle has been applied to all of us. You, too, are just "six degrees of separation" from anyone else on the planet—including Kevin Bacon.

The game underscores that we are all interconnected and that this permits rapid communication—both personal and promotional.

Kinds of Social Media

Here's a rundown of five categories of social and related media. Remember that one medium can link to another medium, each with its own advantages and limitations. For example, Facebook can direct you to a Web site. These links can be woven in such a way that the whole is greater than the sum of its parts.

1. **Social networking sites.** *Facebook* and similar sites are intended to build and maintain relationships, to keep in touch with what your friends or even celebrities are up to. Businesses quickly learned that people also wanted to be "friends" or "fans" of companies and their products. In response, Facebook created an "official" page for business, rather than personal, relationships.

2. **Microblogs.** Microblogs such as *Twitter* allow you to send out instant, short messages, or "tweets." It's a great way to communicate right-now, real-time

But What Do You *Do* with It?

Here are some real-world travel applications of social media networking:

Social Networking Sites

- Three well-known rap artists mention to their fans that they will sponsor a special, fans-only series of performances onboard an upcoming cruise sailing out of Fort Lauderdale, Florida.

- A meeting planner named John Smith asks every John Smith on Facebook to be his "friend." He creates a John Smith group and sponsors a sort-of family reunion for them in Chicago.

Microblogs

- A theme park is experiencing unusually slow attendance because of morning rain. But the weather has cleared. The park blasts out a message to everyone on their customer list and within their geographic area that if they go right now to the park, they'll receive two tickets for the price of one.

- A special computer program flags tweets sent by a hotel guest, who is complaining to friends about his room. The program alerts the hotel manager who immediately contacts the guest and offers to solve the situation—minutes after the complaint was made.

Photo- and Video-Sharing Sites

- A tour company sets up a site where the tour manager and tour members of each specific tour can post their videos and photos and share them with one another. The company later follows up with a special offer to members of the group for a future tour with the same tour manager they had before.

Business Sites

- A cruise line mentions to its suppliers worldwide that they're looking for new, creative ideas for local entertainment performers.

- The hugely successful and well-liked president of a convention and tourist bureau tells her LinkedIn contacts that she has decided to leave her organization, that she'll take a few months off to be with family, and then she hopes to find a fresh new direction for her efforts in a segment of travel different from her current one.

Careers

Careers in Technology

Here are IT-specific positions that are common in the hospitality, travel, and tourism industries:

- Technical support engineers
- Database administrators
- System and network engineers
- Web developers
- Web designers
- Programmers
- IT trainers

- National administrators
- Software quality assurance engineers
- Network engineers
- Webmasters
- Software architects
- Equipment installers

thoughts—including those about travel. For promotion, a tweet can send you to the tweeter's Web site for more information.

3. **Photo-sharing sites.** Sites like *Flickr* permit you (or a business) to post and share photos—something that travelers have done since the very beginnings of photography. Facebook provides a similar photo-sharing function.

4. **Video-sharing sites.** Similar to a photo-sharing site, sites like *YouTube* enable users to share all sorts of videos. For example, a travel agent or meeting planner could post videos of his or her own personal travels to share with clients. Today the line between photo and video sites is beginning to blur, with video sites also accepting photos, and vice versa.

5. **Business sites.** Business sites, like *LinkedIn,* are business-to-business networks. They enable colleagues, suppliers, and similar individuals or groups to communicate about shared issues.

Between the time you began reading this section on social media and now, almost surely someone, somewhere, had an idea that could send the path of social networking in an entirely new direction. In fact, some of what you've just read may already be wrong or obsolete.

But that doesn't mean that it's useless. Often old roads lead to new destinations—and to fresh opportunities. And in that spirit, let's continue our journey through technology and examine a remarkable and now well-established application of computer software: CRM.

CRM

In days gone by, travel companies meticulously wrote down customer information on each of its customers on little index cards, perhaps coded by color. They would then file them alphabetically in drawers of a large metal cabinet.

Check-in technology makes it possible for hotels to address the specific preferences of each guest.

Let's say that company planned to offer a product specifically targeted to families. A clerk would thumb through hundreds of files, pulling every card that represented a family travel customer. They would mail a promotional piece to these families, with addresses typed or written by hand, one by one. It could easily be a day's work.

Now you can do the same thing in less than a minute. The reason: customer relationship management programs, or CRMs. **CRMs** *track buying patterns, demographic and psychographic information, past travel experiences, and key dates, like birthdays and anniversaries.*

Actually, a CRM program isn't so much a computer program application as it is an overall business philosophy that places the individual customer at the center of the company's thinking. Through technology, it "knows" each of its customers' likes or dislikes, then customizes selling based on this key information.

If you have ever received a restaurant promotional piece in the mail for a kind of food you love, if you have ever gone to a hotel where you stayed before and they know what kind of pillow you prefer, if the special photos and stories displayed on your Yahoo! homepage screen seem to be about topics you are especially interested in, a CRM program is probably involved.

CRM Programs

What can a good CRM program help you do? It can:

1. Respond quickly to customer inquiries, requests, and service needs

2. Provide up-to-date information and promotions

3. Organize and manage customer and other valuable information in one place

4. Track a company's or even an individual salesperson's closure rate (the percentage of inquiries that turn into an actual sale)

5. Target promotions specifically to individual customer needs

6. Identify your most profitable customers

7. Strengthen a company's brand image

CRM programs have hundreds of applications in travel. Here are a few of them:

- Airlines, to manage their frequent-flyer programs

- Meeting planners, to follow up to discover what their attendees liked and didn't like about a convention

- Cruise lines, to alert future passengers to changes in their itinerary

- Large travel agencies, to track each of their agent's productivity

Other Travel-Related Technologies

If we were to cover every technology that has an impact on hospitality and travel, this chapter alone would become a book. Consider how:

- GPS devices have enhanced the car rental industry

- iPhones and tablets enable travelers to solve a flight cancellation problem faster than airport staff can

- A downloadable app can help parents locate their kids anywhere on a cruise ship

- A blog can be the place where a chef reveals his latest culinary discovery

- Kiosks help facilitate check-in at a hotel, airport, or train station

© Jacqueline Abromeit/www.Shutterstock.com

Passengers now use self-service check-in stations when they arrive at the airport.

- 3-D movie systems help theme parks fashion incredible rides
- Skype-like technology permits you to see the reservationist you are dealing with on your computer screen—and enable them to see you, if you so choose

Only one thing is for sure: technology will continue to shape the travel industry—and everything else—in ways we cannot even imagine.

More This and That

Here are a few miscellaneous bits of information you should know about travel and technology:

- Most major suppliers and DMOs have special areas of their sites dedicated to travel agents. These sections are sometimes only accessible through the agency's ARC, IATA, or CLIA ID number.

- Some suppliers offer *"Internet-only"* rates that are lower than those available elsewhere. Or they may add a "penalty" fee if you book via a toll-free line or a travel agent.

- Some sites offer a service that continuously monitors offers for dates you want to travel and at prices you specify. If and when your stated criteria are met, the site will notify you by e-mail and ask if you want to purchase.

Review Questions

1. What is a GDS?

2. Give five reasons people like buying on the Internet.

3. Give five reasons people might not like booking on the Internet.

4. What are the five categories of social media?

5. List at least five things a good CRM program can do.

NAME   DATE

It's All About You Questions

1. Have you ever had an experience with social media that made you want to travel somewhere? For example, a friend shares photos of herself on Waikiki Beach—and it makes you really want to go to Hawaii. Describe an example from your experience.

2. Let's say you do decide to visit Hawaii for a seven-day vacation—but you know very little about Hawaii. What steps would you take to make your vacation the best it can possibly be?

Activity 1: Here or Gone?

When you do an online search, it is sometimes difficult to determine whether the information is up to date. That can be a big problem in the travel business. You'll now see why. Look on the Web for the 12 companies listed below. Here's the catch: *some of them no longer exist.* Using your search skills, figure out which ones have gone out of business and which ones still exist. Be prepared to explain how you determined their status.

- Embassy Suites

- Venice-Simplon Orient Express

- Steak and Ale Restaurants

- Delta Queen Steamboat Co./Majestic Lines

- Pan-American Airways

- Radisson Hotels

- Six Flags Entertainment

- Paragon Tours

- Renaissance Cruise Lines

- American Express Travel Related Services

- Mexicana Airlines

- Trafalgar

NAME   **DATE**

Activity 2: What Will They Think of Next?

This chapter opened with *Star Trek* as an example of the technologies that have—or have not—come to pass.

Below are six similar "breakthrough" developments. Select two and explain what you think each would do to the travel or hotel lodging industry. (Remember, the results could be good, bad, or both.)

1. A train that goes 500 miles an hour between New York City and Orlando, Florida

2. The ability to "transport" (as in *Star Trek*) to any spot on the earth instantly

3. A *Star Trek*–like device that creates any food or beverage you want in less than a minute

4. A time machine that could take you to any place and time period on earth, past or future

5. A chair-like device (similar to the one in the movie *Total Recall*) that would permit you to mentally visit any place in the world and think you were there—without leaving the chair-like device

6. A pill that would enable you to stay awake 22 hours a day and only need 2 hours' sleep to remain alert and healthy

Your two choices:

NAME   DATE

Gale Hospitality, Tourism and Leisure Database Assignment

The following assignment requires access to the Gale Hospitality, Tourism and Leisure Database. Check with your instructor to see if you have access to this database.

Find the article *Opinion Pages* in the Gale Hospitality, Tourism & Leisure Collection, then visit three of the opinion sites cited by the author.

Which opinion site did you like best? Why?

Find pages in the Gale Hospitality

Do you think you could trust the site you selected more than the others? Why?

This and That

12

KEY TERMS

- Avatar
- Customs
- Duty
- Immigration
- International driver's permit
- Jet lag
- Passport
- Tourist card
- Traveler's check
- Visa

After studying this chapter, you'll be able to:

- Explain the procedures and documents associated with border crossings

- Interpret and apply the basic principles of currencies and exchange rates

- Address customer health and safety concerns

- Prepare for the changes in travel to come

Photo courtesy of VIP Vacations Inc.

Jennifer Doncsecz

CURRENT POSITION/TITLE:

President, VIP Vacations Inc.

SHORT DESCRIPTION OF WHAT YOUR RESPONSIBILITIES ARE:

I guess I'm a juggler. I juggle sales, marketing, PR, forecasting, etc. Our specialty: destination weddings.

EDUCATION:

BS, Marketing & Communications, Cedar Crest College

FIRST JOB IN TRAVEL/HOSPITALITY INDUSTRY:

Worked in a tiny travel agency

FIRST PAID JOB (IF DIFFERENT FROM ABOVE):

In college, I sold ski trips to fellow students in return for a free trip for me and my friends

FAVORITE PART OF WHAT I DO:

To see a photo of a couple whose wedding I had planned and that went just right. It's like opening up a Christmas present.

THING I WISH I DIDN'T HAVE TO DO:

Deal with airlines

SOMEONE WHO INSPIRES ME:

Marilyn Carlson Nelson, former CEO and now Chairman of the Board, Carlson Companies

STRANGEST OR FUNNIEST CAREER-RELATED THING I'VE EVER EXPERIENCED:

I started getting all these Facebook friend requests from India. Couldn't figure out why. Turned out an old Travel Channel show I did was running in Mumbai.

FAVORITE QUOTE:

"My strength lies solely in my tenacity."

SOMETHING ALMOST NO ONE KNOWS ABOUT ME:

I'm a member of a club in which we go to YouTube, learn a dance, and show up at a prearranged location, do the dance, then walk away.

D o you have a desk drawer—usually it's the middle one—filled with all sorts of small, miscellaneous, and useful things such as pens, rubber bands, Post-Its, a stapler, a ruler, and who knows what else?

Textbooks can be like that too. This chapter serves the same purpose as that drawer: it harbors a collection of diverse topics not yet fully covered in this book but that will prove very useful to you. Frankly, many of these topics could have fit into other chapters, but that might have made those chapters a bit too long and weighty. So here they are: the remaining topics you must know to fully understand and succeed in the travel industry.

Crossing Borders

When traveling internationally, people must cross borders. Sometimes that process is easy, sometimes hard. And for it all to work, travelers must have the proper documents with them.

Documents

Several documents are critical to border crossings. The rules, regulations, fees, and time requirements associated with each document can change and are readily accessible through government Web sites, so these details won't be listed here. You must, however, know what each document is and what it represents:

Passports are essential for international travel.

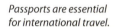

- A **passport** is *a document that a nation's government issues to one of its citizens to establish that person's identity and nationality.* Most countries require a traveler to show a passport to enter their borders. That applies on return too. For example, if you leave the United States, you'll have to show your passport to reenter. Certain countries permit travelers to prove their citizenship through documents other than passports, such as a birth certificate, certificate of naturalization (if born abroad), or even an expired passport. A driver's license or Social Security card does *not* prove citizenship and thus doesn't suffice. U.S. residents who are not citizens must have their *residency cards* (green cards) to reenter the United States.

- A **visa** is *a stamp, imprint, or piece of paper inserted into a traveler's passport, placed there by a foreign government, that indicates the passport's owner may enter and pass through the country that issued it*. In other words, it's an additional step that travelers must take before they can visit certain countries. Not all nations require them; others require them only for people coming from certain countries.

  Why do some countries require visas? Isn't a passport enough? Some governments, for security purposes, wish to do a background check, in advance, of everyone who crosses their borders. Others use visas as an extra form of revenue. Still others do it for political reasons. For example, if the U.S. government requires people from Nation A to have a visa before coming to the United States, then Nation A may retaliate by doing the same to Americans who intend to visit *its* country.

  There are many kinds of visas (such as student or business visas), but the ones travelers use are called *tourist visas*. They can be costly, sometimes take months to obtain, and are often handled in a rather disorganized or highly restricted manner—it differs from country to country. Sometimes they're obtained at the airport upon arrival, but for some countries, visitors must mail in their passport or take it to a local embassy or consulate of the nation they wish to visit. Consulates are local "branches" of a foreign embassy in major cities. For example, China has its embassy in Washington, D.C., and consulates in Chicago, Houston, Los Angeles, New York City, and San Francisco. To find out whether a visa is required to visit a country and what the requirements are, you need only visit that country's consular Web site (found through your search engine) or that of the U.S. Department of State, http://www.travel.state.gov.

- A **tourist card** is *a form that's used instead of or in addition to a passport for entry into certain countries*. Filled out just in advance of arrival, the tourist card must be carried by travelers during their trip and surrendered upon leaving.

- An **international driver's permit** (**IDP**) is *a version of your own driver's license translated into multiple languages*. Although it's not really required for driving in a foreign country, it becomes valuable in the event that you must deal with a non-English-speaking traffic officer, because he or she will probably be able to decipher at least one language on the IDP. IDPs are issued by auto clubs such as AAA.

Immigration and Customs

As you learned in Chapter 3, immigration and customs are integral to any trip where crossing borders is involved. But international travelers often confuse immigration and customs. **Immigration** is *the process by which a government official controls movement of people across its borders*. To do this, it verifies a person's citizenship through a passport, visa, or other document. Most countries try to move travelers through this process quickly, reserving more extended inspections for people coming to their country to work, study, or reside for an extended period. Of course, if a person's documents are incomplete or suspect, the process will be a long one.

Customs is *the procedure by which government agents inspect luggage and other goods entering a country* to check for forbidden items (for example, narcotics) or restricted ones (such as certain kinds of fruits). If the traveler is returning home, Customs assesses whether duties or taxes are due on items purchased on the trip. A **duty** is *a fee imposed on items purchased abroad*. Generally, a U.S. resident may bring back up to $800 worth of items duty-free. In some cases, that "personal exemption" is higher or lower, and certain items (such as art) may be duty-free and therefore won't count toward the personal exemption. Customs regulations are complex and change frequently. For up-to-date U.S. information, you should check the U.S. Customs Web site at http://www.customs.gov.

Cost, Currencies, and Exchange Rates

Each country prints its own money, usually called its *currency*. In a few cases, multiple countries use the same currency (for example, the European countries that use the euro). Each major unit of currency has a name. For instance, in the United States it's the dollar, for Japan the yen, for Mexico the peso. These units of currency are usually further subdivided into smaller units, such as the U.S. cent. Another example is the British currency, the pound, which is divided into 100 pence.

Why is this important to know? Because anyone traveling to a foreign place will encounter prices in local currency and must interpret what that translates to. For example, if it costs 20,000 yen to take a taxi from Narita airport to downtown Tokyo, is that expensive? (Answer: yes, very. It's about US$260.)

So how can you predict whether a place will be an expensive travel destination? One way is to check the official U.S. cost-of-living statistics for U.S. and worldwide cities. Although this information is intended for government workers, it very much reflects current corporate costs worldwide. Go to http://www.gsa.gov/perdiem for U.S. cities or http://aoprals.state.gov for foreign destinations. Here are five guidelines that can also help you:

1. *Big, sophisticated cities are generally more expensive to visit than smaller or less visited ones.* Tokyo, New York City, London, Paris—these typically have expensive lodging, dining, and other travel-related costs (and non-travel-related costs too). Fall River (Massachusetts), Sherbrooke (Quebec, Canada), and Freiburg (Germany) don't.

2. *Rural or suburban areas tend to be less expensive than urban ones.* This applies even to the environs of major cities. Lodging that's just a few miles outside Chicago is much less pricey than in Chicago itself.

3. *Cities with many business travelers cost more than those that attract mostly leisure travelers.* That's why Las Vegas and Orlando, although they are big cities, cost less than Los Angeles and Atlanta do. It's because leisure travelers, as you've learned, are more price sensitive than corporate ones. (After all, for business travel, usually someone else is paying.)

4. *Developing countries have lower overall costs, comparatively, than others do.* In nations such as Turkey, Indonesia, and Honduras, almost everything is a bargain for visitors, at least those from industrialized countries like ours.

5. *It depends on the currency exchange rate.* And to explain this, let's devote at least a few special paragraphs to exchange rates, as follows.

Exchange Rates

The whole issue of currency value is a complex, mysterious one. All sorts of elements affect the value of a nation's currency, including political factors (is the government stable?), economic issues (how productive is its industry?), whether inflation is under control (are prices on day-to-day items going up fast?), how much debt the country has, and a host of other hard-to-figure-out things. In other words, it's not unlike the stock of a company.

The exchange rate between two countries—what one nation's currency is worth in another nation's currency—is extremely critical to travelers. For example, if I want to buy something that costs 60 *zlotys* in Polish currency, how many U.S. dollars is that? Fortunately, it's easy to find out. Many Web sites list the day's accepted exchange rates for virtually every major currency. Most of those sites allow you to fill in the numbers and will do the conversion for you.

A currency exchange counter at New York City's Grand Central Terminal.

© June Marie Sobrito/www.Shutterstock.com

Here's how to do the currency conversion yourself:

To convert foreign currency into U.S. dollars, take the number of foreign currency units (in this case 60 *zlotys*) and divide by the number of foreign currency units per U.S. dollar (at press time three *zlotys* equaled roughly one dollar). So, 60 *zlotys* equal about 20 U.S. dollars.

If this sounds as complicated as the international date line, don't fret. You can use online currency calculators and find their monetary equivalent without having to do the math yourself. Many travel or luggage stores sell little pocket currency converters that enable you to figure things out quite easily. Also, keep in mind that banks, currency exchange offices, and businesses usually offer exchange rates that are slightly different from the "official" ones. The reason for this is that they must earn a profit for the trouble of exchanging the money, so they readjust the rates in their favor. Some also charge an additional commission.

Exchanging Money—and Paying for Things with It

So how do you deal with money when visiting foreign countries? Here are four options:

1. *You can pay with cash in U.S. dollars.* It's rather astonishing, but the U.S. dollar is so respected worldwide that people in many countries are willing to take it for payment. The opposite is quite unlikely. If you work somewhere in the United States, would you be willing to accept payment in Swiss *francs*? Almost surely not, even though the Swiss *franc* is a strong, stable currency. However, the probability that you'll get an accurate or fair exchange rate is slim, whereas the possibility of being cheated is rather large. In general, it's a bad idea to pay in U.S. dollars, except in those few countries (especially in the Caribbean) where even the locals use the U.S. dollar as an alternate form of everyday currency.

2. *You can pay with cash in foreign currency.* This certainly works well, although it's easy at first to confuse the value of unfamiliar paper money and coins. But to get that foreign currency cash, you must do one of the following first:

   - *Convert your dollars into foreign currency before you leave.* You can buy foreign currency online. Some banks and travel agencies also sell foreign currency.

   - *Convert your dollars into foreign currency at the country's bank when you get there.* Most foreign banks will exchange U.S. dollars.

   - *With your debit or credit card, use an ATM to withdraw foreign cash when you arrive.* This is efficient and usually offers the best exchange rate. But you need to know the value of local currency before you do it, or you may unintentionally withdraw thousands of U.S. dollars worth of foreign currency without realizing it.

insider info

The keypads on foreign ATMs often have numbers only. If your password is composed of letters, memorize their numerical equivalents before leaving for your trip.

- *Convert your dollars into foreign currency at the hotel.* This might not work if the hotel doesn't have a lot of foreign currency. Also, its exchange rate will probably not be very good.

- *Convert your dollars at a currency exchange bureau before leaving.* These bureaus are often located at airports and, in some major cities, in downtown locations.

- *Convert your dollars at a currency exchange bureau when you get there.* Currency exchange bureaus are much more common in foreign countries— both at arrival airports and in city locations—than they are in the United States.

- *Convert your dollars with someone on the street, through the "black market."* This is a terrible idea. The rate will probably be worse than anywhere else, and you may be buying counterfeit currency.

3. *You can pay with your credit or debit card.* This has become the preferred way for travelers to buy things abroad. One reason is because the exchange rate is usually favorable. Remember, though, that there will be times when cards may not be accepted for payment (for example, onboard public transportation, at inexpensive restaurants, or in small hotels). Also, most card issuers charge an additional fee on transactions requiring currency conversion. Some charge the fee even when no conversion is required.

4. *You can pay with traveler's checks.* A **traveler's check** is *a check-like form of currency that must be countersigned by the user.* In the United States, it's generally issued in U.S. dollars but can be offered in certain major foreign currencies too. When you get to a country, you use the check in the same way you would use cash. So if you pay for something with a US$50 traveler's check, you'll get the items *plus* the change (in the local currency), based on that day's exchange rate. The advantage of a traveler's check is that, if you lose the check, you can get its value back later, from the issuer. It's not like losing cash. (To be cashed, a traveler's check requires a duplicate signature.) The disadvantages are that many places don't accept them and sometimes there's a fee for buying them and/or for using them (charged by the vendor you're paying). The most common issuers of traveler's checks are American Express and Visa. They can often be obtained from your local bank or from a AAA office.

More About Currency and Exchange

Here are a few more things you should know:

- *Many countries' currencies have the same name.* For example, Canada, New Zealand, Singapore, and Australia all call their currencies "dollars." However, each country's dollar has its own value. So a New Zealand dollar may be worth only 85 cents in U.S. currency.

- *If you prebook travel in U.S. dollars, usually that price will not change, no matter what happens with the local currency.* For instance, in 2002 the

Argentine *peso* began to swiftly plummet. For a week or two, it lost 20 to 30 percent of its value *daily*. However, if you had booked a room in Buenos Aires for US$149, that would be what it would cost, even if during your stay the value of your dollar had doubled vis-à-vis Argentine currency. However, things that weren't purely tourist-related *did* change in value. Within weeks, meals in a local restaurant might go from US$50 per person to US$20. That's because they're typically quoted in *pesos*, not dollars.

- To emphasize what you've learned throughout this section: The exchange rate that a bank, hotel, exchange bureau, or ATM applies when you convert money will be different from what appears "officially," and *those differences will always favor the vendor, not the traveler*. It's the price of doing business with them, plus there may even be an additional exchange fee involved. As a result, you never want to exchange too much cash. If you convert US$1,000 into euros, then exchange your leftover euros into British pounds, then exchange the remaining pounds into U.S. dollars for your return, you've lost money at each transaction. Unless you're paying a fixed fee each time you get money, it's probably better to get a little cash, often, during your trip.

Health Concerns

Wouldn't it be wonderful if we felt perfectly healthy throughout a vacation? That doesn't always happen, though. Long flights and crossing multiple time zones make us tired. Weird microbes may lurk in common tap water. You might go snorkeling and cut yourself on coral, leading to a fierce infection. Or you might boldly dine on something exotic, only to experience days of digestive problems. No wonder overcautious travelers (remember Plog's "Dependables"?) never want to go very far from familiar surroundings.

To have a wondrous trip, though, you sometimes have to take chances. Here are some ways to minimize the risk:

- **Vaccinations** are required or recommended to visit certain foreign nations (especially developing ones). A comprehensive list of guidelines is available at the Centers for Disease Control and Prevention's Web site at http://www.cdc.gov. Physicians are able to access similar information and provide the necessary inoculations.

- **Jet lag** occurs *when your internal body clock is confused by crossing multiple time zones*. Long, tiring flights also help exacerbate the situation. For most people it takes a day per time zone crossed to fully recover. One way to quicken your recovery is to expose yourself to outdoor daylight as much as possible during the first few days of arrival.

This picture says it all.

© mangostock/www.Shutterstock.com

Accessible Travel

Most hospitality and travel businesses are keenly aware of the needs of customers with physical disabilities. Some examples of adaptations include specially designed bathrooms, fewer thresholds on ships, special seating on theme park rides, wheelchair assistance at airports, Braille menus for the sight-impaired, and ramps at convention centers. These accessibility features permit travelers with physical disabilities to enjoy the same travel experiences that others do. In the United States these criteria are called "ADA" standards, for the *Americans with Disabilities Act*. Many countries—especially developing ones—have standards that are less adapted to the needs of this population.

- **Altitude sickness** can occur when visiting a high altitude destination, such as Cuzco, Peru. A physician can provide medication to alleviate symptoms and that you begin taking before you leave home.

- **Motion sickness** can be the result of air, car, or, especially, sea travel. If you know yourself to be prone to sea discomfort, ask your doctor about the Transderm Scop patch, which, when placed behind the ear, helps reduce motion sickness in most people. It does make some people drowsy and dry-mouthed.

- **Food and drink** in foreign countries can lead to mild to serious illness. It's not always a product of unsanitary conditions either: each place's ecosystem may contain microbes that are harmless to locals (who have built up resistance to them) but render visitors quite ill. Some precautions to take include eating only well-cooked food and food you peel yourself. Consume only bottled water. Drink bottled beverages without ice.

Safety and Security Issues

The world has never been a totally peaceful place. At any given time, some country is suffering a revolution, some war is raging, and some cause may lead to terrorism. Such things have always affected travel. People traveling on the roads during the Middle Ages were constantly threatened by thieves. Someone visiting a thriving port might be forced into performing sea labor. Pirates, slave traders, hostile armies—all of these made travel a perilous endeavor.

Travel is far safer today. As a result, any misfortune associated with travel seems especially disturbing in our times, probably because our technologically advanced, presumably civilized society leaves little room for disruption, fanaticism, or disaster. Moreover, the media is attracted to tragedy, bringing it right into our homes.

But disasters do occur, sometimes intentionally. To travel today requires a little more caution, a little more alertness. The chances of something going seriously wrong are, in most cases, as probable as being struck by lightning. Then again, if you avoid trees and hills during thunderstorms, you'll be less likely to be hit, won't you?

So here are some of the things you should tell customers:

- Before selecting a foreign destination, **check for official government assessments** and warnings about the countries you'll be visiting.

- **Keep up to date on recent news**, especially current developments in a region you're thinking of visiting.

- In many countries, **you should be careful of petty theft**. Be wary of pickpockets and purse-snatchers. Park your rental car in a secured lot or structure. Stay at hotels in safe areas. Be alert and cautious. Limit your activities at night anywhere crime is a problem.

- **Go with brands you know.** You're usually safer with a well-known tour company, hotel chain, or cruise line than with one you've never heard of before.

insider info

Politics sometimes influences risk assessments. One country may have a friendly relationship with a certain nation, and another may ban travel to that same nation. Still, advisories are a good reference point for making a decision.

insider info

Some countries have "tourist police" whose job is to protect visitors from harm, hassles, over-aggressive sellers, and con schemes.

Airport security is tighter than ever.

Your Future in Travel

By this point you may have decided that a career in travel might be right for you. If so, what do you do next? Here are some thoughts to guide you:

- **Review the Careers boxes** throughout this book to remind yourself of the numerous job options open to you in travel and tourism.

- **Consider your personality** and how it fits (or doesn't fit) each industry sector. For instance, if you're very outgoing, being a tour guide or concierge might be just right for you. If you're persuasive, a position in sales might be perfect. Enjoy cooking and sharing with others? Being part of the culinary industry may be quite fulfilling.

- **Visit employment sites**, like monster.com to see what's out there. Also, most large companies have job information on their Web sites.

- **Be alert to opportunities**. It's estimated that almost half of all travel and hospitality careers begin through friends, family, or acquaintances—not unusual for a very "people-oriented" business.

- **Project professionalism**. Many Web sites provide excellent "how-to" guidance on effective resumes, cover letters, job interviews, follow-up techniques, and other career-building skills.

- **Time your job quest** to coincide with travel seasonality. Travel-related businesses tend to do the most hiring in early spring, a few months before tourism will peak. But there are notable exceptions. The ski industry, for example, does much of its hiring in the fall.

- **Be alert to what the economy is doing**. When people are optimistic about the future, they tend to travel more. The result: travel-related companies may get more business than expected and start hiring again, often in late spring or early summer.

- **If you have a unique skill, mention it**. For example, if you speak more than one language, that can be a big plus in many sectors of this industry.

- **Apply for an internship** (usually unpaid) in the segment of this business that most intrigues you. Many industry professionals start this way.

- It's okay for free or discounted travel to be one of your job motivators, **but don't give it prominence in your job quest**. Some experts say you shouldn't mention it at all.

- Once in the industry, **get to know not just the people you work with but also those at other companies that you deal with**. The hospitality and travel industries tend to be very "inbred." For example, a hotel front-desk clerk makes friends with a tour manager who regularly brings groups to that hotel. A job opportunity opens up at the tour company. The tour manager then serves as a "connection" for the desk clerk to a job in an entirely different but parallel career.

- A reminder: **travel and hospitality companies are well known for swiftly promoting high-achieving employees**.

- **Be prepared for a series of security checks** at airports and, to a lesser extent, at railway stations, cruise facilities, and bus terminals. This could include passing through full-body scanners, pat-down procedures, questioning from security personnel, luggage and carry-on bag inspections, and even full-body searches.

- **Keep up on restrictions** of what you can bring aboard the plane, such as bottles of liquid, aerosols, and gels.

- Make sure **you know what ID to bring** (for example, a passport).
- **Never leave valuable items openly visible in your hotel room**. Use your room or hotel safe.

Transportation Security and Concerns

Just a few decades ago, a wooden door or, sometimes, only a curtain separated airline pilots and their cockpit from the passenger compartment. Often, the door was left open during flight. The pilots might not even mind if you visited them while they were at work.

Today, the pilot's flight deck is protected by a reinforced, bulletproof, and fireproof door with high-strength hinges, peepholes, and locks. If a pilot needs to go to the bathroom, flight attendants often block passenger access to the area with their galley meal carts.

Natural Disasters

Earthquakes, volcanic eruptions, hurricanes, tornados, tsunamis—yes, nature can be unpredictably dangerous. Still, there are precautions you should keep in mind:

- **Be wary of seasons when weather is most likely to disrupt a trip**.
  For example, hurricanes are more likely in the Caribbean during late summer and fall, and heavy monsoon rains are more likely in India during summer.

Careers

Careers in Other Areas of Travel

Here are careers that are available in the industry segments we cover in this chapter:

- Senior executives, directors, and managers
- Immigration and customs agents
- Safety and security personnel
- Law enforcement and traffic personnel
- Currency exchange personnel

- Travel medical specialists
- Accessibility specialists
- Risk assessors
- Job placement specialists
- Special interest professionals

- **Earthquakes and tsunamis are rare but unpredictable.** Some places, of course, suffer such events more frequently, such as the regions north of the equator that border on the Pacific. It's a good idea to find out what actions you should take if such an event occurs.

- **Volcanic eruptions are sometimes predictable.** Remember that if a volcano erupts, its ashes and smoke can rise high in the atmosphere, disrupting flights to destinations hundreds of miles away.

Keep in mind that major problems like those you've just read about are uncommon. For the most part, careful trip planning results in a safe, orderly, and gratifying experience.

The Future

What can we expect for the future of travel? Here are some probabilities:

- **More and more people will travel.** Although occasional, disturbing events (such as war or terrorism) can reduce travel dramatically, within a year or two it will almost certainly come back and exceed previous levels. The urge to travel has become a powerful one, not easily deterred. In fact, many experts believe that travel never abates; it merely changes. Afraid to fly? Take a drive vacation. Nervous about going somewhere far? Go somewhere near. Think you shouldn't go to a specific city? Bargain air and lodging rates may change your mind.

- **New destinations will emerge.** Cancun. Orlando. Maui. Just about every traveler has heard of these places. But just a generation or two ago, these destinations were virtually unknown. There are places out there, right now, that you've never heard of that will be hugely popular in a decade or two. And some that are extremely popular today will eventually lose their luster and become passé.

- **Special-interest travel will increase.** The "global village" we now live in permits people in diverse places but with common interests to communicate easily. Tie this to the fact that today's travelers often define themselves by their product selection and you have a surge of special-interest travel (for example, diving trips, ecologically oriented journeys, historical tours). Special-interest travel is often called niche travel.

- **"Flash" travel will grow.** Flash travel refers to short trips (called micro-trips) that consumers buy after seeing a pop-up ad, e-mail offer, blog recommendation, or other electronic message. The equivalent of an impulse buy at a store (such as a magazine at a grocery store checkout lane), flash travel purchases tend to be quick, inexpensive getaways that are the result of a spur-of-the-moment decision.

- **Health-oriented travel will be very popular.** The desire to get away from it all and to visit calming, healthy places will become even greater. The popularity of spas is a good example.

insider info

In the 1968 movie *2001: A Space Odyssey*, Pan Am spaceships were shown flying to a Hilton space station. Around the same time, Pan Am took waitlist reservations for their first trip to the moon. (Pan Am went out of business in 1991.)

Preliminary aircraft for Virgin Galactic's space travel program.

- **Space travel is becoming a reality.** Already a few very rich individuals have traveled into space on Russian rockets. Suborbital flights may soon be possible, permitting people to travel from London to New York City in less than an hour.

- **Technology will enhance travel in ways we can't imagine.** Picture this: You're thinking of going to a Caribbean resort. You go to the Internet. After doing some research, you're still a bit confused, so you go to a particular travel agency Web site. You click on the "live agent" icon. A toll-free number appears and you dial it. You get a female voice, who gives you a code to enter online. Suddenly the agent you're speaking to appears onscreen, live. You discuss your ideas with her, and she narrows the options down to two. She asks for permission to use your **avatar**, *a "virtual," electronically encoded version of you.* You e-mail it to her. Then, there *you* are, at each of the two resorts, lying by the pool, dining at a wonderful buffet, dancing the night away. It's like a live TV show, hosted by the travel agent, starring you.

These are just a few predictions. The travel industry always has a few surprises in store that defy forecasting. One sure bet, though: no matter what happens, people will always have a passion for travel. With desire, hard work, and a little bit of luck, you'll almost surely succeed as a travel professional, in an industry that always manages to reward and delight those who commit their lives to it. Our very best wishes for your success.

Review Questions

1. Define the following: passport, visa, tourist card, IDP, Immigration, Customs.

2. What five factors affect the cost of visiting a destination?

3. If you visit a foreign country, what are some of your options for paying for things?

4. How can you access up-to-date information on travel health and security issues?

It's All About You Questions

1. You have unlimited money. What one type of travel company would you buy? An airline? A hotel chain? A cruise line? A tour company? Why?

2. What one business sector would you *avoid* buying into? Why?

Activity 1: Predicting the Future

It's hard to imagine how different travel might be in the distant future. Let's look at some far-fetched, futuristic scenarios. Describe how popular and successful you think each would be (or not be)—and how each would affect the rest of the travel, tourism, and hospitality industries.

1. A "Total Recall" device that would allow people to mentally visit anywhere on earth—without ever actually going anywhere.

2. An aircraft with a fuselage that's completely transparent. The walls are like clear glass, and passengers can look out in almost every direction.

3. A space station hotel in orbit around Earth. It has all the comforts of an Earth-based one—except gravity.

4. A time machine that can take you anywhere in the past—or the future.

5. A one-a-day pill that provides you with all the nutrients you need to be well nourished and healthy. No need any more to eat.

Activity 2: Looking Back

Look back on Activity 2 in Chapter 1. Now that you've completed this book, do you still agree with the answers you gave then, or have they changed?

To help you along, fill out the activity below, based on your current, more advanced level of knowledge of travel. Be prepared to explain your reasons for the differences.

3 = Very interested   **2** = Maybe interested   **1** = Not interested

Job	Amount of Interest	Why?
1. Airport ticket counter representative for an airline		
2. Hotel front-desk person		
3. Travel agent working at a large agency		
4. Travel agent working out of your home		
5. City sightseeing tour guide		
6. Front-desk person on a cruise ship		
7. Front-desk person at a car rental office		
8. Onboard service person on a train		
9. Apprentice chef at a large theme restaurant		
10. Motorcoach driver on multiday, multicity tours		
Other possibilities that you're interested in		

NAME _Hotel_   DATE _27/10/2019_

Gale Hospitality, Tourism and Leisure Database Assignment

The following assignment requires access to the Gale Hospitality, Tourism and Leisure Database. Check with your instructor to see if you have access to this database.

Find the article *Skyscanner Reveals Mass Media Coverage* in the Gale Hospitality, Tourism & Leisure Collection. Do you think the finding from this study is accurate? Why or why not?

GLOSSARY

24-hour-clock system   A system in which time is expressed as a four-digit number.

A

Add-on   See *optional*

Adjoining rooms   Two guestrooms that are near or next to one another but that don't have a door between them.

Avatar   A "virtual," electronically encoded version of a person.

Adventure tour   A tour that features physically active, exotic, and/or sometimes demanding experiences.

Advertising   Promotional information that costs money.

Affinity tour   A tour in which the group members already know each other.

Airport management   The team that makes the operations of an airport efficient, safe, and profitable.

Air-sea package   A cruise product that consists of airfare, airport-to-dock transportation, and perhaps lodging.

All-expense tour   See *all-inclusive tour*.

All-inclusive resort   A resort that includes lodging, food, entertainment, and many activities for one price.

All-inclusive tour   A tour that offers most of its features for one price.

All-suite hotel   A hotel in which all accommodations are suites instead of conventional rooms.

Amenity   (1) An in-room or bathroom extra, such as shampoo, a hair dryer, an iron/ironing board, mouthwash. (2) A hotel's facilities such as a health club, swimming pool, business center. See also *option*.

American Plan (AP)   A room rate that includes three meals daily.

Approval code   A number issued by a credit card company to indicate its authorization of a credit card transaction.

Attractions   Anything that leisure travelers find interesting.

Aviation   The broad term used to describe the industry that builds and flies aircraft.

B

Bed-and-breakfast rate   In England, the Bermuda Plan.

Benefit   The payoff for a feature.

Bermuda Plan (BP)   A room rate that includes a full breakfast daily.

Berth   (1) A bed on a ship. (2) The place where a ship docks.

Booking engine   A function that enables people to make Web-based reservations in real time.

Bow   The front of the ship.

Brand   A highly recognizable name.

Brand-based marketing   Marketing that attempts to establish a brand in the marketplace.

Browser   Software that permits people to access and retrieve documents on the Web.

Bulkhead   A wall separating different passenger compartments on an aircraft.

Bulkhead row   The row of seats immediately behind the bulkhead.

Bumped   When a passenger is not allowed to board the plane because of overbooking.

Business class   On a three-class aircraft, the class of service between first class and coach.

Business hotel   A hotel that targets the needs of business travelers.

Business travel   Travel beyond one's home city for reasons related to work.

C

Cape   A projection of land into the water; smaller than a peninsula.

Carrier   An airline.

Casino resort   A resort that features extensive gaming opportunities in a destination where gambling is legal.

Cay   A sandy coral island that is small and low.

Centrics   In the Plog Continuum, a psychological middle ground between Dependables and Venturers.

Change fee   A fee to change a reservation that is in addition to the difference in price.

Charter   To lease or rent.

Charter flight   (1) A flight flown by a charter airline, which usually sells seats, to or through tour operators, to mass-market vacation destinations. (2) A plane booked by an organization for its exclusive use.

Charter tour   See *customized tour*.

Circle flight itinerary   An itinerary in which the traveler has two or more extended stopovers and returns to the originating city.

Civil aviation   The industry that flies the public from place to place.

Closed-ended question   A question that elicits a brief, usually factual answer.

Club level   See *concierge level*.

Coach class   The more standard level of service on a plane. It features narrow seats, less pitch and recline, simple meals or snacks (sometimes with no menu choice), or even no food service at all.

Code-sharing   When an airline uses the code of another carrier for a scheduled flight.

Commercial flight   A flight whose seats have been sold by an airline to the general public.

Commodity   A product that's simple, similar to other products in its sector, and usually bought based on price and logistic factors alone.

Commuter airline   A carrier that serves a limited section of the country, usually with short flights.

Commuter jet   See *regional jet*.

Computer Reservation System (CRS)   A computer system that allows agents to book travel products.

Concept   The food service elements that together address the needs and expectations of customers.

Concierge   A person who helps guests with special requests, such as obtaining theater tickets, booking restaurant reservations, providing transfer services, and giving sightseeing advice.

Concierge level   A level of hotel guestrooms that features better amenities. It sometimes also refers to a private floor (or floors) with enhanced guestrooms and facilities.

Configuration   The way seating is arranged within an aircraft.

Confirmation number   See *record locator number*.

Confirmed reservation   A reservation that has been entered into an airline's computer system.

Connecting flight   A flight in which the traveler must change planes once, twice, or even more times to get to his or her destination.

Connecting rooms   Two guestrooms with an openable door between them.

Consolidator   A company that specializes in unsold inventory.

Consortium   A group of agencies that works together to obtain and develop marketing tools, accounting systems, training programs, and higher commissions from select, preferred suppliers.

Consumers   People who buy products or services for their personal use.

Continental Plan (CP)   A room rate that includes a daily continental breakfast (for example, rolls, toast, muffins, pastries, and various beverages).

Continents   The world's largest landforms.

Continuing flight   See *direct flight*.

Convention and meeting hotel   A hotel with numerous meeting rooms and large ballrooms that can host groups of any size.

Convention and visitors bureau (CVB)   See *destination marketing organization*.

Convention center   A facility that provides space for conferences and the display booth needs of major associations and corporations.

Converted hotel   An old castle, monastery, or commercial building, etc., that is reconfigured to accommodate tourists.

Corporate hotel   See *business hotel*.

Corporate rate   A special hotel rate offered to businesses that give the hotel volume business.

Corporate travel   See *business travel*.

Corporate travel manager   A person employed by a company to arrange travel for its employees.

Couchette   A bunk in a passenger compartment on a train.

CRM (customer relationship management) program   A computer program that tracks data such as buying patterns, demographic and psychographic information, past travel experiences, and key dates, like birthdays and anniversaries.

Cross-selling   Enhancing a sale by recommending additional products or services.

Cruise consolidator   A company that buys blocks of staterooms from a cruise line and offers them to the public at a discounted price.

Customized tour   A tour tailored for a preformed affinity group at a special price.

Customs   The procedure by which government agents inspect luggage and other goods entering a country.

D

Database   An organized, usually computerized collection of customer information.

Database marketing   Marketing that relies on databases to permit a company to create efficient relationships with its customers.

Day rate   The cost of renting a room for the day, rather than for overnight.

Day tour   A tour that lasts fewer than 24 hours.

Deadheading   (1) Making a trip or a segment of a trip without passengers. (2) Driving an empty motorcoach somewhere.

Debit memo   A request for payment, usually from an airline, when the airline believes that a travel agent or agency made an error on a fare and provided too little money to the airline for that ticket.

Deck   A floor of a ship.

Demand   When people have the desire for something and the money to pay for it.

Demographics   Easily measurable factors, such as age, income, gender, marital status, and the like.

Dependables   In the Plog Continuum, cautious people.

Destination marketing organization (DMO)   An organization whose purpose is to promote and facilitate travel to and within its districts, cities, regions, states/provinces, nations, or continents.

Direct flight   A flight on which a traveler goes from Point A to Point B on the same aircraft but that aircraft stops at an airport in between.

Discretionary money   Money that's left over after paying for the necessities of life such as food, shelter, and clothing and that is used to buy something that a person doesn't necessarily need but certainly may want.

Distribution   The process of making a product available to consumers.

Domestic hub   A hub that handles mostly domestic flights.

Domestic service   When a flight starts and ends within the borders of the same country.

Duty   A fee imposed on items purchased abroad.

E

Economy class   See *coach class*.

Ecotourism   Tourism that is based on travelers' interest in and respect for nature.

Electronic ticket (e-ticket)   An air ticket that exists only as a computer record, much like a hotel or car rental reservation.

Elevation   The height, in feet (or meters), of land.

Equator   The imaginary line that encircles the earth's middle.

Escorted tour   A tour in which transportation, sightseeing, some (or all) meals, lodging, and the services of a tour manager are all prearranged.

European Plan (EP)   A room rate that doesn't include any meals.

Exit row   A row on an aircraft where an emergency exit is located.

Experience   A complex product, one where suppliers in that sector provide different types of vacations.

F

Familiarization (fam) tour   A low-cost, agent-only trip to familiarize agents with a destination.

FAQs   A list of Frequently Asked Questions that consumers are likely to want answers to.

Feature   A fact about a product or service.

First class   The class of service in the compartment at the front of the plane. It usually features wider seats, greater pitch, more recline, more elaborate meals, complimentary alcoholic beverages, and free movies.

FIT   Any trip assembled by an agent from scratch, rather than a package.

Fixed-base operator (FBO)   A company that provides ground services and support to the aviation industry.

Fleet   The makes and models of cars offered by a car rental company.

Flight attendants   Airline personnel who see to the safety, comfort, and needs of passengers on a plane.

Flight record   The information in an airline's computer about a passenger's trip.

Fly-drive tour   A tour with two necessary ingredients only: air transportation and car rental.

Folio   A hotel bill.

Food services   The industry that provides dining and food to people, usually outside their home environment.

Fractional ownership   A setup in which a plane has multiple owners who have a set amount of flight hours they can use.

G

Gangway   The walkway connecting a ship with the dock.

Gate agent   An airline employee who works at the gate where passengers board the plane.

Gate check   Checking in luggage at the aircraft's gate rather than at the check-in counter.

Gateway   A city and/or airport that serves an airline as its departure/arrival point for international travel.

Geyser   A jet of steaming water that shoots high into the air.

Global Distribution System (GDS)   See *Computer Reservation System*.

Great circle route   The shortest route a jet can fly, which is a curved route north or south between destinations.

Gross registered tonnage (GRT)   A measurement of the volume of enclosed public spaces on a ship.

Ground operator   A type of inbound tour operator that specializes in serving other tour companies' arriving groups in a limited geographic area.

Group desk   A division of an airline's reservations department that takes care of group reservations.

Group space   Travel agency's access to special inventory from a supplier.

Group/tour rate   A special rate charged by a hotel to tours.

Groups manager   A one-stop service-person on a cruise ship who facilitates all logistic matters for groups on the ship.

Guidespeak   See *narration.*

Gulf   A large area of water that penetrates into land.

H

High season   When the weather at a place is best and many people get their vacation time.

Homepage   The first page people see on a Web site.

Hop-on, hop-off   A bus tour with predetermined stops; passengers can get on or off at any stop and board another bus later.

Hospitality   The industry that encompasses the lodging and food services industries.

Host agency   An agency used by outside agents for booking travel.

Hosted tour   A tour in which a "host" (a tour representative) meets with the tour travelers only when they need to see him or her.

Hotel   A structure that provides sleeping accommodations to travelers and that usually features dining facilities and daily housekeeping service.

Hotel occupancy   The percentage of rooms occupied in a hotel.

Hotel representative firm   A company that provides Web- and telephone-based services through which potential guests can book their reservations for independent hotels.

Hub   One of an airline's key airports, from which the majority of its flights depart or arrive.

Hurricane   A storm with winds of 74 miles per hour (mph) and above.

Hyperlink   A graphic or series of words on a Web site that, when clicked on, takes the user to another site.

I

Immigration   The process by which a government official controls movement of people across its borders.

Inbound operator   A company that concentrates on tours in a particular city, area, or country.

Incentive trip   A vacation provided by a company as a reward to certain employees for achieving exceptional, preidentified goals.

Inclusive tour   See *all-inclusive tour.*

Independent tour   A tour in which many of the travel components are prearranged but the buyer travels independently of a group or a tour manager.

Informational site   An Internet site that provides details on places, products, and data.

Inside stateroom   A ship's stateroom that is (usually) windowless.

Intangible product   A product that can't be perceived by the senses.

Interline agreement   A formal agreement between two airlines.

Intermediary   A company that acts as a go-between, linking suppliers with the traveling public.

Intermodal tour   A tour that combines different types of transportation into one package.

International drivers permit (IDP)   A version of a driver's license that is translated into multiple languages.

International hub   A hub that features many flights to other countries.

International service   When a flight starts in one country and ends in another.

Internet   A global system of computer networks that enables people to access and communicate with any other computer connected to it.

Inventory   (1) The number of a rental company's available cars. (2) The number of rooms a hotel has available for occupancy.

Island   A landform completely surrounded by water.

J

Jet lag   The feeling that occurs when a person's internal body clock is confused by crossing multiple time zones.

Jet stream   The high-altitude, high-velocity core of the winds that blow from west to east in temperate zones.

Jetway   A movable device that connects the aircraft to the terminal.

Junior suite   A large, oversized hotel room.

K

Key   See *cay*.

L

Lake   A (usually) freshwater body of water that is mostly or entirely encircled by land.

Land operator   See *ground operator*.

Lateral service   When an employee takes the initiative to go beyond his or her job description, when appropriate.

Lead   A person who might be interested in buying a company's travel product.

Legacy airline   One of the major carriers that have been around a long time.

Legroom   See *pitch*.

Leisure travel   Travel for the purpose of enjoyment.

Lines of latitude   The imaginary lines on a globe that go east–west.

Lines of longitude   The imaginary lines on a globe that go north–south.

Link   See *hyperlink*.

Load factor   The percentage of seats filled with people on a plane.

Locator map   A special gridded map, found in travel industry resource books and on Web sites, which represents a small area and helps people locate hotels, attractions, and so forth.

Lot   The place where rental cars are kept.

Low season   When the weather at a place is worst and few people are traveling.

M

Marketing   The process of transferring a product or service from its producer to the consumer.

Mass marketing   Marketing whose purpose is to attract the greatest number of potential buyers.

Mechanical   When a flight is canceled because of a problem with the aircraft.

Meet-and-greet service   A service in which a guide or other greeter welcomes and escorts travelers from the airport to their hotel, assisting them with their luggage as well.

Meeting planner   A specialist who helps plan, negotiate, coordinate, operate, and conduct follow-up evaluations of a convention or relatively large meeting.

Mega-resort   An especially large resort hotel, covering acres of land, which has many facilities and activities.

Microblog   An Internet site such as *Twitter* that allows people to send out instant, short messages.

Military aviation   Aircraft flown by a nation's air force and other branches of its military.

Minimum connecting time   The minimum amount of time needed to transfer from one flight to a connecting one.

Modified American Plan (MAP)   A room rate that includes two meals (usually breakfast and dinner) daily in the room rate.

Motorcoach tour   An escorted tour in which a motorcoach is the main mode of transportation to and from destinations and attractions.

Mountain   A great, high outcropping of rock and soil.

Mystery tour   A tour in which the destination and itinerary are kept secret from the clients until they embark on the tour.

N

Narration   A commentary provided to passengers on a tour.

Narrow-body jet   A jet with one aisle.

Niche marketing   Marketing that targets the needs of a narrow segment of consumers.

Nonstop flight   A flight on which a traveler goes from Point A to Point B on the same aircraft.

Northern Hemisphere   The half of the world north of the equator.

No-show   A person with a reservation who doesn't show up for a flight.

O

Oceans   The world's largest bodies of water.

Ocean-view stateroom   See *outside stateroom*.

One-stop flight   See *direct flight*.

One-way flight itinerary   An itinerary in which the traveler just goes from Point A to Point B.

Open-ended question   A question that usually elicits a longer and more complex response.

Open-jaw flight itinerary   An itinerary in which the traveler flies from Point A to Point B, travels by ground transportation from B to C, then returns by air from C to A.

Opinion site   An Internet site that is subjective, with experts—or self-proclaimed experts—giving their views on everything about destinations and products.

Option   An additional, extra-cost feature on a rental car.

Optional   An additional feature not included in the main tour package.

Outbound operator   A company that takes groups from a particular city or country to another city or country.

Outside stateroom   A ship's stateroom that has a window.

Overbooked flight   See *oversold flight*.

Overrides   Better or extra commissions provided to travel agencies by their preferred suppliers.

Oversold flight   A flight on which bookings exceed the number of seats available.

P

Passenger Name Record (PNR)   The computer reservation system's record of a booking.

Passport   A document that a nation's government issues to one of its citizens to establish that person's identity and nationality.

Pax   An abbreviation for *passengers*.

Peninsula   A large projection of land into the water.

Per-capita tour   See *public tour*.

Perishable product   A product that loses its value if not consumed or used by a certain date.

Phone shopper   A person who phones many different vendors and/or agencies to get the best price and, perhaps, better service or professionalism.

Pied piper   A person within an organization who will spearhead the trip.

Pitch   The distance between an airplane's seat rows.

Port   (1) A place a ship visits. (2) When facing forward on the ship, the left-hand side.

Positioning   The act of making products or services different and distinct from another supplier's products or services in the marketplace.

Preferred supplier   A supplier that a travel agency recommends most often because it gives the agency extra commissions or access to special inventory.

Privately owned jet   A corporate jet that a company or individual owns.

Promotional fare   A discounted fare that usually carries restrictions.

Property   A specific lodging facility.

Prospecting   When a salesperson proactively contacts potential buyers.

Psychographics   Factors that are more difficult to assess, such as attitudes, preferences, and beliefs.

Publicity   Promotional information that's achieved at little or no cost.

Public tour   A tour offered to the public.

Q

Qualifying   The process of asking questions to determine a client's needs.

Queues   A feature of a CRS/GDS to remind the agent of an important action to be taken or message to be delivered.

R

Rack rate   A hotel's official, published rate.

Rate desk   Airline staff who specialize in international fares and help calculate the cost of a ticket.

Receptive operator   See *ground operator*.

Record locator number   A six-digit figure of numbers and/or letters that identifies a reservation.

Recovery   Making right what a customer sees as wrong.

Red-eye flight   An overnight flight.

Reef   A low ridge, usually made of coral, that rises to or near the water's surface.

Regional jet   A small jet that carries fewer than 100 people.

Relationship marketing   Marketing that emphasizes the connection between a business and its customers.

Repositioning cruise   A cruise in which a ship is moving from one general cruise area to another.

Resort hotel   A hotel that caters primarily to leisure travelers.

Revenue ticket   A ticket that has been paid for.

River   A large stream of water that empties into another body of water (for example, an ocean).

Room service   The service that provides in-room dining.

Round-trip flight itinerary   An itinerary in which the traveler flies from Point A to Point B, stays a while, then returns from B to A.

Run-of-the-house rate (ROH)   (1) A rate guaranteeing that the guest will receive the best room available at check-in. (2) A flat rate offered to a group, with the understanding that any rooms in the hotel may be assigned to the group members.

S

Scheduled service   Air transportation that operates regularly at set, advertised times, no matter how many people are booked on the flight.

Sea   A body of water that's usually salty and open to (or even part of) an ocean.

Search engine   An online program that looks for sites containing words, word combinations, subjects, and other information that match what the user has indicated wanting to know more about.

Seating   A set mealtime for dinner and sometimes lunch on a cruise.

Seat rotation   The policy of having passengers on a motorcoach change seats several times per day to ensure seating fairness.

Segment   Each flight of a passenger's air itinerary.

Selling   The process of helping someone buy something.

Service animal   An animal that provides a service to a person, for example a seeing-eye dog.

Shore excursion   A tour at a port.

Shoulder season   An "in-between" time when tourism is neither high nor low.

Site tour   A tour conducted at a specific building, attraction, or limited area.

Ski resort   A resort that provides a site and facilities to serve the needs of winter sports enthusiasts.

Skycap   A luggage handler at an airport terminal's curbside.

Sleeper seat   An aircraft seat that fully converts to a bed.

Social networking site   An Internet site that enables people to build and maintain relationships, to keep in touch with what their friends or even celebrities are up to.

Southern Hemisphere   The half of the world south of the equator.

Space available   If the inventory is not sold out.

Space ratio   A ship measurement that reflects the space or "elbow room" passengers will have onboard.

Spa resort   A resort that provides extensive facilities for massages, facials, fitness activities, and healthy dining.

Split itinerary   An itinerary in which part of the tour group does one thing while the other part does something else.

Stabilizer   An underwater device that helps reduce a ship's motion.

Stall   When a person delays or hesitates to purchase something.

Standby passenger   A waitlisted person who goes to the airport to try to get on a certain flight and is placed on a standby list.

Starboard   When facing forward, the right-hand side of the ship.

Stateroom   A cabin on a ship.

Stateroom steward   The person who maintains a ship's staterooms.

Stern   The back of a ship.

Student tour   A tour involving a preformed school group that visits a destination to enhance the learning experience.

Study tour   See *student tour*.

Supplier   A company that creates, owns, and provides the travel products being sold.

Sustainable tourism   See *ecotourism*.

T

Tariffs   The official rules, regulations, and fares of airlines.

Telemarketing   Prospecting done on the phone.

Temperate zones   The regions between the Arctic or Antarctic circles and the Tropics.

Tender   A small boat that transports passengers to and from shore if the ship is too large or the port is too shallow for docking directly at the pier.

Themed resort   A resort that has a strong identity, often one tied to some other place and time.

Tour   Any preplanned (and usually prepaid) package to one or more places, that includes two or more travel components.

Tour broker   See *tour operator*.

Tour company   See *tour operator*.

Tour conductor   See *tour manager*.

Tour courier   See *tour manager*.

Tour director   See *tour manager*.

Tour escort   See *tour manager*.

Tour guide   See *tour manager*.

Tour leader   See *tour manager*.

Tour manager   On an escorted tour, the person in charge of ensuring that the passengers have an enjoyable travel experience. Also called tour conductor, courier, director, escort, guide, or leader.

Tour operator   A company that contracts with suppliers and attractions to create multiday tour packages. Also called tour broker, company, or packager.

Tour packager   See *tour operator*.

Tourist bureau   See *destination marketing organization*.

Tourist card   A form used instead of or in addition to a passport for entry into certain countries.

Tourist office   See *destination marketing organization*.

Tradewinds   Tropical winds that flow from east to west.

Transcon service   A flight that crosses a continent, as in transcontinental.

Transfer service   The industry segment that specializes in operating buses or vans between airports and hotels.

Transportation   The industry that moves not just people but also things, such as cargo.

Travel advisor   See *travel agent*.

Travel agent   A professional who analyzes a traveler's needs and then prices, recommends, arranges, and sells one or more components of a person's trip. Also called travel advisor, consultant, counselor, or planner.

Travel consultant   See *travel agent*.

Travel counselor   See *travel agent*.

Traveler's check   A check-like form of currency that must be countersigned by the user.

Travel package   A package in which several travel components are bundled together and sold as one product.

Travel planner   See *travel agent*.

Trip director   A tour manager for an incentive company. Larger companies reserve this title for the person who directs all personnel and activities for a particular incentive trip.

Tropical zones   The regions between approximately 23 degrees north of the equator and 23 degrees south of the equator.

U

Unaccompanied minor   A child flying alone.

Unrestricted fare   A fare that permits changes to an itinerary without a penalty.

Uniform Resource Locator (URL)   The address of a Web site.

Upselling   Enhancing a sale by recommending better options than the client had in mind.

V

Venturers   In the Plog Continuum, bolder people.

VFR travel   Travel for visiting friends and relatives.

Visa   A stamp, imprint, or piece of paper inserted into a traveler's passport, placed there by a foreign government, that indicates that the passport's owner may enter and pass through the country that issued it.

W

Waitlist   The list of travelers who cannot be accommodated on their desired flight because it is fully booked.

Walking the guest   When a hotel is overbooked and a guest is transferred to another hotel.

Wholesaler   See *tour operator*.

Wide-body jet   A jet with two aisles.

World Wide Web   A system within the Internet that organizes information—both text and visuals—into pages that can easily be retrieved and displayed.

Y

Yield management   A procedure that enables suppliers to maximize profits by adjusting prices to supply and demand, often at a moment's notice.

Z

Zodiac   A large inflatable rubber boat that is often used in exotic, difficult-to-reach places such as Antarctica.

INDEX

No. **72**

Received from Brenda Powers 24 / 10 / 19

the sum of Fifteen pounds only

VAT No. .... £/€ 15

The Western Hemisphere

ARTIC OCEAN

GREENLAND
(Denmark)

RUSSIA

ALASKA
(U.S.A.)

ICELAND

Arctic Circle

CANADA

UNITED STATES

MIDWAY IS
(U.S.A.)

Tropic of Cancer

Gulf of Mexico

BAHAMAS

HAWAII
(U.S.A.)

MEXICO

CUBA

HAITI

DOM. REP.

PUERTO RICO

GUADELOUPE

BEL.
HOND.

JAMAICA

MARTINIQUE

BARBADOS

TRINIDAD AND TOBAGO

GUAT.
EL SAL.

NIC.

COSTA RICA

PANAMA

VEN.

GUYANA

SURINAME

FR. GUIANA

COLOMBIA

PACIFIC

Equator

ECUADOR

ATLANTIC

KIRIBATI

PERU

BRAZIL

OCEAN

OCEAN

WESTERN
SAMOA

AMERICAN SAMOA

BOL.

Tahiti

FIJI

TONGA

FRENCH POLYNESIA

Tropic of Capricorn

PAR.

CHILE

URUGUAY

NEW ZEALAND

ARGENTINA

FALKLAND IS.

S. SHETLAND IS.

Antarctic Circle

ANTARCTICA

ANTARCTICA

0   5000 km

0   3000 miles

From HUDMAN/JACKSON. Geography of Travel & Tourism, 4E, 4E. © 2003 Delmar Learning, a part of Cengage Learning, Inc. Reproduced by permission. www.cengage.com/permissions

The Eastern Hemisphere

GREENLAND
(Denmark)

Arctic Circle

ICELAND

UNITED
KINGDOM

IRELAND

NORWAY

SWEDEN

FINLAND

EST.
LAT.
LITH.

DEN.

NETH.
BEL. LUX.
GER.
POLAND
BELA.

RUSSIA

FRANCE
SWITZ.
AUS. HUN.
CZ.
SLVK.
SLOT.
UKRAINE

KAZAKHSTAN

MONGOLIA

PORT.
SPAIN
ITALY
CRO. BOS.
YUGO.
ALBA.
ROM.
BUL.

GEOR.
ARM. AZER.
UZBEK.
KYRG.

N. KOREA
S. KOREA

GREECE
TURKEY
CYP.
LEB.
ISRAEL
SYRIA
IRAQ
TURKMEN.
TAJIK.

JAPAN

MOROCCO

TUNISIA

JORDAN
IRAN
AFGHAN.

CHINA

Tropic of Cancer

ALGERIA
LIBYA
EGYPT
KUWAIT
SAUDI
ARABIA
UNITED ARAB
EMIRATES
PAKISTAN
NEPAL
BHU.
INDIA
TAIWAN

PACIFIC

W.
SAH.

MAURITANIA

MALI
NIGER
CHAD
SUDAN
ERITREA
YEMEN
DJIBOUTI
OMAN

BNGL.
MYANMAR
LAOS
THAI.
VIETNAM

PHILIPPINES

OCEAN

SEN.
GAMBIA
G.
BIS.
GUINEA
BURKINA
FASO
BENIN
NIGERIA
CENTRAL
AFRICAN REP.
ETHIOPIA
SOMALIA
CAM.

SRI LANKA
(CEYLON)
BRUNEI
MALAYSIA

SIERRA
LEONE
COTE
D'IV.
TOGO
GHANA
LIBERIA

EQUATORIAL
GUINEA
GABON
REP.
of the
CONGO
DEM. REP.
of the
CONGO
UGANDA
KENYA
RWANDA
BURUNDI
Equator

INDONESIA

PAPUA
NEW
GUINEA

CABINDA

TANZANIA

INDIAN

ANGOLA
ZAMBIA
MALAWI

NAMIBIA
ZIMBABWE
MADAGASCAR

OCEAN

BOTSWANA

Tropic of Capricorn

ATLANTIC

MOZAMBIQUE
SWAZILAND

AUSTRALIA

SOUTH
AFRICA
LESOTHO

OCEAN

Antarctic Circle

ANTARCTICA

0 ————— 5000 km
0 ————— 3000 miles

From HUDMAN/JACKSON. Geography of Travel & Tourism, 4E. © 2003 Delmar Learning, a part of Cengage Learning, Inc. Reproduced by permission. www.cengage.com/permissions

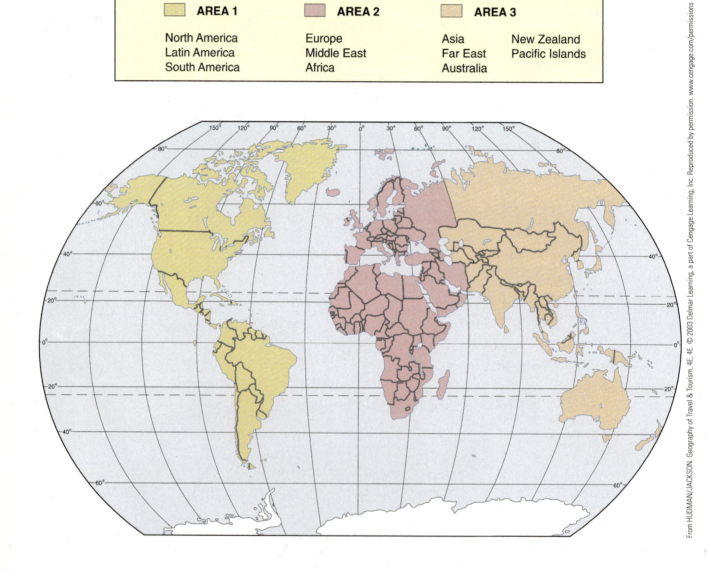

IATA Regions of the World

0 — 5,000 km
0 — 3,000 miles

AREA 1

North America
Latin America
South America

AREA 2

Europe
Middle East
Africa

AREA 3

Asia   New Zealand
Far East   Pacific Islands
Australia